MW01194224

## CONSTITUTIONAL MONEY

This book reviews ten Supreme Court cases and decisions that dealt with monetary laws and gives a summary history of monetary events and policies as they were affected by the Court's decisions. Several cases and decisions had notable consequences on the monetary history of the United States; some were blatant misjudgments resulting from political pressures. The cases included begin with *McCulloch v. Maryland* in 1819 and end with the Gold Clause Cases in 1934–1935. Three institutions were prominent in these decisions: the Supreme Court, the gold standard, and the Federal Reserve System. The final chapter describes the adjustments necessary to return to a gold standard and briefly examines the constitutional alternatives.

Richard H. Timberlake is an emeritus professor of economics at the University of Georgia and an adjunct scholar at the Cato Institute. His research specialties are monetary policy and the history of central banking. Dr. Timberlake's most recent publications include *Monetary Policy in the United States: An Institutional and Intellectual History* and *Money and the Nation State*, edited with Kevin Dowd. He received his Ph.D. from the University of Chicago in 1959.

# Constitutional Money

*A Review of the Supreme Court's Monetary Decisions*

RICHARD H. TIMBERLAKE

A Cato Institute Book

CAMBRIDGE UNIVERSITY PRESS
Cambridge, New York, Melbourne, Madrid, Cape Town,
Singapore, São Paulo, Delhi, Mexico City

Cambridge University Press
32 Avenue of the Americas, New York, NY 10013-2473, USA

www.cambridge.org
Information on this title: www.cambridge.org/9781107032545

© Cato Institute 2013

First published 2013

Printed in the United States of America

*A catalog record for this publication is available from the British Library.*

*Library of Congress Cataloging in Publication data*
Timberlake, Richard H.
Constitutional money : a review of the Supreme Court's monetary
decisions / Richard H. Timberlake.
pages  cm
Includes bibliographical references and indexes.
ISBN 978-1-107-03254-5
1. Money–Law and legislation–United States–Cases.   2. United States. Supreme
Court–Cases.   I. Title.
KF6205.T56   2013
343.73'032–dc23        2012033997

ISBN 978-1-107-03254-5 Hardback

*To*

*Those sovereign people of the Constitution who freely and unwittingly*
*contribute to the undesigned order of human affairs*

# Contents

| | | |
|---|---|---:|
| *Preface* | | *page* ix |
| *Acknowledgments* | | xiii |
| 1 | The Current Condition of Monetary Affairs in the United States | 1 |
| 2 | The Emergence of Money in Civilized Societies | 4 |
| 3 | The Bimetallic Monetary System and Appearance of a National Bank | 10 |
| 4 | *McCulloch v. Maryland,* 1819 | 21 |
| 5 | "To Coin Money and Regulate the Value Thereof ..." | 35 |
| 6 | *Craig v. Missouri,* 1830 | 39 |
| 7 | *Briscoe v. The Bank of the Commonwealth of Kentucky,* 1837 | 47 |
| 8 | Federal Government Issues of Treasury Notes and Greenbacks | 56 |
| 9 | The Track of the Legal Tender Bills through Congress | 62 |
| 10 | *Bronson v. Rodes,* 1868 | 72 |
| 11 | *Veazie Bank v. Fenno,* 1869 | 79 |
| 12 | *Hepburn v. Griswold,* 1870: The Legal Tender Issue | 86 |
| 13 | *Knox v. Lee* and *Parker v. Davis*: Reversal of *Hepburn* | 97 |
| 14 | Monetary Affairs in the United States, 1871–1883 | 114 |
| 15 | The Third Legal Tender Case: *Juilliard v. Greenman,* 1884 | 119 |

16   Commentaries on the Legal Tender Decisions: The Issue of
     Sovereignty                                                    129

17   Other Commentaries on the Legal Tender Cases                   144

18   The [Gold] Currency Act of 1900 and Monetary Affairs in the
     United States before 1914                                      156

19   The Federal Reserve System, 1914–1929                          162

20   The Great Contraction, 1929–1933                               170

21   Gold! Where Did It Go? Why Didn't the Gold Standard Work?      177

22   The Gold Clause Cases, 1934–1935                               182

23   Gold and Monetary Affairs in the Twentieth Century             206

24   A Constitutional Monetary System                               221

*Index*                                                            235

# Preface

*Constitutional Money* examines nine Supreme Court decisions that markedly affected the U.S. monetary system in order to determine how and why money in use today became what it is. The exposition requires attention to three institutions: the Supreme Court because of its interpretations of the Constitution's money clauses, the gold standard and its operations as sanctioned by the Constitution, and the central bank – the Federal Reserve System – and its operations and constitutionality in the presence of a gold standard. The Court decisions begin with *McCulloch v. Maryland* in 1819 and end with The Gold Clause Cases in 1934–1935.

Everyone who thinks critically about the monetary system is aware of the significant difference between the gold-and-silver standard that the Framers originally prescribed and today's central-bank-fiat-money standard. Article 1, Section 8, of the Constitution states: "The Congress shall have power … To coin Money, regulate the value thereof, and of foreign coin, and fix the standard of Weights and Measures." Article 1, Section 10, declares: "No state shall … coin Money; emit Bills of Credit; make any Thing but gold and silver Coin a Tender in payment of Debts." Those passages taken together imply, first, that any legal tender money can only be gold and silver "coin," and, second, that Congress's monetary power is limited to managing the gold and silver contents of those coins. The Constitution does not prohibit banks and other institutions from creating common money managed by "the people," but it clearly denies the states and the federal government, by implication, any authority to change the base of gold and silver.

Barter of goods and services preceded money. Manifestly, any barter-medium that "the people" might use before a general money-medium appears is already "acceptable." Anyone can swap eggs for butter, or labor services for land; no authority in a free society can prohibit barter in any form. Recognizing this principle, the Framers dealt only with the creation of money at the two levels of government – federal and state. The "people," however, could deal with each other on any terms mutually agreeable. That was a significant element of Freedom of Contract.

In spite of these obvious homilies, in 1933 with President Franklin Roosevelt's strong assent and signature, Congress passed a law prohibiting the private ownership of monetary gold. While this law was rescinded in 1974, gold and silver are nowhere to be found in today's monetary system. Their use as money is still illegal. Entrepreneurs who promote them as money are prosecuted, and even persecuted, by U.S. government agencies. The precious metals have become monetary apparitions, futilely reminding Congress of its constitutional limitations and responsibilities.

The Supreme Court's monetary decisions have become a casebook of primary material begging for examination and possible reinterpretation. While the decisions reviewed here are only a small fraction of the total judgments that the Court has rendered over this time span, they have special importance in the economic world of markets because every transaction for goods, services, and capital also includes a sum of money.

The Framers wrote the Constitution for the ages, and they provided for changes by means of simple amendment procedures. Since the Constitution arranges for its own correction, it has no reason to be interpreted differently for different ages, social conditions, or other human circumstances. Judicial decisions that change the original meaning to fit some current social norm are illicit; they violate the substance of the document and destroy its reason for being.

In this book I package an analysis of constitutional cases on money with a summary history of government monetary policies and events through the twentieth century. My account explains how the Federal Reserve System as a central bank has interacted with the later Court decisions to undermine the Framers' monetary constitution, and in so doing has promoted continuous inflation and ongoing public uncertainty regarding the future value of money. I conclude with some suggestions for a constrained monetary system, including the possibility for the reinstitution of an authentic gold standard.

Attempts have been made in the past to treat monetary affairs with some reference to the Constitution. First, Bray Hammond in his book, *Banks and Politics in America* (Princeton University Press, 1957), did a comprehensive study of the operations of the Second Bank of the United States and its struggle to remain in existence after Andrew Jackson became president. Hammond was a historian who spent most of his professional life on the staff of the Federal Reserve Board in Washington. His account is well written and engrossing, but flawed by his misunderstanding of the Framers' monetary constitution and its limits on the monetary powers of Congress. Furthermore, his uncritical acceptance of, and apology for, a central banking institution – The Second Bank of the United States – is highly questionable. The best that can be said for Hammond's work is that it provides a starting point for serious inquiry on the constitutionality of central banking.

Gerald Dunne's short book, *Monetary Decisions of the Supreme Court* (Rutgers University Press, 1960), followed Hammond's work, but did not challenge any of Hammond's analysis or assumptions. Dunne was the legal counsel for the Federal Reserve Bank of St. Louis and a law professor at St. Louis University. His work properly brought the monetary decisions of the Supreme Court into focus for the first time. However, he was not an economist, and he did not question the Court's authority or its clear violations of constitutional monetary precepts in the cases he reviewed.

Much the same is true of James Willard Hurst's work, *A Legal History of Money in the United States, 1774–1970* (University of Nebraska Press, 1973). Hurst, too, was a legal scholar, not an economist. Early in his work, he stated that his research was limited to legal history. He did not try to make "independent judgments that call for expertness [sic] in other than legal matters," and he did "not purport to write an economic history of money in the United States." However, anyone who examines the legal history of monetary decisions must be able to interpret the monetary conditions under scrutiny in order to evaluate the validity of the judicial decisions. Hurst's work therefore lacks economic substance.

A more recent work, *Pieces of Eight*, by Edwin Vieira, Jr. (Devin-Adair, 1983), has much worthwhile legal material in it and addresses critically and validly many of the Court's decisions on monetary affairs. However, Vieira is a legal scholar, so his excellent legal analysis understandably includes only a limited account of the economic events and institutions of the times. Nonetheless, his conclusions correlate highly with my own, even when we emphasize different issues.

A work that focuses primarily on the prohibition of gold ownership in 1934, *The Gold Clause* by Henry Mark Holzer, addresses the constitutionality of gold as the basis of the monetary system, especially with reference to gold clauses in contracts. Holzer's analysis is very useful but limited to the set of circumstances that accompanied the Roosevelt administration's campaign against gold and the resulting Court decision in the Gold Clause cases.

# Acknowledgments

I have several institutions, economists, laypersons, and family to thank for assistance with this project. I begin by thanking the George Edward Durell Foundation for a grant that supported the monetary research I was doing in the 1990s. This Foundation also published my monograph, *Gold, Greenbacks, and the Constitution* (1991), which proved to be a springboard for the present work.

I was also very much helped by being appointed a Visiting Scholar at the Social Philosophy and Policy Center of Bowling Green State University, Bowling Green, Ohio, in 2002, where I developed the first section of this book. I received some excellent legal help and encouragement there from Fred Miller and Jeff Paul.

I also thank the Cato Institute for its monetary conferences, which have been complementary to my own research interests, and in which I have had a modest part. I especially thank Cato for promoting and co-publishing the present work. In that vein, I also thank Cambridge University Press for cooperating with Cato. Both institutions have been exemplary in managing the publication of this book.

I have also benefited significantly from my experience with The Independent Institute in Oakland, California, in editing (with Kevin Dowd) the book *Money and the Nation State: The Financial Revolution, Government and the World Monetary System* (New Brunswick, N.J.: Transaction Publishers). Many of the articles therein, especially those by David Glasner, Leland Yeager, and Frank van Dun are especially relevant to material covered in this book. Van Dun's "National Sovereignty and International Monetary Regimes" is especially useful to the Supreme Court's discovery of "sovereignty," and its decisions in the legal tender cases. I also refer to my own article in that volume, "Gold Standard Policy and Limited Government," when discussing the evolution of the gold standard through the nineteenth and into the twentieth centuries. Other articles in that work are germane to an understanding of the state's relationship to the creation and production of money, and can be read with profit.

Several economist friends and legal counsels have done yeoman service in editing earlier versions of this text. George Selgin and Jim Dorn have been unstinting, unselfish, and constructive critics. I owe each of them a great debt. Others who have contributed corrections to my text and offered constructive comments include: David Boaz, William Beranek, Kevin Dowd, Roger Garrison, Tom Humphrey, Roger Pilon, Richard Salsman, Walker Todd, Larry White, and Leland Yeager. I also thank my good friend and financial analyst, Tom Wilkins, for suggesting useful references and for his stimulating discussions while the book was in progress. My thanks as always to my wife Hildegard for her constructive criticisms and constant encouragement. Finally, I want to thank my grown-up children, Tommy, Chris, Megan, Dave, and Dick, for reading various sections; for their skeptical review of some arguments; and for nagging me to finish. I also thank my brother Allen for one especially important observation on past Court decisions.

# ONE

## The Current Condition of Monetary Affairs in the United States

It is easy to perceive that individuals by agreeing to erect forms of government...
must give up part of their liberty for that purpose; and it is the particular business
of a Constitution to mark out **how much** they shall give up.... which says to the
legislative powers, "Thus far shalt thou go and no farther." A Constitution, when
completed, resolves the two following questions: First, What shall the form of government be? And, secondly, What shall be its power? And the last of these two is far
more material than the first.

Anonymous
*The Founders' Constitution*, "Four Letters
On Interesting Subjects," 1776, Vol. 1, 638

The money clauses in the U.S. Constitution are brief, simple, and explicit;
the humblest mind can understand them without elaborate interpretation.
Article 1, Section 8 states that "The Congress shall have Power ... To coin
Money, regulate the Value thereof, and of foreign coin, and fix the Standard
of Weights and Measures." Section 10 denies the states any monetary powers. It declares that, "No State shall ... coin money; emit Bills of Credit; [or]
make any Thing but gold and silver Coin a Tender in Payment of Debts." Yet
today the U.S. monetary system seems in conflict with those clauses. In particular, it has no place for gold or silver. All of the hand-to-hand currency
in everyday use consists entirely of paper notes – bills of credit – issued
by the Federal Reserve System, and none of it is redeemable in anything
except other "bills of credit." While the U.S. Treasury also issues coin currency for use in smaller exchanges, none of the currency, paper or coin, is
worth anything as a commodity. It is all *fiat*. All checkable bank deposits,
the only other money of any consequence, is based either on bank-held
Federal Reserve note currency or on reserve balances of commercial banks
in Federal Reserve Banks. These reserves are redeemable only for bills
of credit – the aforementioned Federal Reserve notes. In sum, all bank

reserves and hand-to-hand currency are issues that the Federal Reserve System – the U.S. central bank – has created by what is now regarded as standard monetary policy, primarily, purchases of U.S. government securities that the U.S. Treasury has previously marketed to finance the federal government's long-recurring fiscal deficits. None of it is based on gold or silver; none of it can be redeemed for gold or silver. The entire redeeming medium, fiat Federal Reserve notes, is legal tender for all debts, public and private. Federal Reserve notes and "credit" have completely replaced gold and silver. Yet, the words "Federal Reserve" are nowhere to be found in the Constitution of the United States.

Settled and accepted U.S. policy not only flouts the constitutional prohibition against fiat legal tender money – bills of credit – it also fails to provide any gold or silver money in any form.[1] Courts of law will not even hear cases that would challenge this status quo. They throw out attempts to restore constitutional money as "frivolous." Somehow, between the time that the Constitution and the first ten Amendments were ratified and the present, gold and silver money have disappeared, while the prohibited bills of credit – in this era, Federal Reserve notes – have become conventional standard money. Congress and the Executive branch have often initiated the policies that have reversed what once seemed to be eternal verities, while Supreme Court decisions have sanctioned the changes and given them permanence.

This breach of explicit constitutional provisions, which appears illegal on its face, should have an excuse, or at least an explanation, intelligible to anyone and everyone. The present status of the monetary system seems, however, to have been accepted at all levels – from the unschooled layman to the denizens of the Supreme Court – without serious argument, and without embarrassment at the obvious contradiction between what the Constitution specifies and what has come to exist today.

The Supreme Court is a body of legal experts who, understandably, have interpreted the Constitution from legal and political perspectives. When the Court has handed down decisions that call for an understanding of economics, particularly monetary economics, the justices have had to rely on

---

[1] "Fiat money" is any money – always a paper currency – that a government issues on its own authority and without any visible redeeming medium, such as gold or silver. "Fiat" is the vocative form of the Latin verb, "fio," and literally means "Let there be," in this case, "Let there be money." "Bills of credit," discussed both here and further on, are the *fiat* currency that governments have issued at various times in the past and present. They are explicitly prohibited to the states by the Constitution, and by implication as well to the federal government.

"expert" testimony from what are often special pleaders, or from their own superficial knowledge of monetary affairs. At times they have also deferred on these matters to Congress or the Executive branch, who are no better equipped than the justices in either economic doctrine or the analysis of monetary complexities.

The Justices are not to be condemned on this account. They can hardly be both learned legal analysts and accomplished professional economists. Consequently, putting an economics perspective into the briefs for the Court's decisions should add credibility to future judgments that cover similar ground, and may correct for posterity mistaken judgments that are now a part of accepted policy. Such a project may seem politically unrealistic. But if no one suggests corrections to what has been handed down as the ultimate word from the Court, manifestly incorrect or improper arguments become part of accepted law and endure forever.

Any work on the history of monetary affairs must treat explicitly the operations of both metallic standards (gold and silver) and central banking institutions. The money clauses of the Constitution provide legal sanction for a bi-metallic monetary standard, that is, one in which both gold and silver coins are legal tender for all debts public and private. To make such a standard operational, Congress had to specify the terms – that is, the mint prices in dollars – on which the two metals would be legal tender. The two metallic moneys would then reflect an explicit legal ratio of monetary value, that is, an *exchange rate*. The history of how this bi-metallic standard worked, therefore, is also a necessary backdrop to a review of Court decisions, particularly those that abused or rescinded the explicit provisions specifying gold and silver as the only legal tender.

Central banks first appeared during the later nineteenth and early twentieth centuries. During the twentieth century, they acquired a monopoly on the provision of base money and have completely supplanted metallic standards, which are now nothing more than artifacts in the dust-bin of history.

# TWO

# The Emergence of Money in Civilized Societies

Through the ages from ancient times, monetary devices have come into existence spontaneously, in much the same fashion that wheels, levers, writing materials, energy products, languages, and countless other human innovations have appeared. All of these devices make life easier; and by significantly reducing the real costs of man's existence, add to the total product that private institutions can generate and use.

Because money is an economizing agent for any society that exchanges goods and services, it has appeared in many diverse cultures and over many centuries of man's existence. Money, however, has had an evolutionary history somewhat different from that of other commonly used technical devices. Its appearance and use have often given rise to mystical suppositions and superstitions about its nature and those who control it. These traits have accompanied it into the twenty-first century. More importantly, because of its unique properties, money in all ages has been an object of state intervention and control.[1]

Money evolved from commodities that were not money. As primitive peoples began to exploit their productive abilities, they first bartered goods and services directly in order to realize the economic benefits of their specialties. Very soon, they learned to barter indirectly. By exchanging a surplus item for some intermediate good, people could ultimately realize a more desirable end-product or service. These indirect bartering devices were rudimentary media of exchange that had nascent monetary properties.

---

[1]  The following brief history of the evolution of money is well known. For further details, see my account of this evolution in, *Gold, Greenbacks, and the Constitution.* The George Edward Durrell Foundation: Berryville, Va., 1991, pp. 1–12, and my article, "Gold Standard Policy and Limited Government," pp. 167–191, in *Money and the Nation State.*

Carl Menger, a founder of Austrian economics, correctly captured the dynamics of the shift from barter to money in his *Principles of Economics*, published in 1871. "As economizing individuals ... became increasingly aware of their economic interest," he wrote, "they everywhere attained the simple knowledge that surrendering less saleable commodities for others of greater saleability brings them substantially closer to the attainment of their specific economic purposes."[2] While "only a small number of economizing individuals ... recognize[d] the advantage accruing to them from the acceptance of other, more saleable, commodities" in exchange for their own goods or services, others observing the "economic success" of those employing an intermediate good to achieve their ends, adopted the medium themselves. "In this way, custom and practice contributed in no small degree to converting the commodities that were most saleable" into media of exchange.[3]

Besides describing the path by which some common goods became money because of greater "saleability," Menger made three other important observations:

First, money's appearance was "... not the product of an agreement on the part of economizing men nor the product of legislative acts. No one invented it." Rather, money-commodities appeared *spontaneously* as special devices to meet human needs, much like language, the wheel and common law.[4]

Second, "the specific forms in which [money] has appeared were everywhere and at all times the result of specific and changing situations." The emergence of money was scattered over time and place, and primitive moneys took many forms – cattle, weapons, furs, salt, and, only later, metals. Menger correctly noted that what might have become an optimal metallic money, say, gold in an urban-commercial setting, would not have been so viable a money as, say, cattle in a rural-nomadic society.[5]

Third, Menger noted, governments, whether benign or oppressive, had little to do with the development of money from barter. "The origin of money ... is, as we have seen, entirely natural and thus displays legislative influences only in the rarest instances. Money is not the invention of the

---

[2]  Menger, Carl. *Principles of Economics*. New York and London: New York University Press, 1981. Translated by James Dingwall and Bert Hoselitz (German edition first published in Vienna in 1871), p. 262.

[3]  *Ibid.*, p. 261.

[4]  *Ibid.*, p. 271.

[5]  *Ibid.*, pp. 263–266.

state. It is not the product of a legislative act. Even the sanction of political authority is not necessary for its existence."[6]

Although he denied any historic role for the state in the origin of money, Menger suggested that the state might contribute significantly to the acceptability of money. "The sanction of the state," he argued, "gives a particular good the attribute of being a universal substitute in exchange, and although the state is not responsible for the existence of the money-character of the good, it is responsible for a significant improvement of its money-character."[7]

The "sanction of the state" and the "significant improvement" Menger thought possible was for the state to impress upon the money already circulating the additional property of *legal tender* so that everyone would be forced to accept it. A debtor then would be able to clear an obligation to a creditor immediately and without controversy.

Governments have always claimed that monetary systems under their direction require the legal tender provision – that legal tender somehow gilds the gold. The argument is, however, specious on two counts. First, any contract may contain in its text, along with other details, the agreeable medium for its payment. Given this condition, no case exists for a state-enforced legal tender provision. Second, since freely circulating money is already acceptable as far as private volition will take it, impressing it with the legal tender feature can only force it into exchanges where people do not need or want it.

In his section on coinage, Menger embellished his argument for state enforcement of legal tender – an argument that has been common through the ages:

The best guarantee of full weight and assured fineness of [gold and silver] coins ... can be given by the government itself, since [the government] is known to and recognized by everyone and has the power to punish crimes against the coinage. Governments have usually accepted the obligation of stamping the coins necessary for trade. But they have so often and so greatly misused their power that economizing individuals ... almost forgot the fact that a coin is nothing but a piece of precious metal of fixed fineness and weight, for which ... the honesty and rectitude of the mint constitute a guarantee. Doubts even arose as to whether money was a commodity at all. Indeed, it was finally declared to be something imaginary resting solely on human convenience.[8]

[6]   *Ibid.*, 261–262.
[7]   *Ibid.*, 262.
[8]   *Ibid.*, p. 283.

At this point, Menger signed off on the subject.[9] He apparently could not fathom why or how governments that could do so much good in promoting viable moneys ended up doing so much harm. Public choice economics that would explain this seeming contradiction would not appear until 70 years later.

I quote Menger's musings at some length because his analysis of the early progress of money as a medium of exchange from barter is so reliable, and because his presumption of the role of the state in making a good thing better reflects so well common prejudice on this subject, both in Menger's day and in the present. Money, in this naïve Mengerian world of benign governments, is an unusual artifact: When forced upon society by a legal tender law, its quality and utility improve.

Both laymen and trained professional economists unthinkingly presume that governments as functionaries of the state must configure and control any monetary system. Though money in every case came into existence through the private sector, and while experience shows that governments have routinely abused monetary systems, acceptance of state control over money seems assured by default. The momentum of the status quo is overwhelming; the possibility of spontaneous order to regulate monetary affairs appears to have been lost or forgotten.

Primitive moneys initially had no connection to the state. However, once the more rudimentary moneys had evolved into metallic coins, states became interested and, very quickly, a controlling influence. In ancient Greece, for example, the ruling state assumed for itself the prerogative of coinage. The seal stamped on coins became a trademark. Wealthy and powerful merchants whose coins were current, and who themselves could assume political office, used their power to establish coining monopolies. Minting became exclusively a state function.

State authorities realized many benefits from their coinage powers. First, coinage provided a means of exploiting the booty from military conquests and mining enterprises by facilitating expenditures. It also enhanced the state's collection of tribute and taxes, which, noted Arthur R. Burns in his work on ancient money, "the Romans for the first time made efficient." Religious authorities also coined ornaments and temple treasures in order to obtain usable currency.[10]

---

[9] Menger concluded his discussion of coinage by remarking at length on the difficulty of producing smaller denominations of coinage for common use – the problem that the Framers tried to remedy with "coin money and regulate the value thereof." *Ibid.*, pp. 283–284.

[10] Burns, Arthur Robert, *Money and Monetary Policy in Early Times*. New York: Augustus M. Kelley, 1965 (New York: Alfred A. Knopf, 1927), p. 458.

The state did not at first exploit its coinage powers by debasement. The city-state of Athens had a respectable and widely accepted coinage. However, "The Romans," noted Burns, both the republicans and emperors, "attended more to the exploitation than the perfection of coining ... They gave the world the inestimable curse of practical knowledge of all the possible methods of inflation apart from the use of paper money."[11]

In order to make coinage profitable for itself, the state extended the routine practice of stamping coins with a seal of weight and fineness to a stamp of coercive authority that forced acceptance of the coin. Burns noted that Greek coins did not reflect any direct evidence of legal tender, but Roman coins were another matter. As Burns put it:

It is beyond doubt that legal tender regulations existed in some form or other from earliest times. No unit of account could come into general use until it was legally defined, and [legal specification] would involve a statement of the means by which a debt expressed in the unit could be settled. ... The Roman state fixed the rate at which coins were to pass, and presumably at this rate they were legal tender and had to be accepted. They were at no period punch-marked ingots to be placed in the balance at the option of the payee.[12]

Burns's careful study of ancient coinage suggests an answer to Menger's innocent observation on how the state might improve the properties of coined money. No matter how it *might* do so, experience through the ages has confirmed that it will *not* do so. Once state authorities had monopoly control over the coinage – "the prerogative of coinage" – they learned very quickly how to cheapen the gold and silver coins, which they pretended to certify as to weight and fineness, by alloying them with low-cost base metals. Roman rulers, with few exceptions, debased coin currency by this means for four centuries.

Through debasement, state authorities generated *seigniorage*, which is the revenue derived from the excess monetary value of the struck coin over the resource costs of producing it. It is the "profit" earned by any government that issues money. More importantly, it is a tax on everyone who uses the government money.

Only a ruling state, through its power of legal tender, can realize seigniorage. No private person or corporation, even if permitted to produce money, could endow the money with any legal tender provision to force it on the money-using public. Competition in the private production of money would make significant seigniorage impossible.

[11]  *Ibid.*, p. 465.
[12]  *Ibid.*, pp. 378–380.

The state assumed legal tender power, as Menger's account suggests, so that it could specify weights and fineness of particular denominations of coins already exchanged voluntarily. While this simple function may have seemed harmless, it was never necessary. The state does not need a legal tender power over coinage to promote acceptance of its money; the quality of the money itself does that.

Arguing that the legal tender power is necessary to "improve" the coinage system has provided all states, past and present, with vast amounts of seigniorage. This power has also been a confiscatory policy on many occasions when states have generated inflations and hyperinflations with their issues of fiat money. Nonetheless, *legal tender* has become, and is still, an accepted prerogative of the state. It forces acceptance of the paper money that all governments issue, and provides them with significant revenues.[13]

---

[13] For example, the U.S. government has long been realizing approximately $30 billion per year in seigniorage from the money-creating activities of the Federal Reserve System. In the year 2010, however, seigniorage increased to almost $80 billion due to Federal Reserve bail-outs that included the monetization of "junk" bonds.

# THREE

## The Bimetallic Monetary System and Appearance of a National Bank

### BIMETALLISM

Precious metal moneys – gold and silver – first became prominent and widely used in medieval Europe. Silver was the base for most medieval moneys until after the Crusades when trade flourished with Byzantium and other eastern countries that used gold. Since silver was still the common money metal in Europe, the introduction of monetary gold stimulated a movement toward bimetallism.

A bimetallic standard is one in which a political authority makes two metals, usually gold and silver, legal tender. Specified quantities of both metals, coined according to prescribed standards of fineness, are then lawful moneys, and cannot be refused when proffered to liquidate debts. (A transaction can also be defined as a "debt" that is assumed and cleared immediately when the purchaser pays for the goods.) Once both metals are specified as legal tender, they necessarily have a fixed, legal mint value relative to each other – a monetary datum. Actual market ratios between the metals may differ slightly from mint values, but market arbitration keeps this disparity minimal.

To make a metallic standard operational, a legislature must follow certain principles and procedures. First, it must specify the value of the unit of account, say, the dollar, in terms of a weight of gold, and for a bimetallic system also a weight of silver. It does so by prescribing a gold coin of a convenient denomination, and likewise a silver coin. Congress defined the dollar as 24.74 grains of pure gold, and also as 371.25 grains of pure silver. The basic gold coin that Congress specified was the $10 gold Eagle, which contained 247.4 grains of gold, with an additional 10 percent base metal to make the coin durable enough for common use. The silver coin was the silver dollar, which had 371.25 grains of pure silver, plus 41.25 grains of base metal. So it was 412.5 grains total weight. These coins were legal tender in accordance with Article 1, Section 10 of the Constitution.

Once a metallic standard is in place, it becomes self-regulating provided gold and silver are allowed to flow freely in and out of the economy in response to private initiatives. Individuals, banks, and other financial institutions, business firms, foreign exchange dealers, and the world's gold and silver industries unwittingly cooperate to make the system work.

An ongoing metallic standard is a complete commodity-money system, and, therefore, has an appeal not found in other monetary arrangements. Under such a system, the demand for and supply of money react simultaneously, through market prices for all goods and services and for the monetary metals, to determine a given quantity of common money. If market prices tend to fall, say, because of greater production of goods, services, and capital, the value of the monetary metals being fixed in dollar terms rises in real terms, stimulating increases in the production and importation of precious metals and their supply to the mints. Because the monetary metals are the base for currency and bank deposits, the quantity of common money also increases, arresting the prior decline in market prices. No matter in which direction a monetary disequilibrium begins, successive approximations of goods–production and money–production generate an ongoing money-and-prices equilibrium. The system is stable. It provides an economy with a set of rules prescribing the conditions for the supply of common money. When the rules are in place, the system works on the principles of Spontaneous Order. Human design is limited to the details for the framework of the standard, and must refrain from meddling with the ultimate product – the quantities of both base and common money.

The political authority may coin the metals in accordance with the legislature's specifications of weight and fineness, or it may leave the coining to private coin smiths who follow the state's specifications. In either case, the minting enterprise buys the metal and coins it. If the mint is a government institution, as is usually the case, the treasury department that oversees the coinage operation may realize minor amounts of seigniorage for supplying the coinage.[1]

The superior monetary characteristics of both precious metals gave rise to their ubiquitous use as currency and bank reserves. Both were easily

---

[1] For a description of the minting business, see: U.S. Treasury Department, Document No. 1086, Director of the Mint, *Instructions and Regulations in Relation to the Transaction of Business at the Mints and Assay Offices of the United States, Together with the Coinage Laws*. Government Printing Office: Washington, 1888. Brassage is a nominal charge to cover the working costs of coinage.

recognizable, portable, durable, divisible, and limited in quantity. Under the bimetallic system, both metals were minted as full-bodied coins with specific monetary values that corresponded to their weights. Experience revealed, however, that their relative market values would gradually change due to the natural abundance or scarcity of each metal at different times. The "endless change in the [market] ratio of gold to silver," noted W. A. Shaw, "[necessitates] continual revision of the [mint] rate of exchange."[2] However, the social benefit of keeping both species of coin in circulation was significant, for together they provided a denominational spectrum that was essential for household and business transactions.

Governments that legalized and managed full-bodied bimetallic moneys always had a housekeeping problem to contend with. The coins in use – silver for hand-to-hand exchange and gold as a clearing medium for banks, for large purchases, and for clearing international accounts – would in time become worn and abused. Their stated denominations would become illegible, and their reduced weights would belie their full-bodied values. The managers of the coinage system, if acting responsibly, then had two options for restoring the depreciated coin. First, they could, by legislation or proclamation, call in all the depreciated coin and re-coin it, replacing the lost metal from governmental reserves. Or they could re-coin the reclaimed metal into its former nominal quantity by supplementing the lost precious metal with base metal. This action would somewhat reduce the fineness of the coins. According to Luigi Einaudi, this general scheme of coinage was the one actually practiced in Europe during medieval times.[3]

Besides wear-and-tear on the coinage, and more common, were changes in the demand and supply factors determining the coins relative market values – the problem Shaw alluded to. Neither royal prerogatives nor legislative wisdom could prevent market values from deviating from current mint prices. New discoveries of one or the other metal would have this effect. The metal that then became cheaper would tend to buy fewer goods and services. However, its mint value for being coined into money was fixed by the law that made it legal tender. Consequently, a given quantity of the now-cheaper metal would generate just as much money as it did before its market price tended to decline. More and more of it would go to the mint. The other money metal, with its now higher relative market value, would

[2]  Shaw, W. A., *The History of Currency*, second edition. New York: Augustus M. Kelley, 1967 (London: Wilsons and Milne, 1895), p. 13.
[3]  Einaudi, Luigi. "The Medieval Practice of Managed Currency." *The Lessons of Monetary Experience, Essays in Honor of Irving Fisher.* Gayer, Arthur D., ed. New York: Augustus M. Kelley, 1970, pp. 250–268 (New York: Rinehart and Co., 1937).

tend to disappear from circulation as money and be used as a commodity – to make jewelry and fill teeth.

This often observed phenomenon gave rise to the expression: "Bad money drives out good money." It is known everywhere as Gresham's Law, but it was well recognized before Sir Thomas Gresham formalized it in 1560. Reaction of gold and silver coinage systems to Gresham's Law can only occur if both metals are legal tender, and if the coins specified by the legal tender acts are full-bodied.[4]

Over the centuries, silver has been the money metal most given to cheapening owing to ever more favorable circumstances for its exploitation and production. Gold, too, has occasionally enjoyed enhancement of its monetary role because of successful discoveries that lowered its real cost. Sometimes, as well, fallible sovereigns or legislatures valued one or the other money metal too highly at the mint, thus giving rise to the same effect. In any case, the relative market value of gold to silver over the millennia has constantly risen, from perhaps 3-to-1 in ancient times, to 10-to-1 in early medieval times, to 14- and 15-to-1 in the eighteenth and nineteenth centuries, to 40-to-1 by 1900, and as much as 80-to-1 in the twentieth century.[5]

If a government managing a bimetallic system was to maintain coins of both metals in circulation when their relative *market* values changed – say, when silver became cheaper relative to gold – it had either to increase the silver content of silver coins or to reduce the gold content of gold coins. If fractional amounts of silver were now added to each coin of a given denomination, the general increase in silver production could be neutralized so that the quantity of *nominal* money remained constant. Otherwise, the greater quantity of silver would generate more silver money. If the legislature reduced the gold content of the gold coins at the mint, meaning a higher mint price, again, more money would be generated. In general, any reduction in the metallic content of the precious metal coins, that is, any *devaluation*, would have a relatively buoyant effect on the quantity of money and prices, while any increase in the coins' metallic content would be correspondingly deflationary.

A properly managed devaluation that would keep both coins in circulation should have had two features: First, it was supposed to be only a small change, just enough to offset any current market disparity between the two

---

[4] A full-bodied coin is one that has as much precious metal in it as is specified by the coinage law defining its denomination.

[5] Jastram, Roy W., *Silver the Restless Metal*. New York: John Wiley and Sons, 1981, p. 8. Currently, the ratio is around 50-to-one – $1,700 per ounce for gold, and $34 per ounce for silver.

metallic moneys. Second, it was for housekeeping purposes only. It was not supposed to provide any significant amount of seigniorage for the government, or to stimulate business activity.

Another way a political authority could avoid a Gresham's Law adjustment was to change its bimetallic system to either a gold or a silver monometallic standard, supplemented with subsidiary coin that had little or no commodity value. During the nineteenth century, the single-metal standard chosen most often was gold. Silver coins then had to be subsidiary, the value of the silver in each coin being less than the nominal money value the government stamped on it.

Under a monometallic gold standard, the subsidiary silver coins, which were also legal tender, became similar to legal tender paper money. They were redeemable in gold coin, and were limited in quantity, similar to the paper money, so that they would not promote a general increase in prices that would endanger the redeemability of gold money at its fixed mint price. A depreciated silver dollar, which contained less than 100 cents worth of silver, still rang appealingly when tossed on a counter to pay a bill. However, it was just as much a fiat money, and had the same effect on prices, as a scruffy paper dollar dropped soundlessly on the counter for a similar purpose.

Even with a change in market values of the two metals in progress and with Gresham's Law imminent, the tendency for the cheaper metal to go to the mint did not ordinarily mean that the dearer metal would entirely disappear from circulation. Market values usually change gently and incrementally. So even as the cheaper metal began to dominate the coinage, much of the dearer metal would remain in circulation because the costs of removing it from the coinage system exceeded the profits arbitrageurs could realize from their well-publicized swaps.

Indeed, as Milton Friedman noted in his book *Monetary Mischief,* a change in the gold-silver market ratio that began to trigger Gresham's Law was simply a feature of the bimetallic stabilizing strategy. Both metals were used widely for industrial and monetary purposes. So, as one metal became cheaper, the "burden" of monetization would shift to it. The other metal would experience a contrary path: a higher proportion of mined metal would go into industrial metalworking, and less – maybe none – to the mint. Since monetization added significantly to the total demand for either metal, the actual event itself tended to arrest the real decline in the value of the cheaper metal. The greater monetary use of the cheaper metal shifted its market demand outward and increased its real value. Money prices might then stop rising until one or the other metal again became cheaper. The

French experience with bimetallism during much of the nineteenth century, Friedman observed, showed how well a bimetallic system could work.[6]

The monetary system in the United States between 1792 and 1860 provided an example of a working bimetallic system, even though at times it was in partial disequilibrium. Neil Carothers noted in his classic work *Fractional Money*, that gold was undervalued at the mint until 1834, and silver afterward until 1861. During the latter time when silver was undervalued, the disparity between the mint and market ratios of silver and gold was only about one percent. Since many silver coins were worn down by more than one percent of their mint values, and since the costs of converting silver into industrial metal averaged more than one percent, most of the fractional silver coins stayed in circulation. Only when the U.S. Treasury in 1844 started re-coining the worn and defaced silver pieces into new quarters and dimes were they driven out of circulation by the adverse ratio.[7] They then became too precious to be used as currency.

Originally, the case for bimetallism was the fact that it provided full-bodied moneys in usable denominations that all classes of people, banks, and businesses desired and needed for most commercial exchanges. But it also had the advantage of not relying on one substance to provide a base medium for nominal growth of money to finance the economy's real productivity. If one metal became scarce, the other metal would take up the slack so that the common money stock could increase with the growth in real output.

Bimetallism was prominent throughout the world in the nineteenth century. The major exception was the British government, which in 1816 converted to a monometallic gold standard. With German adoption of the gold standard in 1870, the entire trading world, including the United States, experienced a domino effect toward gold. Silver became cheaper and cheaper. By the end of the century, bimetallism had virtually disappeared, although India and China were still on silver standards.[8]

## THE APPEARANCE OF A NATIONAL BANK

Another institution, *the national bank*, unheralded as such but of utmost importance to the workings of the world's monetary systems, began to

---

[6]  Friedman, Milton. *Monetary Mischief: Episodes in Monetary History.* New York: Harcourt, Brace, Jovanovich, 1992, Chapter 6, "Bimetallism Revisited," pp. 126–156. Friedman's account, however, does not treat denominational problems.

[7]  Carothers, Neil, *Fractional Money.* New York: Augustus M. Kelley, 1967 (New York: John Wiley and Sons, 1930), pp. 98–101.

[8]  Friedman, *Money Mischief,* Ch. 6, pp. 126–156.

appear at the same time that metallic standards were so prominent.[9] In the United States, this institution – labeled "The Bank of the United States" – was referred to as a "national bank." It came into existence as a privileged, government-chartered, super-commercial bank with branches that would also function as a fiscal agent for the government. It was *not* a central bank at its birth, that is, an institution that could fundamentally control the economy's stock of money. Rather, it was to be no more than a fiscal auxiliary for the U.S. Treasury. In that guise Congress approved it in 1791 as the [First] Bank of the United States.[10] Its charter was for 20 years, at which time its workings were to be reviewed for possible re-charter. If its charter was not renewed, it would lose its national label and revert to an ordinary state bank.

Alexander Hamilton, who became the first Secretary of the U.S. Treasury, was the famed promoter of the First Bank. His "Report on a National Bank," delivered to Congress in 1790, followed very closely Adam Smith's description of the Bank of England in Smith's *Wealth of Nations*.[11] Smith emphasized that the Bank of England's functions at that time were limited to its fiscal assistance to the Crown and its commercial ventures. It was not at that time a modern-day central bank; it had no statutory or implied authority to control the community's stock of money.

Nor did Hamilton recommend such an institution to Congress. Rather, he emphasized the Bank's fiscal function. The First Bank, he claimed, would "give facility to the Government in obtaining pecuniary aids," that is, loans, and it would assist in financing the various activities of the federal government, such as the sale of public lands.[12] Both Smith and Hamilton emphasized that paper money issued by the government-sanctioned banks they discussed would always be redeemable in gold and silver on demand. Their banks' paper money would only "economize" specie.

---

[9] Much of the following text on central banking is treated in greater detail in my book, *Monetary Policy in the United States, an Intellectual and Institutional History*. Chicago: University of Chicago Press, 1993. See especially pp. 4–50. The first Supreme Court case, *McCulloch v. Maryland*, which follows shortly, centers on the constitutionality of the Second Bank of the United States in relation to states' rights. Consequently, the ensuing treatment of the gold-silver standard and the Bank of the United States is a necessary background for understanding the issues raised in that case.

[10] The Bank did not have "First" in its title because no one knew that another Bank of the United States might follow. "First" has been added to distinguish this Bank from the "Second" Bank of the United States that Congress chartered in 1816.

[11] Adam Smith, *The Wealth of Nations*, ed. Edwin Cannan (New York: Random House, Modern Library Edition, 1937), pp. 651, 883–885.

[12] *Annals of Congress*, 1st Cong., 2nd sess., December 14, 1790, "Report on a National Bank," pp. 2082–2111.

The most controversial feature of the First Bank was that it would need to operate in all the states, that is, across state lines, to fulfill its defined purposes. Since it would have branches in all the states for its fiscal functions, its commercial operations would likewise occur in all the states. Furthermore, its issues of bank notes to finance its commercial loans were sanctioned by its charter to be a tender for all payments due the government.

All these characteristics raised the question of its constitutionality. James Madison, at that time a Representative from Virginia, argued that the Bank "would directly interfere with the rights of the states to prohibit as well as to establish banks, and with the circulation of [state] bank notes."[13] Since a national bank by definition would need to have branches in any state where it operated, state governments could not be allowed jurisdiction over those branches. Because branching is an important organizational means for ensuring the redeemability of note issues, the First Bank had several competitive advantages over its smaller state-chartered competitors.

The proponents of the First Bank based their case primarily on Congress's constitutional power to borrow money and to lay and collect taxes. At that time the federal government had taken over the Revolutionary War debt of the states, and a "Bank" that could absorb some of that debt to support the public credit looked like a good idea. However, by 1810 the federal government's fiscal operations had greatly reduced the national debt to the point where it was no longer an expensive uncertainty. In addition, a sizable number of state and local legislators found the First Bank's presence objectionable because of its inherent advantages over local banking enterprises. The result was that Congress denied its re-charter in 1811.

The War of 1812 required all the extra resources from the economy that wars always do. To provide the fiscal means to carry on the war, Congress duly authorized the U.S. Treasury to issue interest-bearing debt, including both longer term bonds and one-year Treasury notes. The bonds were conventional interest-bearing securities of various terms-to-maturity. The Treasury notes, however, were an interesting combination of debt and money. Most of them bore interest at 5-2/5 percent and were redeemable in one year, but they were also legal tender for all payments due to and from the government. Since they were mostly in larger denominations – very few as small as $20 and most in $100 units – their primary market was the banking system. To banks they were usable as reserves for the notes they issued, and at the same time they paid interest, a perfect combination from the banks' perspective. Their large denominations discouraged their use as

[13] *Report on a National Bank*, pp. 1895–1897.

hand-to-hand currency – even $20 at that time was more than two months wages for a common laborer. However, commercial banks that held them as reserves could increase their own note issues by multiples of the Treasury notes in their vaults.[14] Therefore, households and businesses saw only a few of the Treasury notes. The money they used for transactions was the bank notes the banks issued on the base of their acquired Treasury notes. When the reserve-base was specie – gold and silver – the effect on issues of bank notes was identical.

The Second Bank was modeled along the same lines as the First Bank, but with higher dollar values, because the recent issues of Treasury notes had triggered a war-time inflation. The bill for its creation went through Congress in 1816.

Both Secretary of the Treasury Alexander J. Dallas and his successor, William H. Crawford, supported the incorporation of another national bank. They argued that the new institution would absorb some of the existing government debt in its capital structure and be a restraining influence on the state banks. Both officials saw the state banks as the culprits for the current inflation. "To restore the national currency of gold and silver," Crawford declared, "it is essential that the quantity of bank paper in circulation should be reduced."[15]

Dallas added what should be labeled a "general theory for a national bank." "The national bank," Dallas advised, "ought not to be regarded simply as a commercial bank. It will not operate on the funds of the stockholders alone, but much more upon the funds of the nation.... In fine, it is not an institution created for the purposes of commerce and profit alone, but much more for the purpose of national policy, as an auxiliary in the exercise of some of the highest powers of the Government. Making the bank's notes legally acceptable for government dues and payments," he added, "is the means of preserving entire the sovereign authority of Congress relative to the coin and currency of the United States."[16] Dallas's declaration of governmental monetary power anticipated like remarks from some Supreme Court Justices fifty years later. Here, nonetheless, his notion of

---

[14]  I am referring here to the routine expansion of bank credit resulting in multiple amounts of notes and/or deposits that occurs in a fractional-reserve commercial banking system when the banks get new reserves, whether the new reserves are paper or specie. The banks do not deliberately or consciously "multiply" their demand obligations. Rather, they allow their reserves to decline to a fraction of their deposits. The final effect, however, is a *system* multiplication of notes and deposits.

[15]  *American State Papers: Finance*, vol. 3, p. 60. Dallas to John C. Calhoun, 24 December, 1815.

[16]  *Ibid.*, p. 59

"the sovereign authority of Congress relative to the coin and currency of the United States" is a presumption that has no reference in the Constitution for its validity.[17]

The retirement of the outstanding Treasury notes during 1816–1819 was both a necessary and sufficient condition to force the contraction of bank credit and bank-note currency. It provoked a general deflation to the point where specie payments in gold and silver could resume. The contraction policy continued through 1819 by which time the Treasury notes had for the most part been retired, and bank credit reduced to a specie-redeeming quantity.

The dramatic fall in prices and economic activity prompted a committee in the House of Representatives in March 1819 to ask Secretary of the Treasury Crawford for a report on the relationship of the Bank of the United States and other banks to the currency. Crawford responded by reviewing the inflation and the means by which resumption had been achieved. However, he overlooked – if he even knew – what had made possible the inflationary issues of bank notes. In his view, Treasury notes and commercial bank notes were of equal caliber; he did not acknowledge that the issues of the former made possible the creation of the latter.

The last section of the congressional inquiry asked Crawford to "suggest such measures as, in his opinion, may be expedient to procure a circulating medium, in place of specie, adapted to the exigencies of the country, and within the power of the Government." Crawford replied forthrightly that such a question would not be asked "if the power of Congress over the currency [were] not absolutely sovereign." He elaborated that the primary obstacle to adoption of such a system was not the lack of a sovereign right, but instability, and "lack of integrity and intelligence" of the government. Moreover, he added, the division of powers between the state and federal governments would encourage conflicts of authority. Crawford concluded his testimony by stating: "Coinage and the regulation of money have in all nations been considered one of the highest acts of sovereignty. [However], it may well be doubted whether a sovereign power over the coinage necessarily gives [the government] the right to establish a paper currency."[18]

Shortly after Congress chartered the Second Bank in April of 1816, the Bank became a litigant in a case testing its constitutionality that ended up in the Supreme Court. The decision in *McCulloch v. Maryland* was

---

[17] This issue is treated in depth in the *Legal Tender Cases* below, pp. 123–164.

[18] *ASPF,* vol. 3, pp. 498–504. The Legal Tender Cases 50 years later dealt with this explicit question. (See below, Chapters 12 and 13).

momentous, perhaps more for its assertion of "implied powers" than for what it determined about monetary institutions. However, its monetary impact has been significant, for it contributed to the legitimization of what ultimately became known as a *central bank*. Therefore, the case demands scrutiny for its monetary-institutional implications, as well as for the constitutional controversy it fostered.

# FOUR

## *McCulloch v. Maryland*, 1819

The celebrated case of *McCulloch v. Maryland* came before the Supreme Court in the winter of 1819. It was argued and decided in early March of that year. By that time, the Second Bank of the United States was an ongoing institution, and had established branches in several states, including one in Baltimore. All the branches were fiscal agents for the federal Treasury, and carried on a conventional banking business.

In 1818, the State of Maryland levied a tax on all note issues of banks not chartered by the State of Maryland. (Six other states had done similarly for banks in their states.) When the cashier of the Baltimore branch of the Second Bank, James McCulloch, refused to pay the tax to the State of Maryland, he was hauled into the Baltimore County Court, which returned a judgment against him.[1] McCulloch appealed to the high court of Maryland, but that court upheld the judgment of the lower court. The case then went to the U.S. Supreme Court, which reversed the Maryland court's decision by a vote of 7–0, declaring the Maryland tax to be unconstitutional and void.[2]

The case contained two fundamental issues: First, could a state tax an agency of the federal government that was carrying out one of the rightful

---

[1] *Oxford Companion to the Supreme Court of the United States,* (Eds. Kermit L. Hall and William M. Wiecek.) Oxford, Oxford University Press: 1992, p. 537. The tax was a small percentage tax stamp to be affixed to each note – two percent for lower denominations, and one percent for higher. Or the alien bank could pay a flat fee of $15,000 a year and not pay the stamp tax. Such a tax or fee was prohibitive to the existence of a banking enterprise. To avoid the tax, a prospective bank had to obtain a banking charter from the State of Maryland. The bank in this controversy, however, was a branch of the Bank of the United States, which already had a charter from Congress. Thus, the existence of the Bank's branch became a jurisdictional struggle between the State of Maryland and the federal government.

[2] *McCulloch v. Maryland* (1819), 17 U.S. (4 Wheaton), pp. 316–437.

functions of government? Second, and much more important, was the agency in question constitutional?

The first question virtually answers itself. If the federal agency is legitimate and acting within the category of express powers, no state can be allowed to shackle or even impede its operations by taxation or any other intervention. For example, no state could set up a toll road that would charge a fee on military forces operating within that state's boundaries. If the agency in question is not constitutional, it will cease to exist in the form that is unconstitutional, and the whole argument becomes trivial. Thus, the fundamental issue in McCulloch was the constitutionality of the Second Bank including its branches.

The right of Congress to incorporate an enterprise had been an issue ever since Alexander Hamilton proposed creation of the First Bank of the United States. Since the Treasury's principal function was fiscal, the main argument for incorporation of both Banks of the United States was on the Banks' anticipated utility in assisting the U.S. Treasury in the collection and disbursement of tax revenues. No one ever proposed that either institution would have central control over the monetary system – that either institution would be a central bank.

In fact, proponents of the First Bank, with firm lips and much head-shaking, explicitly denied this possibility. In 1811 Henry Clay, a Whig leader, introduced the idea in Congress only in order to denounce it. "It is mockery," he exclaimed in the Senate, "worse than usurpation, to establish [this institution] for a lawful object, and then extend to it other objects which are not lawful. ... You say to this organization, we cannot authorize you to discount – to emit paper – to regulate commerce, etc. No! Our book has no precedents of that kind. But then we can authorize you to collect revenue, and, while doing that, you may do whatever else you please!"[3] To Clay the very idea of a central bank implied a government owned and operated institution with powers beyond any stretch of imaginable constitutionality.

The Second Bank, as an institution, had many exclusive and unique features[4]:

Not only did the federal government grant it an exclusive charter, but the government also owned twenty percent of its capital and realized twenty percent of

---

[3]  *Annals of Congress*, 11th Cong., 3rd sess., pp. 212–213.
[4]  Catterall, Ralph C. H., *The Second Bank of the United States*. Chicago, University of Chicago Press: 1903 and 1968, Appendix I, *An Act to incorporate the subscribers to the Bank of the United State*, pp. 479–500.

its profits. The President of the United States, with the advice and consent of the Senate, appointed five of its twenty-five Directors.

Second, because the Bank was a fiscal agent of the government, it had to have the right to open branches at its discretion in any state where taxes might be collected and disbursed. Besides collecting taxes, these branches would also do a conventional banking business. Obviously, its required fiscal function made it a truly interstate, that is, national, bank, and thereby allowed it complete geographic license for its commercial operations. By way of contrast, state laws severely restricted the activities of state banks. Some states did not authorize any banks. The ones that did mostly disallowed any branch banking, especially branches from banks in neighboring states.[5]

Congress included a section in the Act promising not to charter any other national bank during the tenure of the Second Bank. This provision confirmed the Bank as a U.S. government-sponsored monopoly enterprise.

Third, the notes of the Second Bank would, perforce, circulate everywhere, since it would be operating in all the states in which the federal government collected tariffs or made disbursements. The Bank's notes were also made a tender for all payments due the federal government. So, while not *legal tender*, the Bank's notes were tender for government payments, and that made them effective tender everywhere.

Fourth, the U.S. Treasury would keep its specie and deposit balances with the Bank and its branches, thereby providing the institution with bountiful reserves and a thriving business regardless of its commercial success.

Daniel Webster, a prominent Whig, presented the U.S. government's case to the Court, arguing for the Bank's constitutionality.[6] Webster had a long-time relationship with the Bank. He was a member of the House of Representatives from New Hampshire during the Bank's formative stages after the War of 1812. Although Webster at first opposed the establishment of the Bank, and voted against final passage of the (First) Bank bill in 1816, after the Bank made loans to him he became a strong supporter both as a Representative and later as a Senator from Massachusetts.[7]

Others who spoke for the Bank were William Wirt, Attorney General of the United States, and William Pinkney, a U.S. Senator from Maryland.

---

[5]   Prohibition of banks from branching whether intrastate or interstate is not a restriction that enhances the health or the efficiency of the banking system. Nonetheless, it was a common restriction of the period.

[6]   I. Also, 17 U.S. (4 Wheat), p. 322.

[7]   Catterall, R. C. H., *Ibid.,* Chapter 1, pp. 1–21.

Pinkney had been U.S. Attorney General under James Monroe, and was renowned for his oratory and persuasive argumentation.[8] All of the spokesmen for the Bank were able lawyers and politicians. Counsels speaking against the Bank, that is, for the respondent, which was the State of Maryland, were Luther Martin, Attorney General of the State of Maryland, Joseph Hopkinson, a congressman from Pennsylvania, and William Jones, who had been president of the Bank for a short period in 1816–1817.

Chief Justice Marshall delivered the opinion of the Court on March 7, 1819. He reported that the Court had decided 7–0 in favor of the Bank's constitutionality. By the same vote, the Court also denied the State of Maryland the power to tax the operations of the Bank in any special way. State taxation of the Bank's notes that seriously interfered with the Bank's *modus operandi* could not be constitutional if the Bank itself was a legitimate agency of the federal government.

In rendering this opinion, Marshall included the gist of Webster's and Pinkney's arguments, but referred very little if at all to Luther Martin's case against the Bank. Of considerable importance in all of the arguments supporting the Bank was the brief Alexander Hamilton had made for the creation of the First Bank in 1791.

Marshall first addressed the issue of whether Congress had the power to incorporate a bank. But that question as posed is insufficient, because the institution under consideration was not just a bank; it was a special kind of bank that had unique privileges. The proper question here should have been whether Congress had the power to incorporate *this kind of bank*. Even though the emergence of the Second Bank as a central bank had not yet occurred, the institution they were sanctioning was very different from just any commercial bank. The Court, instead, ruled under the assumption that the Bank's powers and privileges began and ended with its fiscal role of assisting the Treasury.[9] It could not have envisioned the Bank as a *central bank*, if for no other reason than because no one at the time, including the Justices, knew what a central bank was.

Willy-nilly, the Court ruled that Congress did have the power to incorporate the Bank.[10] The "people," Marshall asserted, had ratified the Constitution. Since the government of "the Union" was a government of the

---

[8]  Hammond, Bray. *Banks and Politics*, p. 264. *Oxford Companion to the Supreme Court*, p. 635.

[9]  *McCulloch v. Maryland*, p. 422. In his argument Marshall stated: "[N]o particular reason can be assigned for excluding the use of *a bank*, if required for [the government's] *fiscal* operations [emphasis added]."

[10] *Ibid.*, p. 403. See also, *Oxford Companion*, p. 537.

people, "its powers are granted by them [the people] and are to be exercised directly on them for their benefit."[11]

Marshall explained that, while the power to incorporate a bank was not enumerated as one of the express powers, "There is nothing in the constitution that excludes it." He could not stop here because of the Tenth Amendment. Certainly, the power to incorporate *a bank* is one reserved to the states or to the people. Never mind that this Bank was a very special blend of "bank"; even a simple bank was not within the range of express powers. Marshall noted that the Constitution could not provide for every exigency. Its subsidiary or implied powers had "to be deduced from the nature of the objects themselves."[12]

The power to charter the Bank, Marshall continued, was valid as an incidental or implied power in furtherance of Congress's fiscal operations. But that argument, too, is insufficient, for it allows too much. The incidental or implied power must have some definition, description, and limitation. What exactly is the license for an implied power that is clearly not express?

Following the legal counsels in favor of the Bank, Marshall found the answer to this question in Article 1, Section 8, which allows Congress to make "all laws which shall be *necessary and proper* for carrying into execution the [express] powers, and all other powers vested by this constitution in the government of the United States." He asserted that the Bank was indeed both necessary and proper. "Necessary," he wrote, meant "convenient, useful, and essential." While the first two of those interpretations hardly sufficed, Marshall insisted that they "import [imply or justify] the use of 'necessary' as commonly understood and used."[13]

Marshall concluded with what is often hailed as "a ringing declaration of federal authority."[14] In his words: "Let the end be legitimate, let it be within the scope of the Constitution, and all means which are appropriate, which are plainly adapted to that end, which are not prohibited, but consist with the letter and spirit of the Constitution, are Constitutional."[15]

---

[11] *Ibid.*

[12] *Ibid.*, p. 407.

[13] *Ibid.*, Webster, in his statement as Counsel for the plaintiff, had provided synonyms "*suitable* and *fitted* to the object," and "such as are *best* and *most useful* in relation to the end proposed." My thesaurus gives only "essential," "imperative," "indispensable," "obligatory," and "required" as synonyms for "necessary." No mention is made of "convenient," "useful," or "suitable."

[14] Dunne, Gerald T., *Monetary Decisions of the Supreme Court*. New Brunswick, Rutgers University Press, 1960, 31. See, also, Hammond, *Banks and Politics*, p. 265.

[15] *McCulloch*, p. 421.

To say "*all* means which are appropriate" violates the entire spirit in which the Constitution was written and ratified. In Article 1, the words "necessary and proper" afford Congress the means not expressly granted, but necessary and proper "for carrying into execution" powers that are expressly granted. The phrase's presence there cannot be a license for extending any and all governmental powers. Otherwise, Congress's implied powers would have no limit. The Ninth and Tenth Amendments counter such an interpretation.[16]

The issue of a national bank's "necessity" does not depend on the rhetorical arguments that came before the Court. Since the Bank had already existed for 20 years as the First Bank (1791–1811) and would exist for another 20 years as the Second Bank (1816–1836), the actual experience of the monetary system and the government with the Bank tells whether the Bank was a necessary. If it were, how did the government manage without it between 1811 and 1816, and again between 1836 until 1914, when the Federal Reserve System began operations? Even if "convenient and useful" or "proper," experience surely denied its necessity as a fiscal agent to the government.

One might well ask how the Marshall Court in 1819 could have determined that the Bank was necessary when the government had had so little fiscal experience to guide it. Marshall and the Associate Justice Bushrod Washington were Federalists, sympathetic to "national" institutions and a relatively strong central government. Their vote, therefore, was logical in terms of their political beliefs.

The other five members of the Court, however, were Democrat-Republicans (Jeffersonians) of a different political persuasion. They were more concerned with states' rights. Consequently, the unanimous 7–0 decision allowing the Bank's constitutionality is somewhat puzzling. The Justices' acquiescence suggests, first, that none of the Justices had any serious objection to the Bank as it then existed: to them it was only a subordinate department that would assist the Treasury to carry out allowable fiscal functions. Perhaps they also believed it would have some utility in helping the banking system recover from the Panic of 1818. They may also have thought that future congresses would re-argue the Bank's constitutionality when its "necessity" waned. Then another court could re-try the case if circumstances warranted.

---

[16] See especially, Randy E. Barnett, *Restoring the Lost Constitution*. Princeton: Princeton University Press, 2004, Chapter 7, "Judicial Review: The Meaning of the Necessary and Proper Clause," pp. 153–190. Barnett's analysis of this phrase is definitive. See also, Herbert J. Storing, *The Complete Anti-Federalist*. Chicago, University of Chicago Press: 1981. Vol. 2, p. 390.

Finally, since the Bank would have to obtain a new charter in a few years –
by 1836 – no matter what was decided in 1819, the question of the Bank's
legitimacy would soon re-appear in congressional debates.[17]

The Bank bill had passed Congress in 1816 by votes of 80 to 71 in the
House, and 22 to 12 in the Senate after seven attempts.[18] Given this legislative history with all its attendant debate, it perhaps would not have been
prudent for the Court to negate years of legislative effort with so little evidence of any mischief on the Bank's part. To the Court in 1819, the status
quo seemed harmless and, if necessary, reversible.

The *McCulloch* decision gave the Bank license to continue unmolested
by legal roadblocks for another 10 years. During that time it thrived, carrying on its banking business with discretion and aplomb. How could it do
otherwise with all the privileges and advantages it had over rival private
institutions? Always in the background, however, was the knowledge that
its charter had a time limit, and would have to be renewed before 1836 if
the Bank were to continue operating as a national bank. For this reason
Nicholas Biddle, the Bank's controversial President, and the Bank's directors were careful neither to claim nor to do too much.

## JACKSON'S COURT ON THE BANK ISSUE

After his election as president in 1828, Andrew Jackson reopened the
issue of the Bank's constitutional legitimacy. In his inaugural address, he
remarked that, "Both the constitutionality and the expediency of the law
creating this Bank are well questioned by a large portion of our fellow citizens."[19] Jackson also claimed that the Bank had failed to provide a sound
and uniform currency, an assertion that was undeniably political pretense.
The Bank's influence over the currency was not really at question, only its
constitutionality. Moreover, its instrumentality in promoting a sound currency – its central banking role – dominated the debate, and was the primary argument for the Bank's legitimacy after 1828.

The Bank's privileged fiscal-banking position gave it entrée for carrying
out rudimentary monetary policies. If the Bank were collecting and sequestering money for the Treasury, it had to be a depository for the government's
money. If it were a Treasury depository, it had sizable amounts of deposit

---

[17] Catterall, *The Second Bank,* Ch. 1, "Establishment of the Bank," pp. 1–21, *et passim,* on the
Bank's constitutionality, and its torturous journey through Congress.

[18] *Ibid.*, pp. 20–21.

[19] Hammond, Bray, *Banks and Politics in America, from the Revolution to the Civil War.*
Princeton, N.J., Princeton University Press: 1957, p. 374.

balances and its own notes outstanding, as well as many other banks' notes flowing through it. And if it had all that money within its reach, it necessarily had many opportunities to manipulate that money in ways that could be both good and evil. Under Biddle, the ways were mostly good. Nonetheless, neither the Constitution nor Congress had delegated to the Bank the circumstantial powers it now assumed.[20] Clearly, the "necessary and proper" crutch that had supported the case for the Bank as a fiscal agent of the Treasury could not justify it as a central bank, no matter how restricted the powers and activities of such an institution would be in that era.

Congressional supporters of the Bank now based their case on Congress's undeniable right under Article 1, Section 8, "to coin money and regulate the value thereof." Their former argument on the Bank's "necessary" fiscal role to the Treasury had disappeared, probably because the national debt was almost paid off and by this time of little fiscal consequence. However, the Bank's dominant role in the banking system, suitably restrained as it had been, argued to many congressmen the desirability of keeping the institution intact.[21] The Bank was now seen as "necessary and proper" for maintaining a sound banking and monetary system. On this new ground in 1832, and again in 1834, Congress passed bills to re-charter the Bank, but President Andrew Jackson vetoed both of them.

Jackson's veto message in 1832 was a re-argument of the McCulloch decision written 13 years earlier. Whereas Marshall's words became a panegyric for federal authority, later critics have bemeaned and discredited Jackson's arguments as nothing more than the embittered prejudices of an ignorant backwoodsman who favored states' rights.

Nonetheless, Jackson's prejudices concerning purported evils to society from predatory commercial banking practices, even if exaggerated, do not affect the main issue – that is, the Second Bank's constitutionality. In fact, Jackson's veto message is relatively free of his personal animosities.[22]

One might imagine Jackson's Cabinet assembling as an "Executive Court" to decide the issue from the Executive's perspective. Roger B. Taney, Jackson's Attorney General and soon to be appointed Chief Justice of the Supreme Court (1836), is reported to have written much of the message.[23] It seems only fitting that the man who was to replace Marshall as Chief Justice

[20]  See Timberlake, *Monetary Policy*, pp. 28–46.
[21]  Catterall, *The Second Bank*, pp. 215–313.
[22]  *The Founders' Constitution*. Eds. Kurland, Philip B., and Ralph Lerner. Vol. Three. "20, Andrew Jackson, Veto Message," July 10, 1832, pp. 263–267.
[23]  See, Hall and Wiecek, eds., Oxford Companion. "Roger B. Taney," pp. 857–861. Jackson nominated Taney as Chief Justice after Marshall died.

should have been the major figure in rearguing the Bank's constitutionality. No explicit record exists of the various opinions of other Cabinet members, although at least two favored approval of the re-charter act.

The veto message that Jackson delivered to Congress contained at least ten objections to the national bank. First, it challenged the idea that the precedent of the Supreme Court's earlier decision in 1819 settled the constitutionality issue for all time, and that the very existence of the two Banks of the United States for four decades had established their legitimacy.

Jackson's message began by stating, "Mere precedent is a dangerous source of authority, and should not be regarded as deciding questions of constitutional power except where the acquiescence of the people and the States can be considered as well settled." The record of opinions in both the courts and Congress, he noted, did not support treating the matter at hand as such an exception. Various Congresses had both supported and denied the Bank's legitimacy at different times. Even more telling, executive and judicial opinions in state governments had been approximately four-to-one against the Bank.[24]

More generally, one act of Congress or one Court opinion could never answer the question of legitimacy for all time. Many conditions of the moment – depressions, bank panics, inflations, or wars, with their difficult fiscal pressures – may easily sway the most objective jurists and legislators. While the *McCulloch* decision had been unanimous, many Court opinions are almost evenly divided, as are congressional divisions, and these narrow balances of majority voting that determine critical issues of constitutionality can never be decisive. Reconsideration and review are surely primary functions of any court, particularly the Supreme Court. As Chief Justice Joseph Story put the matter in one of his *Commentaries*, "The expediency of exercising a particular power at a particular time must, indeed, depend on circumstances; but the constitutional right of exercising it must be uniform and invariable; the same today as tomorrow."[25]

Jackson's second argument, related to the first, was that no Court decision controlled the opinions of the other branches of the government:

Congress, the Executive, and the Court must each … be guided by its own opinion of the Constitution. Each public officer … swears that he will support [the Constitution] as he understands it, not as it is understood by others.…The opinion of the [Supreme Court] judges has no more authority over Congress than the opinion of Congress has over the judges, and on that point the President is independent

---

[24]  *The Founders' Constitution*, "Veto Message," p. 263.
[25]  *Ibid.* "Joseph Story, Commentaries on the Constitution, 1833," p. 268.

of both. The authority of the Court [can] have only such influence as the force of their reasoning deserves.[26]

While Jackson's veto message aired out the "necessary and proper" provision that Marshall had leaned on so heavily, it also treated the related issue of exclusivity – that is, whether either Congress or the Court had the expertise to judge unilaterally the degree of necessity or propriety of the case in question. The Court opinion, Jackson stated, had asserted that the degree of the Bank's necessity was

a question exclusively for legislative consideration.... Under the decision of the Supreme Court, it is the exclusive province of Congress and the President to decide whether the particular features of this act are necessary and proper in order to enable the Bank to perform conveniently and efficiently the public duties assigned to it as a fiscal agent, and therefore constitutional, or unnecessary and improper, and therefore unconstitutional. [27]

By shunting the ball of decision making to Congress and the Executive as the exclusive authorities to judge what is "necessary and proper," and thereby debarring the Court from judging that which it ought to have prepared itself to judge, the Court established an untenable precedent. It implied that Congress knew something that Justices did not know – perhaps that financial or banking specialists in Congress had some arcane insights that mere mortal Justices on the Bench could not fathom. It also ignored the political compulsions among congressmen that may have been important in creating the Bank. It also gave Congress some license to expand the government's powers in as yet unforeseen ways.

This claim of exclusivity was, furthermore, on its own merits both false and improper. Legislators have no more information on difficult subjects than jurists, and what they glean from private sources is also available to the Court. Indeed, the Court is there for the very purpose of analyzing and digesting such information. As a Supreme Court, it cannot defer such responsibility.[28] The danger of the precedent it wanted to establish – that is, alleging its own incompetence or inadequacy as reason not to

---

[26] *Ibid.*, "Veto Message," p. 263.

[27] *Ibid.*, p. 264.

[28] Vieira, Edwin, *Pieces of Eight, The Monetary Powers and Disabilities of the United States Constitution*. Devin-Adair Publishers: Old Greenwich, Conn., 1983, pp. 148–149. Vieira reasons tellingly, "No rule of law requires, or could rationally require, that 'we must consecrate the mere blunders of those who went before us, and stumble every time we come to the place where they have stumbled'. ... Whether a decision is consistent or inconsistent with the Constitution depends on whether it satisfies certain legal principles, not in earlier 'precedents', but only in the organic law itself."

challenge Congress – became manifest in the *Legal Tender Cases* later in the century. Moreover, if only Congress and the President could properly decide the technical complexities of monetary and fiscal policies, Jackson, as President, was there to tell them that the Second Bank was not "necessary and proper."

A related argument, the Jackson opinion stated, was that in passing the re-charter act, "the Congress of 1832 proposes to abolish [the power of deciding the necessity and propriety of the Bank] for fifteen years more." It cannot be necessary or proper, Jackson argued, "for Congress to barter away or divest themselves of any of the powers granted them by the Constitution.... They may properly use the discretion vested in them, but they may not limit the discretion of their successors." To do so, Jackson declared, is unconstitutional.[29]

The most decisive of Jackson's arguments consisted of two points. The first emphasized the shift in justification for the Bank from its fiscal function of collecting taxes to its regulation of the currency. Many congressmen now favored the Bank, Jackson observed, because it was a "necessary" means for executing Congress's express power "to coin money and regulate the value thereof." Jackson corrected this presumption. "Congress," he stated, "have established a mint to coin money and passed laws to regulate the value thereof. The money so coined, with its value so regulated, [is] the only currency known to the Constitution." Furthermore, he added – his second point – "If [Congress] have the power to regulate the currency, it was conferred to be exercised by themselves, and not to be transferred to a corporation. If the Bank be established for that purpose, with a charter unalterable without its [the Bank's] consent, Congress have parted with power for a term of years, during which the Constitution is a dead letter. It is neither necessary nor proper to transfer legislative power to such a bank, and therefore unconstitutional."[30] His veto also included other valid objections to the Bank's operations – its monopolistic status and its right to violate some of the states' fiscal powers.

Jackson's message emphasized the hybrid nature of the Second Bank. By its original chartering in 1791, the Bank was both a commercial bank and a fiscal agent of the government. At first it operated in the role designed for it, but it eventually extended its activities to those of a *central bank*, albeit one that had to function within the confines of a gold-and-silver standard. In any event, the Bank's fiscal "necessity," even if granted, could not also serve

[29] "Veto Message," p. 264.
[30] *Ibid.*, p. 265.

to establish the Bank's pragmatically acquired power to regulate the banking and monetary system.

Proponents for the Bank never acknowledged the change in its role as fiscal agent to monetary regulator, blatant though the change was. Instead, they rested their case on the phrase "regulate the value thereof." Regulation, they argued, ought to include control over bank-issued notes. Since the Bank had been discreet in its regulatory practices, its advocates could argue that the commercial banking system's conduct had become safer and more stable under the Bank's careful shepherding. Its policies, they insisted incorrectly, were no more than "what was intended by its charter, and what was specified by the Constitution." No one ever admitted that the Bank's monetary-banking powers were a circumstantial result of its privileged position, or that neither the Constitution nor the Bank's charter provided any license for such a controlling agency. For the Bank to have become genuinely constitutional as a regulator of the nation's bank-issued paper currency, Congress or state legislatures would have needed to amend the Constitution in the manner prescribed by that document. In view of the antipathy of the states to the existence of the Bank, an amendment providing for a national bank to regulate the monetary system would surely have failed, as the controversy over the National Banking System that came in during the Civil War made clear.

Jackson concluded by saying that he would have "cheerfully" supplied suggestions as to how a Bank of the United States "might be so organized as not to infringe on our own delegated powers or the reserved rights of the States." Since he had not been asked to do so, "it was obviously proper that he should confine himself to pointing out those prominent features in the act presented which in his opinion make it incompatible with the Constitution and sound policy.... The upcoming election [of 1832] will bear to the Capitol the verdict of public opinion, and bring this important question to a satisfactory result."[31]

Jackson added one more observation. "The Bank," he noted, "is professedly established as an agent of the executive branch of the Government, and its constitutionality is maintained on that ground." But, he wrote, "[The executive] had no opportunity to say that it neither needs nor wants an agent clothed with such powers and favored by such exemptions. There is nothing in its legitimate functions which makes it necessary or proper."[32]

---

[31] *Ibid.*, p. 266.
[32] *Ibid.*

History has been neither charitable nor objectively analytical in reviewing Jackson's veto message. The vitriolic denunciation it has received in light of the substantive merit of his arguments is astonishing. More puzzling is the fact that no historian, political scientist, or jurist seems to have recognized the unique feature of this entire episode: to wit, that the Bank experience served as an exemplary model of check-and-balance within the three main branches of the federal government. First came the original chartering of the two Banks of the United States after much controversy and debate, where action initiated in the *Legislative Branch* of the government became law. Second, the dynamics shifted to the *Judicial Branch* when the Bank's operations provoked a court case on the constitutional propriety of the legislature's action. The case went to the Supreme Court, and the *Judicial Branch* had the opportunity to adjudicate the question of constitutionality. To do so, the Court had to use a lever – "necessary and proper" – that had been put into the Constitution to afford Congress the means to carry out its enumerated ends.

Throughout the 1820s, the Second Bank operated as a national-commercial-central bank. However, the Jackson Administration, by rejecting its central banking role, challenged its existence as a "necessary and proper" governmental institution. It did so by presidential vetoes of acts that would have re-chartered the Bank as a quasi-governmental institution. The dynamic thereupon shifted to the *Executive Branch* of the government. The veto message became the obligatory judgment on the institution when the *Legislative Branch* could not override Jackson's vetoes, and the subsequent election in 1832 returned Jackson to the presidency.[33] All three branches of the government had the spotlight at different times, and all three debated and decided on the Bank's constitutionality. Regardless of the outcome, the whole episode from 1791 to 1836 became an excellent example – perhaps a "model" – of the check-and-balance principle in the tripartite division of powers.

The only remaining issue was the experience of the Treasury's financial operations after the Second Bank and its branches were parceled out and sold off in 1835–36. Beginning in 1833, the Treasury began depositing its fiscal balances in approved state banks. These institutions became known as "pet banks" since they were seemingly chosen because of political favoritism.

---

[33] Succeeding Congresses and presidential campaigns kept the bank issue alive. The last attempt came in 1841 under President John Tyler. After Tyler's agonized vetoes of the institution, the issue was quiescent until the Civil War period when Republicans (erstwhile Whigs) legislated a national banking system as a war measure.

No doubt they were, but that fact is largely irrelevant. Before it could become a Treasury depository bank, a pet bank had to have proven to be a viable business enterprise. At least pet banks were not endowed with special advantages to bring them into existence, even though they were undoubtedly chosen in part because of their political leanings.

But what of it? How was any government-selected bank going to be free of political compulsions? The Second Bank was itself the extreme example of a "pet bank." It had numerous legal privileges that the pet state banks, subsequently appointed by the Jackson administration, did not have and never could have had.

After ten years of controversial operation, the "pet bank" system also proved unsatisfactory. So, in 1846, Congress passed the Independent Treasury Act that had the Treasury keep all its specie and other money balances in Treasury and sub-Treasury offices, with no connection at all to commercial banks. This legislation became known as "the divorce of bank and state."[34] The Independent Treasury system operated unexceptionably until 1861, when the momentous changes provoked by Civil War legislation raised new problems and controversies for Congress, the Executive, and, eventually the Supreme Court. Nonetheless, the twenty-five year experience following Jackson's veto proved beyond question that the Second Bank was very *un*necessary, and therefore fundamentally *im*proper to the government's fiscal and monetary operations.

---

[34] Congress passed The Independent Treasury Act twice, first in 1841, and then in 1846. For an account of this institution and its operations, see, Timberlake, *Monetary Policy*, pp. 65–82.

# FIVE

# "To Coin Money and Regulate the Value Thereof ..."

The characteristics of coined money under a bimetallic system had an important bearing on the money clauses in the Constitution. Congress's power "to coin money" meant that Congress should provide the practical facility for minting coins. "Regulate the value thereof," meant that Congress would specify a weight of fine gold or fine silver as a precise quantity of dollars. "Regulate" was an unfortunate choice of words for the meaning it was supposed to convey, because its meaning in this day and age has been so seriously warped from what the Framers intended. Back then it could not have meant, by any stretch of the imagination, "determine the supply of," nor could it have been a license for Congress to issue any kind of paper money or to control the banking system by means of a discretionary central bank.

After the original specification of the metallic content and fineness of coins, "regulate" only authorized Congress to adjust very marginally the metallic content of either or both metals so that their mint values approximated their relative market values. That they both remain in circulation was the ultimate desideratum, so that all necessary denominations would be available. "To regulate the value thereof," therefore, meant no more than to *specify* and then to *adjust* marginally the precious metal content of given coins.

Congress's 6.6 percent devaluation of the gold dollar in 1834 was a good example of the legislature's proper regulatory power over the coinage. At that time, gold was undervalued at the mint, with the mint value of gold-to-silver being almost exactly 15-to-1. The Gold Coin Act of 1834, as the measure was labeled, reduced the gold content of the ten-dollar gold Eagle at the mint while leaving the minted silver dollar unchanged. It thereby raised the relative mint value of gold-to-silver to approximately 16-to-1, a 6.6 percent increase, and incidentally overvalued gold at the mint.

The estimated market ratio at the time was 15.625-to-1. So the new mint ratio was slightly more than 2 percent too high for gold to be market neutral. The important practical effect was that a given amount of gold could now be minted into 6.6 percent more dollars than before, while a given quantity of silver could now buy a somewhat larger quantity of gold in the market, and therefore was too valuable as a means for that purpose to be coined.[1] Large quantities of silver coin were still in circulation, but as long as they were somewhat worn so that they did not have their full-bodied weights, they would be cheap enough to remain in circulation.[2] To emphasize the rarity of this devaluation event: it would not happen again in the United States for 100 years.[3]

Gold devaluation in 1834 had a buoyant effect on prices and business activity. During the next few years, prices rose about 35 percent as gold flowed into the economy to balance the outflow of traded goods and services. In the first six months of 1834, gold coinage at U.S. mints was over $4,000,000, which was ten times the average amount coined between 1825 and 1834.[4]

In England this same kind of change had occurred on a number of occasions over the centuries for the same reason. S. P. Breckinridge noted in her excellent work *Legal Tender*, how the English crown from 1326 to 1527 had altered the precious metal content of both gold and silver coins to keep both species current. However, Henry VIII during his notorious reign initiated serious abuses of the content and fineness of the coins. Nonetheless, from 1603, the year of Elizabeth's death, to 1816, when silver coin officially became subsidiary, that is, not full-bodied, "the weight and denominations of gold coins were altered to secure the concurrent circulation of the coins of both metals; but no change was made by law in the character of the silver coins.... From this time the value of gold bullion changed rapidly in terms

---

[1]    For a brief account of this devaluation, see, Timberlake, *Monetary Policy,* pp. 46–47. See also, J. Huston McCulloch, "The Crime of 1834: Comment," in *Money and Banking: The American Experience,* John Robbins, ed., pp. 57–67. (Durell Foundation: George Mason University Press; Fairfax, Va., 1995.) See also, Vieira, *Pieces of Eight,* pp. 101–115.

[2]    Carothers, Neil. *Fractional Money.* New York: Augustus M. Kelley, 1967 (New York: John Wiley and Sons, 1930), pp. 88–101. Carothers's account is a fascinating documentary on the machinations and complexities of coinage valuation under a bimetallic standard. His style is tart and realistic as well as exquisitely documented.

[3]    The gold dollar had contained 24.75 grains of fine (pure) gold, with an additional 12 percent copper to give the coin durability. The devalued dollar of 1834 contained 23.22 grains of gold, with 10 percent copper. Only a few one-dollar coins were minted because they were too small to exchange expediently. Five- and ten-dollar gold pieces were minted, the former being a half-Eagle and the latter one Eagle. Silver dollars were never devalued.

[4]    Carothers, *Ibid.,* p. 93.

of silver, and although the mint ratios were frequently altered, all efforts to retain both metals in circulation failed."[5]

While the efforts ultimately "failed," the English experience emphasized that the Framers, in allowing Congress to "regulate the coinage," had nothing more in mind than the kind of marginal adjustment Congress enacted in 1834. It could not have meant more. For one thing, the clause, "coin money and regulate the value thereof," is immediately followed by the clause, "and fix the standard of weights and measures," with hardly a breath between them.

This placement indicates what the Framers were thinking when they put the coinage power under the jurisdiction of Congress. "Fix the standards of weights and measures" did not include the power to alter the linear value of a foot to eight inches or a yard to 25 inches, or somehow to change the gravitational force of a five-pound bob. It meant to "fix" for all practical purposes so that households and institutions could use these physical measures with practical certainty that they would stay constant. This same principle applied to the bimetallic coinage, but here it had to allow for minor real-life changes in the production and availability of the precious metals.

Indeed, the very act of adopting a specie standard contradicts the idea or the possibility that "regulate the value" meant anything more extensive or profound than what is argued here. A specie standard by its very nature is self-regulating, as all the Framers knew, and as all the antecedents of English law that they relied on so fundamentally implied.

The contention of the Second Bank's supporters that the Bank was constitutional in assisting Congress in its regulatory role with respect to money, therefore, was wrong on at least five counts:

(1) English and American tradition and experience with bimetallic standards;

(2) the clear meaning of "regulate" as "specify," in the context of Congress's power to fix the standard of weights and measures;

(3) the self-regulating character of the specie standard, for which hands-on control of the monetary system was a contradiction;

(4) the opportunistic switch of the Bank's supporters from arguing the Bank's "necessity" as a fiscal agent to its "necessity" as a bank-regulating agency – that is, as a de facto central bank; and

[5] Breckinridge, S. P., *Legal Tender, A Study in English and American Monetary History.* New York: Greenwood Press, 1969 (Chicago: University of Chicago Press, 1903), p. 43. (Emphasis added.). See also, Vieira, *Pieces*, pp. 39–46.

(5) the fact that the U.S. Treasury, government, and commercial banking system all continued to function soundly for the next 25 years without a national bank.

After Jackson's executive veto in 1832, the Supreme Court did not again have an opportunity either to reverse or approve the Bank's existence, or that of any such similar institution. However, the momentous changes in the monetary system resulting from Civil War legislation again provoked instances of monetary adjudication that were significant, and which became permanent. Their judicial acceptance, unfortunately, came to rest on "precedents" that the Court had established for itself in *McCulloch v. Maryland*.

# SIX

# Craig v. Missouri, 1830

Two other monetary controversies came before the Supreme Court in the decade following *McCulloch v. Maryland*. The first became known as *Craig v. Missouri* and the second as *Briscoe v. Bank of the Commonwealth of Kentucky*.

On June 27, 1821, just 2 years after the *McCulloch* decision, the legislature of the newly admitted state of Missouri passed an act for the establishment of loan offices that were to issue a total of $200,000 worth of paper notes – "certificates" – signed by the state's auditor and treasurer, and in denominations between fifty cents and ten dollars. Each county in the state was to get a share of the notes to be loaned in proportion to the population of that county. The notes in the Missouri case, similar to the U.S. Treasury notes issued during 1812–1814, would bear interest at the rate of two percent per annum, where the earlier Treasury notes bore interest of 5.25 percent per annum. The notes were to be issued for loans of less than $200 for no longer than 1 year, bearing an interest rate no greater than six percent.[1] In addition, the notes were to be "receivable at the treasury ... and by all tax gatherers ..., in payment of taxes or other moneys due ... to the state or any county or town therein; and ... also received by all officers civil and military in the state, in charge of salaries and fees of office." Finally, the Act stated that it was the duty of the auditor and treasurer "to withdraw, annually, from circulation one-tenth part of the certificates [notes issued]."[2]

The loan offices thus established were quasi-state banks and the loan certificates functioned as a lower denominational currency, such as were issued routinely by commercial banks of the time. However, Missouri

---

[1]  *Craig v. Missouri*, 4 Peters (29 U.S.) p. 410 (1830).
[2]  *Ibid.*, pp. 413–414.

had no commercial banks then, and would have only one until 1855, due to pervasive anti-bank sentiment. (The State of Arkansas was similarly deprived.)

In accordance with this new law, a consortium of three men, Hiram Craig, John Moore, and Ephraim Moore of Chariton County, Missouri, borrowed $199.99 on August 1, 1822. Their note was to run for one month beginning October 1, 1822, and be paid off with interest by November 1, 1822. However, the borrowers paid neither the principal nor any interest on the note. So, in 1823 "an action of trespass on the case" was instituted in the circuit court of Chariton County, Missouri, against Hiram Craig and others. The case was decided against Craig et al., and the court ordered the consortium to pay principal and interest totaling $237.79. In 1825 Craig et al. appealed their case to the Supreme Court of Missouri, "where the judgment of the Circuit Court was affirmed."[3] Undaunted, the trio then appealed the case to the United States Supreme Court, claiming that the Act providing them the notes was unconstitutional. The high Court considered and decided the case in January 1830.

The counsel for Craig et al. was Mr. Sheffey, a local attorney. Sheffey argued that the certificates were "bills of credit [paper money] … that they were 'emitted' by the state of Missouri, payable to no specific person, and that they were a 'tender in payment of debt.'" Although not declared *legal* tender, the notes, Sheffey stated, "[would] circulate as freely and extensively" as if they were. "The states are especially prohibited such issue by the Constitution." Therefore, the plaintiffs' promissory note to pay principal and interest, he contended, was void: "The state cannot receive [payment] upon such notes."[4]

Thomas Hart Benton, who was Missouri's newly minted United States Senator and who was to become a major ally of Andrew Jackson in Jackson's "war" against the Second Bank of the United States a few years later, argued the case for the State of Missouri. Benton noted that the act establishing the loan offices sought to relieve the "deficiency of currency in the state," a reference to the fact that the state had no banks and suffered from a dearth of small denominational notes. The certificates were not made a legal tender, he emphasized, and, "So long as no objection to receive them is imposed by the law which directs and authorizes their emission, they can injure no one." Benton added an important qualification: "All bank notes issued under state charters are equally within the constitutional prohibition, if the

---

[3]　*Ibid.*, p. 412.
[4]　*Ibid.*, pp. 416 and 423.

construction assumed by the counsel for the plaintiffs [that is, respondent Craig et al] … is correct."[5]

Benton then compared the Missouri state notes with the Treasury notes authorized by Congress during the War of 1812. "Congress," Benton recounted, "had no express authority to issue [U.S.] treasury notes, but they were issued. These notes were precisely like the Missouri certificates…. [They] were not bills of credit; for they were not made a legal tender. They were freely circulated throughout the United States without objections." Also, similar to the Act providing for U.S. Treasury notes, the Missouri Act made sufficient and certain provision for the ongoing redemption of the notes – retirement of one-tenth of the notes annually, while the U.S. Treasury notes were issued for 1 year, and paid no interest after that time. Benton's brief emphasized states' rights: If the federal government could issue such notes, as indeed it had, then the states could do the same thing, simply because the states had a higher order of rights than the federal government under the Tenth Amendment.[6]

In the January 1830 term, the Marshall Court decided the case 4–3 in favor of Craig et al. Chief Justice John Marshall, who had given the opinion supporting the Second Bank of the United States, read the opinion, with Justices William Johnson, Smith Thompson, and John McLean dissenting.

The majority opinion argued that the Constitution prohibited emissions of bills of credit or making anything except gold or silver a legal tender. The certificates, Marshall charged, "are as entirely bills of credit, as if they had been so denominated in the Act itself." The fact that they were not explicitly declared a legal tender made no difference: "Both are forbidden," Marshall emphasized, and neither prohibition – bills of credit or legal tender – depended for its judgment on the fact that the other condition was absent.[7]

Since the law that brought the notes into existence "is against the highest law of the land," Marshall concluded, "… the note [the plaintiffs owe the state] is utterly void…. The judgment of the Supreme Court of the state of Missouri … is reversed; and the cause remanded with directions to enter judgment for the defendants."[8] The substance of the decision was that Craig et al. did not have to repay their debt, and that the State of Missouri could no longer emit such notes.

---

[5]  *Ibid.*, p. 422.
[6]  *Ibid.*, p. 423.
[7]  *Ibid.*, p. 433.
[8]  *Ibid.*, p. 437.

The majority opinion, as read by Marshall, did not deign to address the important argument Benton had made – that the United States had issued Treasury notes very similar to Missouri's certificates to help finance the War of 1812–1814, and that these notes, too, bore interest, were issued for a limited time, and were legal tender only for payments to and from the government. Most of the Treasury notes, however, were in larger denominations – $100 or more, and therefore were used by banks as reserves. Only a few were as small as $20, while Missouri's certificates were between fifty cents and $10, and more suited for use as hand-to-hand currency.

How could Marshall argue that the federal government could issue such notes, but that a sovereign state could not? He was able to avoid the issue formally because no legal case had arisen over the issue of the Treasury notes. Two of the three dissenting Justices, however, explicitly referred to them.

The first of the dissenting Justices, William Johnson, re-argued the question of whether the loan certificates were bonds or bills of credit. If the certificates had been in larger denominations, he observed, say, $20 to $100, their issue would have been unobjectionable, as was in his opinion the issue and sale of the former U.S. Treasury notes. But, he continued, if during the next year the state would authorize "these certificates to be broken up into ten, five, and even one dollar bills [to facilitate the payment of taxes], [w]here would be the objection? Thus far the transaction partakes the distinctive features of a loan; and yet it cannot be denied that its adaptation to the payment of taxes does give it one characteristic of a circulating medium. ... Forcing the receipt of it upon those to whom the state had incurred the obligation to pay money" also contributed to the certificates monetary "similitude." However, they also bore an interest rate, so that they "[varied] in [dollar] value every moment of their existence," something that an ordinary bank note would not do. He concluded from his reasoning that the certificates were of an "amphibious character," with features of both bonds and an issue of money. Such a doubtful case, he concluded, should be presumed "innocent." "The judgment of the State Court should be affirmed." The U.S. Treasury notes were similarly "amphibious."[9]

Justice Smith Thompson, also dissenting, agreed with Johnson that the certificates had some properties as a circulating medium, but that they were limited in this function being unable "to answer the purpose of a circulating medium to any considerable extent." Because the certificates were issued for an interest-bearing loan that had to be repaid, they were not issued

---

[9]   *Ibid.*, pp. 437–443.

on the credit of the state but upon a "fund" that insured their ultimate redemption.

Thompson also agreed with Benton that if the certificates were "bills of credit," then "all bank notes, issued either by the states, or under their authority and permission, are bills of credit falling within the prohibition [of the constitution].... I am unable to discover any sound and substantial reason why the prohibition does not reach all such bank notes, if it extends to the certificates in question."[10]

Justice McLean presented the final dissent. He agreed that the State of Missouri issued the certificates as a currency. He, too, argued that the lower denominations in which the certificates were issued should have had no bearing on their constitutionality – that is, they were just as constitutional when issued in smaller denominations as they would have been in hundred-dollar denominations. The problem was that they appeared to be more like "money" in small denominations because in that form they could be used as hand-to-hand currency. This property, McLean argued, should not bias their acceptance. "Their circulation was not forced by statutory provision; [T]here was no promise on their face to pay at any future day; ... but a simple declaration that they will be received in payment of public dues."[11]

McLean entered an additional issue: "If the certificates under consideration were 'bills of credit,' within the meaning of the constitution, is the [promissory] note on which this suit is brought, void?" He argued forcefully over many pages that, even if the issue of the certificates was held "invalid," the debt-contract of the plaintiffs who had borrowed the money was "not void, even admitting that the certificates were bills of credit." Emission of the notes and the validity of the debt, McLean concluded, were two separate issues.[12] On this point, McLean was entirely correct. Craig et al. had used the money to command resources in some way, and having reaped they should have repaid.

McLean finished his brief by contrasting the powers of state governments with those of the federal government:

The federal government is limited in its powers, and can in no case exercise authority where the power has not been delegated. The states are sovereign, with the exception of certain powers, which have been invested in the general government, and inhibited to the states ... It would be as gross usurpation on the part of the federal

---

[10]  *Ibid.*, pp. 445–450.
[11]  *Ibid.*, p. 463.
[12]  *Ibid.*, pp. 458–463.

government, to interfere with state rights, by an exercise of powers not delegated, as it would be for a state to interpose its authority against a law of the union.[13]

The Founding Fathers themselves could not have expressed the philosophy of the Constitution more accurately.

The three dissenting Justices, arguing that no significant harm seemed likely from issues of the certificates, were willing to allow the state of Missouri the authority to issue a small amount of nonlegal tender currency that would have enhanced the efficiency of the payments system. State loan offices would have operated as quasi-banks for 10 years, and the notes would have been retired when paid as taxes into state offices. It is also possible that the law may have been repealed and the certificates phased out if commercial banks had appeared.[14] In any case, the Marshall majority, consistent with their decision in the *McCulloch* case, denied the State of Missouri the power to do what the federal government had done and would continue to do from time to time until the Civil War. They were more ready to advance the federal government's powers than they were to allow the states similarly limited powers. While *Craig* confirmed this tendency, albeit with a bare 4–3 majority, it was more pronounced 11 years earlier in the unanimously decided *McCulloch* case. The *Craig* decision suggests that the Court was not as sanguine about centralized government powers by 1830 as it had been in 1819.

## A NOTE ON BILLS OF CREDIT: WHAT THEY WERE AND ARE, AND WHAT THEY ARE NOT

The *Craig* case was the first to emphasize the term "bills of credit" and its relevance to the constitutional prohibition of state currency issues. The term became common during the Revolutionary War when many of the colonial states issued "bills of credit" to finance military expenditures, although several of them had earlier issued such bills as ordinary fiscal expedients.

The proper definition is implied by the discussion in the debates in the Philadelphia Convention of 1787 over the question of whether to prohibit bills of credit explicitly or to imply their prohibition by not making their

---

[13] *Ibid.*

[14] However, this argument is questionable in light of the severe distaste that many politicians, such as, Thomas Hart Benton, had for commercial banks and bankers. Western states of that day were notorious for their laws prohibiting banking, or making banking enterprise very difficult, and for prohibiting small denominational currencies.

issue an express power of the central government. The delegates all decried "paper money," and some, including Madison, used the word *tender,* which meant *full legal tender,* in discussing the issue. Some argued that their issue had been essential in prosecuting the war. Thus, the majority of the delegates decided not to prohibit them to the federal government, while presuming that the clause for "borrowing money" would make the issue of bills unnecessary. James Madison agreed to the motion not to prohibit bills of credit when he "became satisfied that striking out the words [to prohibit bills] would not disable the Gov't from the use of public [Treasury] notes as far as they could be safe and proper; & would only cut off the pretext for a *paper currency,* and particularly for making the bills a *tender* either for public or private debts."[15]

The experience with bills of credit issued by the states, however, moved the delegates to prohibit state issues by a specific provision. Article 1, Section 10, declares that, "No State shall … emit Bills of Credit; make any Thing but gold and silver Coin a Tender in Payment of Debts, etc.…" This explicit prohibition, together with the debate on a similar proscription to the federal government and while not explicitly denying the federal government the power to issue bills of credit, implied prohibition barring some unforeseen catastrophe.

Putting all the evidence together from the experience with state bills of credit and the debates in the Convention, *bills of credit* are government issues of paper money, declared legal tender for all debts public and private, not redeemable in anything of material value, reissuable indefinitely, and redeemable only at the discretion of the government issuing them. The colonial governments that issued bills had much difficulty repaying them, often with greatly depreciated currency. The new United States government eventually consolidated the states' obligations, including their bills of credit, and paid them off at varying rates of discount.

The case of *Craig* just discussed raised the question of whether state-issued paper currency, alleged to be "bills of credit," had to be both full legal tender and not redeemable in any real commodity. Chief Justice Marshall decreed that *either* property made the currency issued "bills of credit," but the dissenting Justices argued otherwise. They claimed that because the Missouri "bills" were not full legal tender, they could not be forced on private

---

[15] Madison, James, *The Debates in the Federal Convention of 1787 which Framed the Constitution of the United States of America,* pp. 413–414. Prometheus Books: New York, 1987.

parties by other private parties or the State of Missouri. Therefore, their redeemability into gold or silver was not an issue.

This writer agrees with the dissenters. Full legal tender – *forcing* private parties to accept them – is the one necessary and sufficient property of "bills of credit."

# SEVEN

## Briscoe v. The Bank of the Commonwealth of Kentucky, 1837

The *Briscoe* case, which emerged a few years later, was very similar to the *Craig* case. In fact, its initiation and evolution seemed clearly to be a "moral hazard" stemming from the Court decision on *Craig*.

The legislature of Kentucky passed an act establishing the Bank of the Commonwealth of Kentucky on November 20, 1820, several months prior to the Missouri act that created that state's loan offices. However, the Kentucky act created a state-owned *bank*, not loan offices, and the state legislature appointed the bank's president and directors. The bank had a capital of two million dollars, and could issue notes for loans it made up to a total of two million dollars in denominations of one dollar to $100. So its monetary capacity was precisely ten times that of Missouri's loan offices ($200,000), though the money-issuing powers of the two institutions were similar.[1] The Commonwealth Bank started operations a few months earlier than the Missouri institution.

Approximately 9 years later, on February 1, 1830, and just weeks after the Court's *Craig* decision allowed debtors of a Missouri loan office to renege on their debt to the state, a consortium of four men, George H. Briscoe, Abraham Fullerson, Mason Vannoy, and John Briscoe, signed a promissory note for $2,048.37. The note was issued by the Bank's branch at Harrodsburg, Kentucky, and was due by June 1, 1830. The Briscoe group, undoubtedly informed by the *Craig* decision, did not repay the note when due, and the Bank brought suit against them in the circuit court of Mercer County on April 15, 1831.[2] The circuit court gave judgment against the Briscoe group, just as the Missouri circuit court had done against Craig in the first airing of that dispute, and the *Briscoe* case went to the Kentucky appeals court. On

[1]  *Briscoe v. Bank of the Commonwealth of Kentucky* (1837) 36 U.S. (11 Peters) p. 257.
[2]  *Ibid.*, p. 259.

May 5, 1832, the appeals court affirmed the judgment of the circuit court, so the Briscoe group likewise took their case to the United States Supreme Court.

The Court, however, did not hear the case until January 1837, by which time the Court had three new members, including a new Chief Justice, Roger B. Taney, a close political ally of Andrew Jackson and, like Jackson, an advocate of states' rights.[3]

The case was argued by Mr. White and Mr. Southard for the appellants (Briscoe et al.) and for the state of Kentucky by a Mr. Hardin and Henry Clay, the famous Whig presidential nominee and senator, and a leading supporter of the Second Bank against Andrew Jackson's attacks to disallow its re-charter. Clay's support for the Commonwealth Bank was entirely consistent with his support of the Second Bank of the United States.

The primary argument of Briscoe's attorneys was that the notes issued were unadorned bills of credit, and therefore prohibited by the Constitution. Both attorneys cited the *Craig* decision innumerable times. They exhaustively reviewed the history of colonial bills of credit, as well as those issued during the Revolutionary War. White noted that Missouri's notes bore interest, while those of the Kentucky bank did not, but he observed that this feature made no practical difference between the two. Both were effectively "tenders" for debts owed the states, even though not *legal* tenders: "The bills of the Commonwealth's Bank were a qualified tender [sic]. If the plaintiff did not [agree to] receive them [to satisfy a debt]," White noted with some exaggeration, "his execution was stayed."[4]

Hardin, arguing for the "defendants in error" (that is, the Bank), noted that the Bank's notes were payable for taxes and land purchases. By this time (1837) almost the entire issue of notes had been returned to the state for such payments and had been destroyed, thereby proving the notes' limitation as well as their utility as a medium of exchange. Hardin repeated an important argument that the dissidents in the *Craig* case had emphasized: " ... [I]f the notes of the Bank of the Commonwealth of Kentucky are 'bills of credit,' and the issue of them was prohibited by the constitution of the United States, the notes of all state banks are equally prohibited."[5] The

---

[3] Taney was Attorney-General in Jackson's Administration from 1831–1833, and acting Secretary of the Treasury for a short time in 1833. He ordered the controversial "Removal of the Deposits" from the branches of the Second Bank of the United States after two previous Treasury Secretaries had refused to do so. The Senate then would not confirm Taney's appointment. See, Timberlake, *Monetary Policy in the United States*, Ch. 4.

[4] *Ibid.*, pp. 263–275.

[5] *Ibid.*, pp. 275–277.

implication was clear: if the Court were to declare this Bank's notes "bills of credit" and therefore illegal, it had to prohibit *all* state bank note issues on the same grounds. Such a far-reaching outcome seemed too momentous to justify solely because the notes were embryonic bills of credit. They had to be something more objectionable than that.

Henry Clay, agreeing with Hardin, presented two questions for the Court's consideration:

1st. Were the [Bank's] notes issued by the state of Kentucky?

2nd. If so issued, are they bills of credit within the meaning of the Constitution?

Contrary to Chief Justice John Marshall's argument in *Craig*, Clay claimed that "the Constitution requires both properties to be features in the note ... upon which suit was brought." The notes had to be issued by a state on the credit of the state, and they had to be declared a legal tender. Clay argued that the "issues of the bank were not those of the state." They were issues of a bank. If not constitutional, all banks incorporated by states and their note issues would be subject to the same censure, and "all state banks [would be] unconstitutional ... These are bank notes," he repeated, "redeemable and redeemed by specie, and payable on demand." [6]

The stratagem of the Bank's counsel obviously leaned heavily on the practical fact that hundreds of commercial banks already existed and furnished the bulk of the country's exchange media. However, a state-owned bank was not a commercial bank. So the Briscoe counsel had to show that this difference negated the constitutionality of the Kentucky bank's issues.

Attorney Southard for the "plaintiffs in error," – Briscoe et al. – undertook to argue this point. In his brief, Southard developed an interpretation of the constitution that reflected a fundamental dichotomy in its implications, and so is worth reviewing.

The Constitution, Southard stated, has two provisions that are connected with and that control the issue of a state bank issuing money: "The one gives power to Congress; the other restrains the power of the states." Southard cited the oft-quoted Section 8: "Congress shall have power to coin money and regulate the value thereof.... This [provision] gives power to the Union [central government]." Then, "the 10th section of the same article declares, that no state shall ... coin money; emit bills of credit; make any thing but gold and silver coin a tender in payment of debts....This [section] restrains the authority of the states." These sections, Southard continued, "grant

---

[6]    *Ibid.*, pp. 280–284.

power to one portion of our government, that of the Union; and the restrictions upon the other, that of the states.... Thus, 'Congress may coin money' ... is one power substantive and different from the rest. 'May regulate the value thereof, and of foreign coin' is another power; 'may fix the standard of weights and measures' is still another. Each may be exercised without the rest."[7] Nowhere in this section does Southard indicate what monetary powers the federal government did not have nor which powers the states did have, nor did he even mention the implications of the Tenth Amendment. The Framers, he claimed, imposed "their prohibition [on the states] in the same mode and form as they granted the correlative powers of the general government."[8] Treasury notes issued during the War of 1812, Southard claimed, were bills of credit. "The government had the authority to issue them; its necessities justified their emission.... Will it seriously be debated that they were not, therefore, bills of credit; and that if the states had issued them, [the notes] would have been constitutional?.... Hence the power of creating and regulating the currency was given to the Union, and withdrawn from the states.... The authority is fully and absolutely given to the Union, without restriction or limitation." Provision of a common currency, he emphasized, "is, indeed, a natural, inalienable, indispensable, attribute of sovereignty, in all nations."[9] He embellished his main point: "The duty of Congress is to create and to protect a common currency of the Union. The power to create, embraces the power to regulate, and the means of regulation.... Congress has the entire control of the currency, and with it, as a necessary consequence, the power to regulate the circulating medium."[10] He concluded: "I am unable to perceive a distinction between the cases, which will justify the condemnation of the Missouri paper, and the support of that of Kentucky." The former paper currency of Missouri was signed by the state auditor and treasurer, and that of Kentucky, by "persons called The Commonwealth Bank of Kentucky: a distinction without a difference. Both were agents of the state."[11] Therefore, he concluded, the *Briscoe* case should have the same judgment as the *Craig* case.

Southard's review of the Constitution's assignment of powers to the Union relative to the states does not heed the fundamental doctrine of the Tenth Amendment. His assertion that the Framers gave "absolute" money power to the "Union," and denied it to the states and that "Congress has

[7] *Ibid.*, pp. 286–287.
[8] *Ibid.*, pp. 288–289.
[9] *Ibid.*, p. 290. (Emphasis added.)
[10] *Ibid.*, p. 293. (Emphasis added.)
[11] *Ibid.*, p. 310.

the necessary power to control the currency, etc.," is the first time that such a blanket grant of power appeared in a Court opinion.[12] It is fundamentally discreditable on two counts – in addition to the fact that Southard cited no antecedent evidence to support such a sweeping claim. First, the Constitution, according to the Tenth Amendment, delegated only specific coinage powers to the "Union." Congress could "regulate" the quantities of gold and silver metal in the gold and silver coins in order to keep both gold and silver current, but its authority over the monetary system ended there. Nowhere in that document are the far-reaching powers with respect to federal control over the monetary system that Southard claimed, unless some such action was "necessary and proper" to the exercise of some other express power. Moreover, Southard's argument that the clauses concerning the coinage of money were distinct and independent is also inaccurate. The coinage clause, followed by "and to fix the value of weights and measures," allowed Congress to fix units of measurement for both coins and common physical quantities. What could be more logical than to place them together? And if so, they were written in stone, and not to be altered by the whims of Congress.

Finally, Congress could not create a national bank, such as the Second Bank of the United States, which could print bank notes, while denying the same power to the states. If the Bank of the United States was constitutional, as it was in Southard's eyes, so should have been a Commonwealth of Kentucky Bank.

The Court decision was 6–1 against Briscoe et al. Justice McLean, who had been in the minority on the *Craig* decision, read the majority opinion of the Court that seemingly reversed the *Craig* decision from 7 years earlier.

The term "bills of credit," the opinion stated, covered a wide variety of paper money issued by different colonial and state governments. The *Craig* case was the first attempt by the Court to decide what features determined a bill of credit. Given all the variations in paper money that had been issued over the previous century since colonial times, the Court had developed a definition, McLean read, that included "all classes of bills of credit emitted by the colonies or states: [It] is a paper [currency] issued by the sovereign power, containing a pledge of its faith, and designed to circulate as money."[13]

---

[12] But it would not be the last. See below, Chapters 12 and 13 on the Legal Tender Cases.

[13] *Ibid.,* p. 314. "Pledge of faith" implied that the government issuing the bills of credit would use the taxing and borrowing powers of the state, if necessary, to redeem the notes. It was more a "pledge of taxes" than a "pledge of faith." McLean should have included as a necessary feature the *legal tender* provision.

The opinion next considered the question of whether the Commonwealth Bank notes came under this rubric. Congress, within the framework of the Constitution, McLean continued, regulates the gold and silver currency, and prohibits states from emitting bills of credit. If the paper medium was intended to be made subject to this same power, and if a "state cannot do indirectly what it is prohibited from doing directly, ... then it must follow, as a necessary consequence, that all banks incorporated by a state are unconstitutional.... This doctrine strikes a fatal blow against the state banks, which have a capital of near four hundred millions of dollars, and which supply almost the entire circulating medium of the country."

The opinion thus agreed with Clay's argument: if Congress could prohibit state bank notes in the form in which they already existed because they were bills of credit, ordinary commercial banking enterprise was seriously threatened. As a general principle to the contrary, the opinion parried, a state "may grant acts of incorporation for those objects which are essential to the interests of society. This power is incidental to sovereignty, and there is no limitation in the federal Constitution on its exercise by the states, in respect to the incorporation of banks.... At the time the Constitution was adopted, the Bank of North America, and the Massachusetts Bank, and some others, were in operation. It cannot, therefore, be supposed that the notes of these banks were intended to be inhibited by the Constitution, or that they were considered as bills of credit, within the meaning of that instrument.... " [14] This argument was reasonable and incontestable.

The remaining question was whether the state-owned Commonwealth Bank of Kentucky had enough of the characteristics of a state-owned institution to taint the notes it issued as bills of credit. The majority again argued to the contrary.

A bank note that was a bill of credit "must be a paper which circulates on the credit of the state; and is so received and used in the ordinary business of life," the opinion read. The people who issue the bill must "act as agents, and of course do not incur any personal responsibility, nor impart, as individuals, any credit to the paper." The opinion admitted that the Commonwealth Bank had some of these features, which could "imply that the bank was a mere instrument of the state to issue bills.... That there is much plausibility, and some force in this argument, cannot be denied."[15]

The ordinary lending operations of the bank, however, confirmed that its notes were not issued on the credit of the state. The opinion continued:

[14]  *Ibid.*, p. 317.
[15]  *Ibid.*, p. 319.

In making loans, the bank was required to take good securities, and these constituted a fund, to which the holders of the notes could look for payment, and which could be made legally responsible. In this respect the notes of this bank were essentially different from any class of bills of credit....The notes were not only payable in gold and silver on demand, but there was a fund [reserve] ... to redeem them. This fund was in possession of the bank ... independent of the state, and was sufficient to give some degree of credit to the paper of the bank.... The notes of the bank which are still in circulation are equal in value, it is said, to specie.

The notes had not lost any real value through bank-credit management. Moreover, the bank could be sued, and a depositor who had done so had obtained "the full amount of his judgment in specie."[16]

The majority's final argument contrasted the *Briscoe* decision with the *Craig* case. McLean speaking for the Court noted that the state of Kentucky was but a stockholder in the Commonwealth Bank (albeit a 100 percent stockholder), while the state of Missouri owned the loan offices outright:

If the Bank of the Commonwealth is not the state, nor the agent of the state, if it possess no more power than is given to it in the act of incorporation, and precisely the same as if the stock were owned by private individuals, how can it be contended, that the notes of the bank can be called bills of credit, in contradistinction from the notes of other banks?... Under its charter the bank has no power to emit bills which have the impress of the sovereignty, or which contain a pledge of its faith. It is a simple corporation, acting within the sphere of its corporate powers, and can no more transcend them than any other banking corporation.... We are of the opinion that the act incorporating the Bank of the Commonwealth was a constitutional exercise of power by the state of Kentucky; and consequently, that the notes issued by the bank are not bills of credit, within the meaning of the federal constitution. The judgment of the [Kentucky] court of appeals is, therefore, affirmed, with interest and costs.[17]

This judgment meant that Briscoe et al. had to ante up the $2,048.37, plus costs that they had hoped to see forgiven. If they had won, their reward would have been approximately $500 per litigant, which was more than double an average family's annual income of that era.

Justice Joseph Story, the remaining Justice from the *Craig* decision's majority, and a close associate and ally of the late Chief Justice Marshall, presented the lone dissenting opinion. He did not, however, repeat or use Southard's argument featuring the absolute sovereignty of the Union over the creation and supply of money.

Story agreed that all bank notes are bills of credit. However, he continued, they "are not in a legal and exact sense money," but issued on the credit

16    *Ibid.*, pp. 320–321.
17    *Ibid.*, p. 327.

of the bank, which has a "capital fund or stock for their redemption." Story cited Marshall's words from the *Craig* decision. Marshall claimed that the two constitutional prohibitions – "against bills of credit *and* the enactment of tender laws, as distinct operations, are independent of each other, [and] may be separately performed. Both are forbidden. To sustain the one because it is not also the other; to say, that bills of credit may be emitted, if they be not a tender of debts, is in effect, to expunge that distinct independent prohibition, and to read the clause, as if it had been entirely omitted. We are not at liberty to do this."[18]

Story referred pointedly to the issues of Treasury notes during the War of 1812–1814, but he regarded the federal government's issues of these notes benignly. He allowed that the Kentucky bank's notes were "receivable in payments at the Treasury … in all payments of taxes and other debts to the state … and … payable and redeemable in gold and silver."[19] Nonetheless, they were issued by the state; the bank was nothing more than a façade, since the state was ultimately responsible for their payment. No persons – managers or stockholders – had any personal responsibility for their redemption.[20] He concluded his case by repeating that "these bank bills are bills of credit, within the true intent and meaning of the Constitution; that they were issued by, and in behalf of the state, upon the credit of the state, by its authorized agents, and that the issue is a violation of the constitution." Finally, he emphasized his "profound reverence and affection for [the late] Mr. Chief Justice John Marshall," with whom Story had concurred in the *Craig* decision. Marshall, he implied, would also have concluded that the Kentucky act was unconstitutional.[21]

While the notes issued by the Missouri loan offices and the Commonwealth Bank of Kentucky were similar in design, they had differences. The Missouri notes bore interest, copying the Treasury note issues of the federal government in 1812–1814. Both sets of notes were redeemable in specie, and both were tender for taxes, sales of state property, and even for some state salaries. Neither was a general tender in any sense for private parties. Since both were redeemable in specie – a fact that Court opinions only noted in passing – neither issue was harmful in the bills-of-credit sense that the Constitution condemns.

---

[18] *Ibid.*, pp. 331–333. All "bills of credit" *were* legal tender. That is what made them "bills of credit" to start with. If it was not full legal tender, it was *not* a 'bill of credit.'

[19] *Ibid.*, pp. 342–343.

[20] *Ibid.*, pp. 343–348.

[21] *Ibid.*, p. 350. Undoubtedly.

The *Craig* decision, similar to *McCulloch v. Maryland*, reflected the tendency of the Marshall Court to tolerate and even approve an approach to constitutional principles that favored the power of the national government relative to the powers of state governments. The Court was willing to allow the federal government to create a bank that it deemed "necessary and proper" for the conduct of other government functions, but would not sanction the states to create similar institutions. Surely, if a government-owned bank is unconstitutional and a threat to a stable monetary system, it is much more dangerous at the federal level than at the state level.

The question of whether the Missouri notes or the Kentucky notes were unconstitutional cannot be either affirmed or denied strictly on what the Constitution says because it does not precisely treat this issue at the state level. It prohibits only "bills of credit." In this case, both states' issues were limited in quantity, limited in tender, and constrained by redemption in specie and tax payments. Therefore, they did not fully fit the description of "bills of credit." Moreover, the notes had supplied useful small denominational currencies to the states' payments systems, and no harm resulted from their issue. Therefore, why impose a hostile ruling from on high prohibiting state institutions from doing something that worked benignly and did not plainly violate the Constitution?

# EIGHT

# Federal Government Issues of Treasury Notes and Greenbacks

## PRE-CIVIL WAR ISSUES OF TREASURY NOTES

The notes of the Second Bank of the United States had been legal tender for all payments due the federal government. After the Bank's denationalization resulting from Jackson's vetoes of its re-charter in 1832 and 1833, the federal government's shares in the Bank were sold off, and the Bank became an ordinary state bank in Philadelphia with no branches. Its bank notes thereafter had no legal tender status.[1]

The only other national paper currency of any consequence in the antebellum period was Treasury notes, issued or sold by the U.S. Treasury. On several occasions beginning with the War of 1812 and up to the beginning of the Civil War, Congress authorized such notes as short-term fiscal expedients. They covered unexpected demands on the Treasury before revenues could be raised through the conventional channels of tariffs and borrowing at term. Nominal amounts of the notes appeared in 1812–1815, 1837–1842, 1846–1847, and 1857–1861.[2]

The monetary properties of Treasury notes stemmed from the fact that they were a legal tender for any payments due to or from the federal government. The Treasury sold most of them in denominations of one-hundred dollars and higher, and only rarely in denominations below twenty dollars. All the notes very much resembled conventional bank-note currency, and when issued, that is, not *sold*, in lower denominations, were routinely exchanged in hand-to-hand transactions. Because the Treasury sold most

[1] Ralph C. H. Catterall, *The Second Bank of the United States*. Chicago: University of Chicago Press, 1902, pp. 358–375.

[2] Dunbar, Charles. *Laws of the United States Relating to Currency, Finance, and Banking from 1789 to 1896*. New York: Augustus Kelley, 1969 (Boston: Ginn and Co., 1891, revised edition, 1897), pp. 7 and 155.

of the notes in large denominations, and because most of them paid market rates of interest, some observers questioned whether they were money or "investments," that is, bonds.[3]

Their dual nature made larger-denomination Treasury notes especially attractive to commercial banks, which used the notes as reserves for extending bank credit. In this capacity the notes were not only properly "money," but also "high-powered" money, that is, note-reserves, on which the commercial banking *system* issued multiple quantities of bank notes in the lower denominations that households and businesses ordinarily used for their daily transactions. Consequently, almost all of the paper currency that the public saw was notes of commercial banks. Because no one then, and very few people even now, understand how the commercial banking system creates bank money – checkable deposits, and, in those days, bank notes – the banking system came to bear popular opprobrium for price level fluctuations. No one could see the Treasury notes doing their monetary multiplications as reserves in the banks' vaults. On one occasion, a Secretary of the Treasury actually *deposited* the Treasury notes in commercial banks that the Treasury used as depository banks, and then checked against the balances thereby created. This operation emphasized the notes' high-powered reserve feature, and raised an alarm in Congress that resulted in a fiscal about-face by the Secretary who had initiated the venture.[4]

Congress's Treasury note authorizations were usually on a year-to-year basis to help finance a temporary fiscal deficit, so the notes appeared only in limited quantities and were not reissuable. Seldom did the volume of Treasury notes outstanding exceed ten percent of the federal government's annual expenditures, which in that era were twenty-five million to fifty million dollars per year.[5]

No court cases ever tested the constitutionality of the Treasury notes because no private party ever had to accept them. Their use as bank reserves and their acceptability for taxes by the Treasury made them an acceptable medium for virtually any private transaction.

---

[3] When Treasury note denominations were small, i.e., below twenty dollars, the interest rate they paid was less than .01 percent. Since banks faced no legal reserve requirements back then, they used any asset as "reserves" that in their view could be liquidated quickly enough to provide redemption for the banks' current demand obligations.

[4] Timberlake, *Monetary Policy*, pp. 71–73. See also, S.P. Breckinridge, *Legal Tender*. Greenwood Press: New York, 1969, pp. 101–115. (Originally published, University of Chicago Press, 1903.)

[5] Timberlake, *Monetary Policy*. pp. 71–74.

## DEFINITIONS OF CIVIL WAR ISSUES OF UNITED STATES NOTES – GREENBACKS, NATIONAL BANK NOTES, AND SILVER CURRENCY

The full legal tender United States notes, commonly known as greenbacks, that Congress authorized during the Civil War were of an entirely different *genre* from the Treasury notes that preceded them during the first half of the century.[6] Congress authorized the first issue of $150 million of these notes in February 1862, another $150 million in July 1862, and an additional $100 million in January 1863.[7] This currency was known as *United States notes*, or *U.S. notes*, and popularly as *greenbacks*, because the notes' back-side was green. Occasionally, greenbacks were also called *legal tenders*, because they were fully legal tender for all debts public and private. This last feature also made them *bills of credit*, although that term was not often used except to condemn them as unconstitutional. Since the Treasury issued the new legal tender currency, some people also referred to them as "Treasury notes." But here, to avoid confusion, that term refers only to the limited tender notes that the Treasury issued before 1860.

Table 8.1 contrasts the characteristics of the earlier Treasury notes and the new greenbacks. The new notes were issued in massive quantities, were not interest-bearing, were reissuable indefinitely, and were legal tender for virtually all debt payments both private and public, including debts made before as well as after the dates on which the Acts became laws. The property of being full legal tender even for debts incurred before they were authorized was the greenbacks' most questionable and controversial feature. Their legality was bound to be challenged in the courts, and it was, first in lower courts and subsequently in the Supreme Court.

The question of how to finance the Civil War posed major problems for the governments of both the North and South, although only the North's experience has historical relevance to subsequent monetary affairs. The three time-worn methods of answering this question were: (1) tax whatever part of the national product that was taxable; (2) borrow by issuing interest-bearing fixed dollar claims (government debt) redeemable sometime in the indefinite future; and (3) print paper money in the necessary amounts to be spent by the government agencies actively engaged in the war effort.

---

[6]   National bank notes and silver certificates came into the national monetary picture some years later than the greenbacks. They both were limited legal tender paper currencies. I treat them below as they appeared.

[7]   Dunbar, *Laws Relating to Currency*, pp. 163–170.

Table 8.1 *Treasury notes, 1812–1861, and United States notes, 1862–1865*

| Treasury notes | United States notes ("Greenbacks") |
|---|---|
| (1) Legal tender only for payments of debts due government, i.e., taxes, duties, and public lands. | (1) Full legal tender for all debts public and private, except for interest on public debt and tariffs. |
| (2) Interest bearing. | (2) Noninterest bearing. |
| (3) Issued for 1 year, after which interest payments ceased. | (3) Issued for an indefinite period – in practice, forever. |
| (4) Not reissuable when received at Treasury. | (4) Reissuable when received as revenue at Treasury. |
| (5) Issued in very limited quantities – average amount outstanding in years issued was $5 to $10 million. | (5) Issued in massive quantities, $400 million by 1863, plus $50 million in other legal tender forms. |
| (6) Large denominations, most above $100, some at $20, and a few as low as $5. | (6) All denominations of $5 or greater, with a few as low as $1. |

Taxes at the time, and throughout the nineteenth century, were primarily tariffs on imported goods and services. But trade hates wars, and the revenues from tariffs were likely to decrease as any war began – the very time when a government needed quick money.

Internal taxes were another possibility. But new tax programs were slow to take effect and could not produce revenues quickly. Sales of government securities – notes, bills, and bonds of all tenures and denominations – were a natural and legitimate means, too. and for the long-run conduct of the war, bond sales raised the bulk of the necessary revenues. For quick revenue, however, nothing could match the printing of money.

When a government treasury department, or central bank in the present day, "prints"[8] money and spends it into circulation, it realizes all the proceeds from what the money buys minus the trivial cost of printing the money. Most such money-printing-and-spending programs cause inflations of various magnitudes, up to the astronomical multiples of a hyperinflation. However, even if Treasury creation of money is just enough to keep prices stable, a money-printing policy is a *tax*. The government realizes all the revenues from such money creation by spending the money for real

---

[8]  Contemporary central banks print money in the form of currency; but they also create bank reserves by buying outstanding government securities in financial markets, and creating the means for payment by crediting the sellers' accounts at the central bank. Thus, the creation of most "money" is by accounting legerdemain.

goods and services that are related to its fiscal operations. By buying these things with new money, the government bids them away from private consumers and investors. If it openly taxed the money from private households and business firms and then spent the tax money, the action would have a similar effect but would be recognized as conventional taxation. The contrast is between *issuing* newly created money to buy things and *taxing* with "old" money to do the same thing. In either case the goods and services go to the government for its purposes and are no longer available to the private sector.

The money the government realizes by money creation is called *seigniorage*. In modern times governments use paper notes or bookkeeping entries in central bank balance sheets to realize their seigniorage. However, ancient kings and emperors who did not have paper money to play with would get their seigniorage by simply calling in all coined money, melting and diluting the precious metal with base metal, and re-issuing the increased volume of coins with the same weights and denominations on their faces. Paper makes the operation simpler, easier, and cheaper, but any kind of governmental money debasement is a tax, whether it is done by mixing the precious metals with base metals, or simply printing paper with a legal tender mandate.

The stock of common money in the United States in 1860 was approximately $500 million, composed of roughly equal amounts of hand-to-hand bank-note currency and bank deposits. Even though the U.S. Treasury coined gold, silver, and fractional coin, the bulk of the currency in use was issued by commercial banks based on their reserves of precious metals. As the greenbacks began to appear, they, too, served as bank reserves as well as hand-to-hand currency.[9] Banks received the greenbacks as deposits, then routinely made loans and expanded their balance sheets in the mode of fractional reserve institutions everywhere, thereby creating multiples of bank money for every unit of newly acquired greenbacks. Prices duly began to rise in the customary fashion, including the market prices of gold and silver bullion as well as the prices of the baser metals, such as copper and nickel, used to make fractional coins. Because gold and silver were the standard metals that governed the monetary system, Congress had long ago fixed their mint prices.

---

[9]   Most of the greenback denominations were five dollars or higher. Since the fractional coins became more valuable as commodities than their fixed coinage values, when market prices rose they disappeared from circulation. Their hiatus provoked huge difficulties for making transactions. No one could "make change" for the humblest of sales. (See, Carothers, *Fractional Money*, Chapters XII–XV, pp. 151–214.)

Inflation of market prices for goods and services in the presence of fixed mint prices for gold and silver induced people to accumulate ("hoard") the precious metals in anticipation of similar increases in their prices. Foremost among the gold hoarders was the U.S. Treasury, which demanded gold from the banks in return for bank-issued currency that it acquired from tariffs, and as payment for interest-bearing securities that it sold to banks. Secretary of the Treasury Salmon P. Chase stocked this gold in the Treasury's vaults so the banks could not continue to use it as reserves. When the banks complained of difficulties in maintaining gold and silver payments, Chase roundly criticized them, never intimating that the issues of Treasury notes and his gold stock-piling policy might have caused their problem. Nonetheless, given the ongoing inflationary pressures of the government-issued greenbacks, specie payments were destined to end. That moment came on December 30, 1861, when government and banks together announced the suspension of specie payments.[10] Not until January 1, 1879, 17 years later, would paper money again be freely redeemable in gold.

---

[10]  White, Horace. *Money and Banking*, 6th edition, revised and enlarged by Charles S. Tippets, and Lewis A. Froman. New York and London: Ginn and Co. 1935, pp. 224–226.

# NINE

# The Track of the Legal Tender Bills through Congress

Wesley C. Mitchell, in his comprehensive analysis of the greenback episode, *A History of the Greenbacks* (1903),[1] examined critically the initiation of the legal tender bills in Congress, including the arguments that accompanied their passage. Mitchell drew much of his account from Elbridge G. Spaulding's *History of the Legal Tender Paper Money Issued during the Great Rebellion*, published in 1869.[2] Spaulding, a Representative from Buffalo, New York, was the principal architect of all three Legal Tender Acts, a position he fell into largely by chance.

A new national bank was a favorite idea of many Whig-Republicans who were now a commanding majority in Congress. Such an institution was a close relation to the Banks of the United States that had appeared in the early part of the century. But now, with the outbreak of hostilities, the Whig-Republicans, who had a penchant for a strong federalist government, had become a working majority in Congress. All the Southerners, who were mostly Democrats, had gone home. So the Whig-Republicans could promote a national banking system with much confidence that it would become a reality.

The first legal tender bill came into existence as a provision in the first national bank bill in late 1861, just as the Treasury's fiscal necessities became serious. Treasury Secretary Salmon P. Chase had suggested, in his *Annual Report to Congress* that year, the desirability of a government-sponsored currency. Chase deplored state bank notes – the common currency at the time – for being of questionable constitutionality, and for representing

---

[1] Mitchell, Wesley Claire, *A History of the Greenbacks*. Chicago: University of Chicago Press, 1903.

[2] Spaulding, Elbridge G. *History of the Legal Tender Paper Money Issued During the Great Rebellion being a Loan without Interest and a National Currency*. Westport, Conn.: Greenwood Press, 1971 (Buffalo. N.Y.: Express Printing Co., 1869).

"loans without interest from the people to the banks." He suggested that the "advantages of this loan be transferred ... from the banks, representing only the stockholders, to the Government representing the aggregate interests of the whole people."[3] With these remarks, Chase implied the centralized track that government monetary policy would take.

Elbridge Spaulding was chairman of the Ways and Means Sub-Committee on Banking in the House of Representatives, and by virtue of this office was preparing a national bank bill. He repeated Chase's pejorative remarks about commercial bank notes as an introduction to the bank bill he was sponsoring. His bill intended to collect all the state-chartered banks into a national system for issuing national bank notes. It also provided for a Treasury issue of United States notes redeemable in coin on demand that the federal government would monitor, regulate, and control through the Treasury Department. His bill also anticipated the nationalization of note issue through a provision that would tax state bank notes out of existence.[4]

While working on his bank bill, Spaulding wrote Chase a letter asking him to suggest measures to support it, as it would also include provision for issues of "Treasury notes" – that is, greenbacks.[5] Chase agreed, and requested in turn that Spaulding make up the note bill for him. Upon reflection, Spaulding concluded that a bank bill would take too long to get through Congress to be of much help in meeting immediate government payments. He thereupon "drafted a legal tender Treasury note [that is, a greenback] section to the bank bill, hoping ... that [these notes] might be made available ... while the bank bill was put into operation."[6]

Upon still further and more "mature" reflection, Spaulding calculated that a comprehensive bank bill would also take too long. The state banks had recently suspended specie payments owing largely to the Treasury's fiscal mismanagement and prior suspension of gold payments (although Spaulding did not refer to this fact). Consequently, he "changed the legal tender section, intended originally to accompany the bank bill, and on his own motion introduced it into the House by unanimous consent on the 30th of December 1861." The Committee on Ways and Means almost rejected

---

[3] Spaulding, *History*, pp. 8–9. Many people had this view. It ignores the role that competition plays in creating consumer surplus in contrast to the seigniorage the government gets through its banking monopoly profits.

[4] *Ibid.*, pp. 9–10.

[5] When government officials first talked or wrote about the new currency that would eventually appear, they still used the older term, "Treasury notes."

[6] *Ibid.*, pp. 11–12.

the bill outright, but one congressman on the committee who opposed the bill voted for it just so it could go before the full House for debate.[7]

Spaulding became the bill's principal advocate in the House. His all-important argument for it was its "*necessity.*" "The bill before us," he declared, "is a war measure of *necessity*, and not of choice." Yet, on the next page and in the same speech, he stated, "We have the alternative [that is, the choice] either to go into the [securities] market and sell our bonds for what they will command, or to pass this bill, or to find some better mode to raise means to carry on the war." [8]

When bankers subsequently met with House and Senate committees, they recommended two alternatives to the issue of legal tender paper money – "vigorous taxation and selling [government] bonds at their market value." Spaulding replied that "selling bonds below par was more objectionable than issuing paper money.... Thus," commented Mitchell, "the argument for the legal tender bill was shifted from the ground of necessity to that of expediency."[9]

The subsequent debates in the House and Senate reflected congressional opposition to selling government securities below the par value – that is, below the stated value of the security with its nominal rate of interest, say, a $1,000 bond for 20 years at 5-2/5 percent. If the Treasury then marketed the security, but could sell it for only $900 – that is, at a discount from its par value – it meant that investors wanted 6 percent, not 5-2/5 percent. This disposition to try to flout the democratic "law of the market" has appeared throughout fiscal history. The U.S. Congress of 1862 simply repeated this ages-old practice.

In spite of their anti-bank and anti-market prejudices, many congressmen were decidedly uncomfortable with the clear-cut unconstitutionality of the legal tender measure. To counter this objection, Spaulding and other supporters of the bill continued to declare its "necessity." Spaulding also argued that "the degree of a [law's] necessity is a question of legislative discretion, not of judicial cognizance."[10] Congress, he claimed, could properly judge the necessity of a bill; the judiciary was not up to the task.

Congress's constitutional power "to borrow money" also entered the debate. Congress does indeed have the express power to "borrow money, on the credit of the United States [government]," meaning that it has the fiscal

---

[7]  *Ibid.*, p. 14.
[8]  *Ibid.*, pp. 29–31.
[9]  Mitchell, *Greenbacks*, p. 49.
[10]  *Ibid.*, p. 35.

authority to authorize the selling of government debt for money that will then be used to buy goods and services used by government agencies for legitimate government functions. Senators John Sherman and J. M. Howard argued that this express power to borrow money implied the power to make the U.S. notes legal tender. But Senator Collamer of Vermont countered that notion. "Where there is an express power to do a thing [borrow money or tax money]," he corrected, "there can be no implied power to do the same thing."[11] In short, the government's express power to borrow precluded any assumed implied power to avoid borrowing by creating legal tender paper money. If Congress was to authorize the issue of paper money, it had to be done because the action was both "necessary" and "proper."

Congressional opponents of the bill seemed to win all the debates. They denied its expediency, its constitutionality, and its morality. Yet, the bill's sponsors prevailed by means of an argument that trumped all reasoned debate. "This argument," Mitchell reported, "was the plea of absolute necessity" that Spaulding had initiated when he introduced the bill in the House.[12] With its fiscal "necessity" giving it excuse in the minds of many legislators, the bill worked its way through Congress by a process of reluctant acceptance. The House Ways and Means Committee was evenly divided on it, but allowed it to go out of the Committee to the full House because of one otherwise negative vote (noted above). The full House, however, treated the bill as if the Committee had recommended it.[13]

Secretary Chase did everything he could to promote the bill and move it through Congress. As the House and Senate debated and almost stalled on the bill, Spaulding's Ways and Means Committee asked Chase "to communicate ... his opinion as to the propriety and necessity of [the bill's] immediate passage by Congress." Chase replied that it was impossible at that time (late January 1862) "to procure sufficient coin for disbursements; and it has therefore become indispensably necessary that we should resort to United States notes." Since some people might not accept the notes if they were a tender only for government dues, he argued, everyone should be forced to accept them to prevent "discrimination."[14] His letter concluded: "The legal tender clause is a necessity ... and I support it earnestly."[15] Of course, if the

---

[11] Spaulding, *History,* p. 104; Mitchell, *Greenbacks,* p. 54.

[12] Mitchell, *Greenbacks,* p. 61.

[13] Barrett, Don C. "The Supposed Necessity of Legal Tender Paper Money," *Quarterly Journal of Economics (QJE),* 16, May 1902, p. 326.

[14] Spaulding, *History,* pp. 45–46.

[15] I., p. 50. Also see, Simon Newcomb, *Examination of Our Financial Policy during the Southern Rebellion.* New York: Greenwood Press, 1969. (New York: D. Appleton Co., 1865, p. 161.)

notes were made full legal tender, the Treasury would not need to disburse any "coin." By this time, some of the old style limited legal tender "Treasury notes," issued in July 1861, were in circulation, and they suffered no lack of acceptance.

Chase was ill-fitted for the Treasury post.[16] His anti-bank prejudices were patent. When influential bankers recommended that he use the banks as governmental depositories and leave the specie in the banking system when the banks made loans to the government, he adamantly refused. Spaulding and many other congressmen also objected to using the banks as a means to economize Treasury operations – not that it would have ultimately prevented inflation and suspension of specie payments.[17]

Even at this early stage of the war, people could deposit demand notes, which were a form of interest-bearing currency similar to earlier Treasury notes, in Treasury and sub-treasury offices for five percent Certificates of Deposit (CDs). Unfortunately, the rate of interest the government paid on the CDs was at the discretion of the Secretary of the Treasury. When he observed the popularity of the CDs, Chase promptly reduced the rate to four percent and "attempted, unsuccessfully, to force holders of loanable funds to convert to 5–20 bonds," which the Treasury could redeem in 5 years, and had to redeem in 20 years. But the investing public did not want such bonds; it wanted CDs. If Chase had encouraged the CD option, according to Barrett, the Treasury might have floated loans that returned the government "more than the entire amount of legal tender notes authorized by the three legal tender acts."[18]

All the prominent economists – Don Barrett, Wesley Mitchell, and Simon Newcomb – who commented on the Legal Tender Act at various times agreed that its full legal tender provision was completely unnecessary. For one thing, the alternative of taxation had not even been tried, in spite of the sentiment that the public was "ready" to be taxed. Additionally, the 6 percent bonds that the Treasury was marketing remained nearly at par as late as the summer of 1862, 6 months after the oratorical hyperbole in Congress. In fact, Congress debated the greenback bill for six weeks after it

---

[16] Barrett, *QJE*, p. 333. According to Barrett, Chase was one of Lincoln's chief rivals for the presidency, and was appointed to the cabinet in the interests of preserving party unity. He was "spurred on by his own notion that the administration in general would fare better in his hands than in the President's." In 1868 he coveted the *Democratic* nomination for President, even though Lincoln appointed him Chief Justice of the Supreme Court in 1864. All accounts agree that Chase's ambitions had no upper limit, just as his fiscal competence had no lower bounds. More on his tenure as Chief Justice follows.

[17] Barrett, *QJE*, p. 347.

[18] *Ibid.*, pp. 330–332.

was alleged to be a "pressing necessity," but only a few greenbacks appeared before May 1862.[19]

Many congressmen tried to wash their hands of the legal tender taint by righteously promising their colleagues and themselves that the bill was a temporary expedient: they would allow legal tender paper only for the duration of the war, after which they would repeal the law. Spaulding was one such. The provision was clearly constitutional as a war measure, he wrote after the war in 1868 to Hugh McCulloch, who had become Secretary of the Treasury. "I am equally clear that as a peace measure it is unconstitutional. No one would now think of passing a Legal Tender Act making the promises of the Government ... a legal tender in payment of 'all debts public and private.' Such a law could not be sustained for one moment."[20] Well might Spaulding say so after the fact, but just how was the act to be undone when the "necessity" was past? How was the post-war Congress going to ensure that the monetary system would be rid of legal tender paper and return to a gold (or bi-metallic) standard? No provision in anticipation of this event was discussed.

Opponents of the bill proposed, first, the issue of Treasury notes of former times – receivable for government dues, but not legal tender for private debts; and, second, sales of 6 percent 20-year bonds, but at rates not less than par. Minor variations of these proposals were also discussed. In spite of these alternatives, the bill passed the House by a vote of 93 to 59, or by a 61 percent majority. In the Senate the bill passed by about the same margin, and was signed into law by President Lincoln on February 25, 1862. The "bill authorized the issue of $150,000,000 in United States notes in denominations not less than five dollars.... The notes were declared to be 'a lawful money and a legal tender payment of all debts, public and private ... except duties on imports and interest on the public debt,' which were expressly made payable in coin." The bill also authorized $500,000,000 of 6 percent 20-year bonds, for which the notes were exchangeable.[21]

Hardly had the Legal Tender Act become law when demands upon the Treasury prompted Secretary Chase to request another legal tender bill. The new bill appeared in the summer of 1862, with Congressman Spaulding again serving as its primary spokesman.

The debates featured many of the same arguments that had appeared during discussion of the first bill. Three arguments were common: first, the

[19]  *Ibid.*, pp. 349–353; Mitchell, *Greenbacks*, p. 73; Newcomb, *Financial Policy*, p. 161.
[20]  Spaulding, *History*, Appendix, pp. 24–25, and pp. 202–203.
[21]  Mitchell, *Greenbacks,* pp. 78–80.

"necessity" argument; second, that issuing legal tender paper money was "better" than selling government securities below the arbitrary "par" that the Treasury Secretary and lawmakers assumed was proper; and third, that many congressmen and Secretary Chase found much satisfaction in making commercial bankers whipping boys for all monetary problems. Their specific prejudice was that government issues of irredeemable paper money were preferable to bank issues of irredeemable paper money. They delighted in blaming the banks for the suspension of specie payments. The banks, of course, were completely innocent of such a charge; they could not create their own reserves. The government was doing that by issues of greenbacks that the banks had to use as reserves, and on which the banks routinely extended credit and issued bank notes.

The second legal tender bill came to a vote in the House on June 24, 1862. It passed there by a 61 percent majority, and by a similar majority in the Senate.[22]

Both Legal Tender Acts catered to the prejudices of lawmakers of the times not to allow banks or the Treasury to issue small denomination currency. Neither bill permitted the issue of any notes of a lower denomination than five dollars, which was about the weekly wage of a good worker of the time. Metallic market values of almost all coins had appreciated beyond their nominal stamped values, so the coins had become more valuable as commodity metals and disappeared from circulation. While banks had issued small denomination notes in the past, many states had been hostile to the practice and had passed laws forbidding it. The new Legal Tender Acts provided for the issue of only $35 million of one-dollar notes. In terms of money prices of the times, a minimum denominational value of $1 for the medium of exchange meant that millions of small transactions could not take place with paper currency, but would require inefficient substitutes, barter, and, inevitably, the use of illegal currencies.[23]

The shortage of official fractional money – coins and notes worth less than $1 – prompted the immediate passage of another act. To deal with the shortage, Chase reported to the House Ways and Means Committee what he regarded as the only options: recoining all the existing fractional coins into higher valued coins – an impossible logistical operation, or issuing postage stamps as currency. The latter option was the one he favored,

[22]  *Ibid.*, p. 98.
[23]  Carothers, *Fractional Money*, pp. 150–155.

and Congress passed the ludicrous act to issue this ghastly currency on July 17, 1862.[24]

The results of this act were both bizarre and counterproductive. The stamps still had the mucilage on them, anticipating their one-time use as postage. So their substance was flimsy and sticky, just the opposite of what good coin should be. Neil Carothers aptly described this episode. The country, he wrote,

> … found itself, in the midst of a war boom, virtually without a currency between the 1 cent piece and the $5 note. It is not possible to visualize all the disorder and demoralization in business and social life such a situation entails.… Among the less obvious and visible results in 1862 was a heavy decline in the volume of retail trade, especially in the case of business establishments that sold for cash, such as groceries, confection-eries, saloons, barber shops, street car and bus services, and ferries.[25]

In today's world, an equivalent situation would be the complete absence of a currency denomination smaller than $40, and prohibition of all digital money. No one would believe that such a law could be passed, much less accept a "reason" for it.

The last *Legal Tender Act* came into existence in 1863. In his *Report* for 1862 (December), Secretary Chase argued against further authorizations of greenbacks, and suggested that the Treasury market bonds to obtain the necessary revenues. He now had a captive depository for the additional securities – the new national banks. The recently authorized national banks were required to purchase United States bonds both as part of their capital and as security for their note issues. With national banks required to buy bonds, the government would be able to borrow from the market on better terms. Once again, a war was an excuse for a national bank, only this time it was used to justify a system of national banks.

*National bank notes* issued by national banks were legal tender for all payments due the government, so they became another prominent currency. Like the pre-Civil War Treasury notes, national bank notes were only a limited tender, but were accepted everywhere. The total quantity was originally limited by the National Bank Act to $300 million. (More on these notes in the following section.)

Meanwhile, payments to the armed forces had fallen in arrears. Consequently, after much sparring among Chase, the House Committee

[24] Mitchell, *Greenbacks*, pp. 98–99.
[25] Carothers, *Fractional Money*, p. 160.

on Ways and Means, and the Senate Finance Committee, expediency again became the order of the day. Thaddeus Stevens, Chairman of the House Committee on Ways and Means, introduced a "Joint Resolution to provide for the immediate payment of the Army and Navy of the United States." This bill authorized $50,000,000 additional greenbacks. The amount was soon amended to $100,000,000, and the measure passed without any discussion. The next day the Senate "acted upon it with similar expedition, and President Lincoln signed it on the 17th [of January 1863]."[26]

This Resolution, however, was not the last of the legal tender measures; still more financial resources were needed to carry on the war. The House was already preparing to raise another $900,000,000. Congress debated the third Legal Tender Bill for three weeks. As finally passed on March 3, 1863, the Act provided for an additional issue of $150,000,000 U.S. notes, but this amount included the $100,000,000 previously authorized by the Resolution. Therefore, the total amount of greenbacks authorized and put into circulation by the three acts was $450,000,000. Also included in the last bill was an authorization for $400,000,000 of 3-year Treasury notes bearing not more than 6 percent interest. These notes were similar to the pre-war Treasury note issues that were legal tender only for payments to the government. The remainder of the total authorization – $50,000,000 – was to consist of 6 percent, ten-forty bonds issued on the best terms available, that is, at market prices. Unlike previous measures that prohibited the sale of bonds below their statutory values, this act allowed the newly issued securities, as well as all the previous authorizations of U.S. bonds, to be sold at market prices. Its passage signaled a victory for market forces over government edicts.[27]

The remaining years of the war required many more resources than the initial activities of 1862–1863, but did not give rise to further issues of greenbacks. Government expenditures rose from $470,000,000 in 1862 to $719,000,000 in 1863, to $865,000,000 in 1864 to $1,297,000,000 in 1865. The first $1,189,000,000 of war expenditures, therefore, necessitated $450,000,000 of legal tender greenbacks, but the remaining expenditures of $2,162,000,000 required no additional legal tenders.[28] These data confirm that the supposed "necessity" for legal tender notes was nothing more than crisis hyperbole. If greenbacks were unnecessary during the last 3 years of the war, neither were they necessary in the war's first years.

---

[26] Mitchell, *Greenbacks*, p. 109.
[27] *Ibid.*, p. 118.
[28] *Ibid.*, pp. 119–120.

To impress the President with his own necessity, Secretary Chase offered his resignation to Lincoln in mid-1864. But Lincoln accepted the resignation much to Chase's discomfiture, and appointed Senator Fessenden of Maine to the post. Fessenden did a creditable job, but he also resigned after Lincoln was re-elected. Lincoln then appointed Hugh McCulloch, who had been president of the State Bank of Indiana, as Treasury Secretary. McCulloch was an able banker who understood fiscal affairs and markets far better than Chase. Once the war ended, he "set himself to reducing government finances to more manageable shape." He proposed a plan to retire the $3,000,000,000 national debt to zero in 32 years. His first priority, however, was to reduce the outstanding volume of the greenbacks as "a preliminary to resuming specie payments at an early date." He noted in his *Report of the Secretary of the Treasury to Congress, 1865,* that the legal tender notes "ought not to remain in force one day longer than shall be necessary to enable the people to prepare for a return to the constitutional currency."[29]

A three billion dollar government debt, with $450 million in greenbacks serving as the monetary base of the payments system, was almost incomprehensible to the general public. Prior to 1861, no one in his most deranged moments considered a government paper currency as a defensible alternative to gold and silver, especially if the paper was irredeemable. Yet here it was, and it worked after a fashion, even though everyone knew that government paper money could not become a *standard*. No matter how many greenbacks stayed in the monetary system, specie payments of gold and silver had somehow to be resumed.

[29]  *Ibid.*, p. 127.

# TEN

## *Bronson v. Rodes,* 1868

The Legal Tender Acts had legitimized government-issued, fiat paper money for all debts, public and private. They did not, however, address the "gold clauses" in already-existing contracts or prevent their use in new contracts. Gold clauses required debtors to pay the gold-standard equivalent of the value of the debt when it became due. Gold value for the debt was an approximate means for retaining the real value of the debt. It was a quasi-price index adjustment for inflated currency values, using the price of gold as the price index.

Ordinary transactions or short-term debts, private or public, were payable in the new greenbacks, with no allowance for the greenbacks' depreciation – that is, for the general rise in prices. However, many debts were contracted before the Legal Tender Acts appeared, and one issue that had to be decided was whether the debts in those contracts could be paid off with depreciated greenbacks. Though the Court was not yet ready to consider this question, it brought up and decided a less difficult case. This one was a contract for a debt between private parties that *explicitly* called for payment of the debt and interest by a sum of money equivalent to the gold value of the money-dollars in the contract. This case, *Bronson v. Rodes,* came to the Court in 1868.

The venue was New York. Rodes, a borrower, incurred a mortgage debt of $1,400 from Bronson in 1857, "payable in gold and silver coin," or, presumably, its equivalent in ordinary bank notes. Annual interest on the debt was seven percent, also payable in either gold or silver coin. Until 1865, payments on the debt were satisfactory. Then, the text of the case reports:

In January, 1865, ... Rodes tendered to [Bronson] United States notes [greenbacks] to the amount of fifteen hundred and seven dollars, a sum nominally equal to the principal and interest due upon the bond and mortgage. These notes had been declared, by the acts [in 1862 and 1863] under which they were issued, to be lawful money and a legal tender in payment of debts, public and private, except duties on imports, and interest on the public debt. At the time of the tender by Rodes to Bronson, one dollar in gold coin was equivalent in market value to two dollars and a quarter in United States notes. The tender was refused; whereupon Rodes deposited the United States notes in the Merchants' Bank [of New York] to the credit of Bronson, and filed his bill in equity, praying that the mortgaged premises might be relieved from the lien of the mortgage, and that Bronson might be compelled to execute and deliver to him an acknowledgment of the full satisfaction and discharge of the mortgage debt.[1]

Although the bill was at first dismissed by the state court, "on appeal to the state supreme court in general term, the decree of dismissal was reversed, and a decree was entered, adjudging that the mortgage had been satisfied. and directing Bronson to satisfy the same of record." After the lower court's decree was affirmed by the state Court of Appeals, Bronson brought the case to the U.S. Supreme Court.[2]

The Supreme Court's opinion, read by Chief Justice Chase, began by noting: "It is not pretended that any real payment and satisfaction of an obligation to pay fifteen hundred and seven coined dollars can be made by the tender of paper money worth in the market only six hundred and seventy coined dollars. The question is does the law compel the acceptance of such a tender for such a debt?"[3]

The opinion reviewed the circumstances under which the debt had been contracted:

The currency of the country, at that time [1857], consisted mainly of the circulating notes of state banks, convertible, under the laws of the states, into coin on demand. This convertibility, though far from perfect, together with the acts of Congress which required the use of coin for all receipts and disbursements of the national government, insured the presence of some coin in the general circulation; but the business of the people was transacted almost entirely through the medium of bank notes. The state banks had recently emerged from a condition of great depreciation and discredit, the effects of which were still widely felt, and the recurrence of a like condition was not unreasonably apprehended by many. This apprehension was, in fact, realized by the general suspension of coin payments, which took place in 1857.[4]

The opinion correctly described the monetary situation: banks did not always redeem their notes on demand, but their continuing existence depended upon their ability ordinarily to do so. Likewise, the federal

---

[1]   *Bronson v. Rodes,* 74, U.S. 7 Wall, 1868, p. 229.

[2]   *Ibid.,* p. 245.

[3]   *Ibid.,* p. 246.

[4]   *Ibid.*

government operated with an "independent treasury" system, and all government payments had to be in specie or its equivalent. In 1857, a credit stringency with some bank failures occurred in New York City. To insure against bank note depreciation, Bronson's contract included the gold clause now at issue. As the opinion stated the case:

> It is not to be doubted, then, that it was to guard against the possibility of loss to [Bronson's] estate, through an attempt to force the acceptance of a fluctuating and perhaps irredeemable currency in payment, that the express stipulation for payment in gold and silver coin was put into the bond. There was no necessity in law for such a stipulation, for at that time [1857] no money, except of gold or silver, had been made a legal tender. The bond without any stipulation to that effect would have been legally payable only in coin. The terms of the contract must have been selected, therefore, to fix definitely the contract between the parties, and to guard against any possible claim that payment, in the ordinary currency, ought to be accepted. The intent of the parties is, therefore, clear. Whatever might be the forms or the fluctuations of the note currency, this contract was not to be affected by them. It was to be paid, at all events, in coined lawful money.[5]

The opinion then reviewed the succession of statutes that regulated the weight, purity, and fineness of the coinage. It cited in exhausting detail the laws establishing gold and silver coinage, and the alloys of metals to establish .900 fineness in the coins. It noted that the gold dollar had been devalued in 1837, but that the technology of minting coins had resulted in a coinage system for gold and silver that made them a nearly perfect means for expressing values between debtors and creditors. Some regulations concerning the tender of fractional coins of less weight and purity for small loans had been made, but otherwise "no other provision than that made in 1837, making coined money a legal tender in all payments, now exists upon the statute books." Moreover, the opinion postulated, the precious metals, gold and silver, are valuable commodities, "and being such, and being in other respects best adapted to the purpose, are the only proper measures of value; [and] these values are determined by weight and purity; and that form and impress [of the coins] are simply certificates of value, worthy of absolute reliance only because of the known integrity and good faith of the government which gives them."[6]

The Justices regarded the propositions just stated as incontestable. If they were so in fact, the opinion declared, the inquiry concerning the legal meaning of the phrase "dollars payable in gold and silver coin, lawful money of the United States" could be answered without difficulty:

5   *Ibid.*, p. 247.
6   *Ibid.*, p. 249.

We cannot suppose that it was intended by the provisions of the currency acts to enforce satisfaction of [the] contract by the tender of depreciated currency of any description equivalent only in nominal amount to the real value of the bullion or of the coined dollars. Our conclusion, therefore, upon this part of the case is that the bond under consideration was in legal import precisely what it was in the understanding of the parties, a valid obligation to be satisfied by a tender of actual payment according to its terms, and not by an offer of mere nominal payment. Its intent was that the debtor should deliver to the creditor a certain weight of gold and silver of a certain fineness, ascertainable by count of coins made legal tender by statute, and this intent was lawful.[7]

The opinion referred briefly to the "partial demonetization [that is, the suspension of specie payments] to which the gold and silver money was reduced by the introduction into circulation of the United States notes and national bank currency," but thought it "unnecessary to pursue this branch of the discussion further. Nor do we think it necessary now to examine the question whether the clauses of the currency acts, making the United States notes a legal tender, are warranted by the Constitution."[8] That momentous argument would come later.

The opinion went another step to discuss the question of whether, "upon the further assumption that engagements to pay coined dollars may be regarded as ordinary contracts to pay money rather than as contracts to deliver certain weights of standard gold, it can be maintained that a contract to pay coined money may be satisfied by a tender of United States notes." That is, could paper dollars pay off contracts that had been circumscribed with a gold clause just because the contract also called for the payment of "money"?

The opinion noted that gold and silver coinage at the mints had continued uninterrupted, and in the last year had amounted to over $19 million. Nor had "those provisions of law which make these coins a legal tender in all payments been repealed or modified." Therefore, the opinion stated: "There were two descriptions of money in use at the time the tender under consideration was made, both authorized by law, and both made legal tender in payments." Although both moneys were legally "dollars," they were

... essentially unlike in nature. The coined dollar was, as we have said, a piece of gold or silver of a prescribed degree of purity, weighing a prescribed number of grains. The note dollar was a promise to pay a coined dollar; but it was not a promise to pay on demand nor at any fixed time, nor was it in fact convertible into a coined dollar. It was impossible in the nature of things that these two dollars should

---

[7]   *Ibid.*, p. 250.
[8]   *Ibid.*, p. 251.

be the actual equivalents of each other, nor was there anything in the currency acts purporting to make them such. How far they were, at that time, from being actual equivalents [in value] has been already stated [i.e., 100:225]. Both descriptions of money had been issued by the same government, and contracts to pay in either were equally sanctioned by law.[9]

The several statutes relating to money and legal tender, the opinion argued, make coined dollars and note dollars legal tender in all payments. "Coined dollars are now worth more than note dollars; but it is not impossible that note dollars, actually convertible into coin at the chief commercial centers, receivable everywhere, for all public dues, and made, moreover, a legal tender, everywhere, for all debts, may become, at some points, worth more than coined dollars." If this situation developed, the Justices asked, "What reason can be assigned now for saying that a contract to pay coined dollars must be satisfied by the tender of an equal number of note dollars, which will not be equally valid then, for saying that a contract to pay note dollars must be satisfied by the tender of an equal number of coined dollars?" Then, the opinion offered the only reasonable conclusion possible, one that covers all contracts and reflects their ultimate reason for existence: "It is not easy to see how difficulties of this sort can be avoided, except by the admission that the tender must be according to the terms of the contract."[10]

The opinion noted that the Legal Tender Acts themselves provided for some payments in coin – duties on imports and interest on the public debt. These payments required contracts of one sort or another for their fulfillment. The very fact that the Acts allowed for such exceptions meant that contractual agreements were still paramount before the law. Depositors of gold bullion at the mints, the opinion continued, likewise have a contract with the government, yet are paid in greenbacks according to the paper money value of what will be coined money. "Can judicial sanction," the opinion asked rhetorically, "be given to the proposition that the government may discharge its obligation to the depositors of bullion by tendering them a number of note dollars equal to the number of gold or silver dollars which it has contracted by law to pay? ... It seems to us clear beyond controversy ... that express contracts to pay coined dollars can only be satisfied by the payment of coined dollars." Unaccountably, however, the Justices added an *obiter dictum* that was not only gratuitous but opened

---

[9] *Ibid.*, p. 252.

[10] *Ibid.*, (Emphasis added.) This opinion thus implied that the medium for payment was whatever was agreeable at the time the contract was *signed*, an issue that became very important in the Legal Tender cases a few years later.

the door to a re-argument that could have contradicted the logical opinion just rendered. This contract, and others with similar wording, they stated categorically, "are not *'debts'* which may be satisfied by the tender of United States notes."[11]

What was the majority thinking? Virtually every contract, including those entered into by the U.S. Mint, had a debtor as well as a creditor, so had to include a "debt." The only conclusion possible is that the majority wanted to allow this contract to stand as intended, payable in coin according to its original terms, but did not want to address the larger question of what its response would have been if the contract had not included the words "payable in gold and silver." Most contracts did not include these words, but instead took it for granted that "dollars" meant the kind of dollars current at the origin of the contract. Surely the Justices knew that this question was going to come up for adjudication, and wished to set the stage for future cases without prejudicing the current opinion.

The opinion concluded: "It results that the decree of the Court of Appeals of New York must be *Reversed and the cause remanded to that court.*"[12] The decision of the lower courts, therefore, was overruled.

Two justices wrote concurring opinions, and one wrote a dissenting opinion. All were Lincoln appointees, that is, Republicans. The two concurring opinions, by Justices Swayne and Davis, agreed with the majority, but insisted that their approval said nothing to the question of the constitutionality of the legal tender acts.[13]

Justice Samuel Miller alone fully dissented from the majority opinion. He admitted that gold and silver were the lawful money of the Constitution, but "the special reference to them in the contract … gave no effect to that contract beyond what the law gave." The "law" he referred to was the Legal Tender law. Given that law, Miller argued:

This contract … did not differ in its legal obligation from any other contract payable in dollars. Much weight is attached in the opinion to the special intent of the parties in using the words gold and silver coin, but … that intent … is only what the law would have implied if those words had not been used. I cannot see their importance in distinguishing this contract from others which omit these words. Certainly every man who at that day received a note payable in dollars, expected and had a right to expect to be paid 'in gold and silver coin, lawful money of the United States,' if he chose to demand it. There was therefore no difference in the intention of the parties

---

[11]  *Ibid.*, pp. 254–255. (Emphasis in original.)
[12]  *Ibid.*, p. 255. (Emphasis in original.)
[13]  *Ibid.*

to such a contract, and an ordinary contract for the payment of money, so far as the right of the payee to exact coin is concerned.

Miller's reasoning was perfectly sound. What this particular contract stated explicitly, other contracts implied. However, for him the Legal Tender Acts trumped the Law of Contracts; and *all* private contracts, no mater how written, were in effect rewritten by the Legal Tender Acts. "If I am asked why these words were used in this case," Miller said, "I answer, that they were used out of abundant caution by someone not familiar with the want of power in the states to make legal tender laws.... As I have no doubt that it was intended by those [Legal Tender] acts to make the notes of the United States to which they applied a legal tender for all private debts then due, or which might become due on contracts then in existence, without regard to the intent of the parties on that point, I must dissent from the judgment of the Court, and from the opinion on which it is founded."[14]

Miller's dissent is an unqualified affirmation for the constitutionality of the Legal Tender Acts. It left no doubt as to what his opinion would be when the Legal Tender Acts were formally adjudicated. It was the confirmation of the power of consolidated government to do whatever it wished, regardless of the Constitution – perhaps not "regardless of the Constitution," but rather in distortion of some phrase in it, which would alter the Constitution's original meaning to fit some current political preference.

[14] *Ibid.*, p. 258.

# ELEVEN

## *Veazie Bank v. Fenno,* 1869

The end of the Civil War and the corresponding enhancement of federal powers were bound to witness conflicts over the provisions of war-time laws that would have to be resolved in the courts. *Veazie Bank v. Fenno* [75 U.S. (8 Wall.) 533, 1869] was one such case.

By the war's end, the national banking system had gained a substantial foothold in the banking industry.[1] However, state-chartered banking in most states was simpler and more profitable than banking under a national charter. State banks issued their own bank note currency as they had been doing since the Revolution, and were subject to state laws and regulatory requirements. National banks under the new law were required to buy and hold U.S. government securities both as collateral for their issues of national bank notes and as a percentage of their capital structure. They were also subject to statutory reserve requirements and other regulations administered by the Office of the Comptroller of the Currency. These restrictions were much more onerous than those for many state banks. While larger banks in the major population centers may have had some reason to become national, banks in towns and small cities had little incentive to do so.[2] Many banks

---

[1]  The National Banking System differed from the two Banks of the United States that had appeared in the first part of the century. The earlier Federal Banks enjoyed significant federal connections. Each was a privileged monopoly, had many state branches, issued bank notes from every branch, and had all the machinery in place to become a central bank. National Banks after the Civil War lacked these unique privileges. Consequently, they could not create base money, which was still gold, silver, and, at this time, greenbacks. However, non-national state banks on their own initiative did come to use national bank notes as reserves. (On this issue, see, George Selgin and Lawrence White, "National Bank Notes as a Quasi-High-Powered Money." *Money and Banking: The American Experience,* George Mason University Press: Fairfax, Virginia, 1994, pp. 169–200.)

[2]  For an excellent discussion of national banking, see, A. Barton Hepburn, *A History of Coinage and Currency in the United States,* Macmillan: New York, 1903, 1915, and 1924, pp. 306–341.

had established themselves as sound, productive, and profitable. They had no incentive to become "national."

Most quarters believed that national bank notes would gradually supplant the greenbacks as the latter were retired after the war ended. However, national banking was not at all popular with the cheap money "Greenback Movement" that was gestating. This movement coalesced into the Greenback Party in 1867. Its advertised mission was to counteract the ongoing Republican policy of greenback retirement. The new Greenback Party, Hepburn wrote, "favored the substitution of legal tender notes for bank-notes, and in fact the national system suffered a precarious existence for the next ten years, with strong probabilities of its abandonment."[3]

To enhance the prospects for the national banking system, Congress, in 1865, passed an amendment to the National Bank Act in the form of a revenue law that imposed a 10 percent tax upon state bank notes paid out by any bank, state or national, no matter which bank had issued them. In 1866, the tax was extended to state bank notes used in payment by anyone at all. By this measure, the ruling majorities in Congress hoped to end all issues of state bank notes, and thereby force the remaining state banks to become national banks.[4]

Although the measure occurred as a revenue bill, the tax that Congress imposed was a *prohibitory* tax as opposed to a *revenue* tax. No state bank could conceivably make loans at an interest rate high enough to recover the costs of a 10 percent tax on its outstanding notes, so the tax effectively prevented state banks from issuing any notes at all. State banks would be compelled to become national banks, and thereby to enlarge the market for the huge stock of outstanding government debt issued during the war, or to find some new means for extending credit, or just go out of business altogether. After August 1867, state banks stopped all issues of their bank notes, thus confirming the prohibitory nature of the tax.

Some state banks now became national banks, but others discovered the second option cited. Instead of becoming national, they perfected another payment mechanism – demand deposits, or "checkbook banking," that had seen only very limited use until this time. Rather than paying out their own notes as substance for the loans they made, state banks began to issue check books to borrowers with deposits of dollars accounted in them, which the banks would redeem on demand in whatever reserves of "lawful money"

---

[3] Hepburn, *History of Coinage and Currency*, p. 313. Hepburn's comment reflects the political force that had emerged to counteract the policy of greenback retirement.

[4] *Ibid.*, pp. 310–311.

they had. At this time, only greenbacks were circulating, and they were the common lawful money. But, presumably, the gradual extension of national bank note issues and growth in the economy would ultimately witness the retirement of the greenbacks and the return of specie payments.

When the 10 percent tax on state bank notes passed Congress in 1866, deposit banking was in its infancy; it was not yet a viable means of providing bank credit to borrowers. Knowing only note issues as a means of extending credit to customers, state banks were very much opposed to such a restrictive tax and were prepared to contest the new law. Shortly thereafter, not surprisingly, the case of *Veazie Bank v. Fenno* challenged the constitutionality of the tax.

The Veazie Bank was a commercial bank chartered by the State of Maine, with authority to issue state bank notes for circulation. The notes on which the 10 percent tax was levied were issued in 1867. Veazie declined to pay the tax, alleging that it was unconstitutional. The collector of internal revenue, a man named Fenno, proceeded to make Veazie's refusal a court case, so Veazie paid the tax under protest. When the collector did not agree to the protest, Veazie brought suit against the collector, Fenno, claiming that the Ninth section of the Act of Congress of July 13, 1866, was not a valid and constitutional law.[5] The case came before the Supreme Court in 1869, and was decided in December of that year.

Two propositions were argued on the question of the constitutionality of the tax. First was the question of whether the tax was a direct tax. If it were, then it would have to be apportioned among the states "agreeably to the Constitution," that is, "on the basis of population." The second issue was whether the tax impaired a franchise granted by the state: whether Congress had power, under the Tenth Amendment, to pass any law with that intent or effect. The implication was that the constitutional authority to charter commercial banks belonged to the states, and could not be abridged by the federal government.[6]

The Court at this time had only eight members. Three of the Justices, Samuel Nelson, Nathan Clifford, and Robert Grier, had been appointed by past Democratic Presidents before the Civil War. The other five, including the Chief Justice, Salmon P. Chase, were Lincoln appointees. Despite being a Lincoln appointee, Chase's political stance was ambiguous; sometimes, he seemed to be a Republican and sometimes a Democrat. Stephen Field, who had been Chief Justice of the California Supreme Court, was

[5]  *Veazie Bank vs. Fenno* [75 U.S. (8 Wall.) 1869]. Preview, p. 535.
[6]  *Ibid.*, p. 540.

a Democrat, as well as a most controversial political figure. On balance, however, the Court's eight members were evenly split: four Democrats and four Republicans.

The majority decision, approved by a vote of 6–2 and read by Chief Justice Chase, was agreed to by three Republican and three Democratic Justices. It affirmed the power of Congress to tax state bank notes at any rate, prohibitory or not. It based its decision, first, on Congress's power to tax. Most of the argument treated the nature of the tax, that is, whether it was or was not a "direct tax." If the tax had been a direct tax, its incidence would have had to be "apportioned among the several states, according to their respective numbers." The decision concluded that it was not a direct tax and need not be so apportioned. The majority's second argument had nothing to do with taxation. It declared that the federal government had "undisputed constitutional power to provide a currency for the whole country ... by appropriate legislation, and to that end may restrain, by suitable enactments, the circulation of any notes not issued under its own authority."[7]

While the definition of a direct tax has never been agreeably settled, the proposed tax on state bank notes surely was not one such. It was more in the nature of a prohibitory sales tax on the issue of bank notes. The opinion reviewed the government's policy of taxing both national and state bank note circulations during the war, first at 2 percent of the value of the notes issued, and later at 1 percent. Banks also bore a tax of 2 percent on their capital.

No one denied Congress's right to levy taxes to generate revenue during the war. However, a more fundamental question, which the majority opinion did not treat, was whether the Constitution provided for a tax policy to be used for causes other than the collection of revenue. Obtaining revenue for the government was one thing; preventing an operation of a banking or business enterprise in pursuit of Congress's "undisputed constitutional power to provide a currency for the whole country" was something else. The majority opinion did not treat this issue with argument, but presumed it *a priori*.

Justice Samuel Nelson, who had been appointed by President James Polk in 1846, read the dissent, Justice David Davis[8] concurring.

---

[7]  *Ibid.*, p. 554. Here again was the sweeping presumption of Congress's monetary powers stated by Attorney Southard in the *Briscoe* decision.

[8]  David Davis was appointed by Lincoln in 1862. He was a personal friend of Lincoln, and had been Lincoln's "indefatigable" campaign manager. Hall, Kermit L. (ed.), *Oxford Companion to the Supreme Court of the United States*, "David Davis" by Gregory Levh, pp. 218–219.

Nelson began his case by noting that the power to incorporate and regulate commercial banks was a power belonging to the states not to the federal government. It had not been given to the federal government, and it had not been denied the states. True, the incorporation of the Banks of the United States had affirmed that the federal government also had that power, as the *McCulloch* decision had affirmed. Nelson, however, did not mention Jackson's denial of this power to the federal government, and his veto of the bill to recharter the Second Bank. Rather, he based his argument on the Tenth Amendment. This particular tax on the banks, Nelson emphasized, "… cannot be upheld as a tax upon property; neither could it have been so intended. It is simply a mode by which the powers or the facilities of the states to incorporate banks are subjected to taxation, and which, if maintainable, may annihilate these powers."[9]

Nelson agreed that the real property of the banks – buildings, land, and equipment, like all other property – was taxable. Such a tax on banks was "consistent with the power of the states to create the banks, and … is the only subject of taxation, by this government, to which these institutions are liable." Just as the Court had denied the power of the states to tax U.S. government securities, so should the Court deny the federal government the power to implement a tax that threatened the existence of the state banks. The powers reserved to the states, Nelson continued, "… are as supreme as before they entered into the Union.… The bonds of the federal Government have been held to be exempt from state taxation. Why? Because they were issued under the power in the Constitution to borrow money, and the tax would be a tax upon this power [and] the power to borrow might be destroyed." U.S. notes, Nelson added, were exempt from state taxation for the same reason. "[But] we learn from the [majority] opinion of the Court in this case that notes of the national banks are to be regarded as … issued indirectly by the government, and it follows, of course, from this [assumption] that the [national] banks used as instruments to issue and put into circulation these notes are also exempt [from taxation]. We are not complaining of this. Our purpose is to show how important it is to the proper protection of the reserved rights of the states, that these powers and prerogatives should be exempt from federal taxation and how fatal to [the state banks'] existence if permitted." To tax state bank notes, Nelson added, is a "tax upon the powers and faculties of the states to create these banks," and therefore unconstitutional. "Indeed," he said, "the purpose is scarcely concealed, … namely, to encourage the national banks.… The burden of

9   *Veazie Bank v. Fenno*, p. 555.

the tax … has proved fatal to [the state banks], and this consequence was intended."[10]

Nelson made an important argument here. However, he could have elaborated the tax's impropriety. After noting that "the consequence was intended," he might have asked why Congress did not simply pass a law decreeing that state banks could no longer issue any bank notes at all, unless they rechartered themselves as national banks. Obviously, the federal government, no matter how presumptuous of its own authority, was unwilling to exercise so blatant a disregard for states' rights. Nonetheless, since both the intent and the effect of the tax were just what such a law would have furthered, the dissent could have put the case in this light. It would have emphasized more forcefully the important distinction between Congress's power to tax in order to raise revenue and the possible unconstitutionality of the taxing power employed to do other things, such as inhibit state-sponsored enterprises.

Nelson's dissent made it clear that using the taxing power as a means to regulate enterprise set a dangerous precedent. "No person can fail to see," he warned, "that the principle involved affects the [states'] power to create any other description of corporations, such as railroads, turnpikes, manufacturing companies, and others." He concluded with a fundamental observation concerning the sovereignty of the states that in itself should have voided the majority opinion. "The taxation of the powers and faculties of the state governments, which are essential to their sovereignty and to the efficient and independent management and administration of their internal affairs," he stated, "is, for the first time, advanced as an attribute of federal authority. It finds no support or countenance in the early history of the government or in the opinions of the illustrious statesmen who founded it. These statesmen scrupulously abstained from any encroachment upon the reserved rights of the states, and within these limits sustained and supported them as sovereign states."[11] One or another of the majority Justices in this case should have attempted to answer Nelson's compelling argument, but none did.

Neither Nelson nor the majority opinion referred to the parallel case in 1818 when the State of Maryland levied a tax on the Baltimore branch of the Second Bank of the United States. Chief Justice John Marshall, famously observed in this case – *McCulloch v. Maryland* (decided in 1819, see above, Chapter 4) – that "The power to tax is the power to destroy." The Court denied Maryland the right to destroy a federally sponsored bank that

---

[10] *Ibid.*, pp. 555–557.
[11] *Ibid.*, p. 557 (Emphasis added).

issued notes. *Veazie v. Fenno* put the shoe on the other foot. Now it was a question of the federal government destroying state banks of issue. Surely, the Framers of the Constitution did not sanction taxes as a means of controlling enterprise, either for the states or the federal government. Taxes for revenue? Yes, as a necessity for the functioning of government. Taxes to prohibit legitimate enterprise at the state level in order to foster the same enterprise at the federal level, or vice versa? No, not if the Constitution of the United States was to govern institutions in the light of what the Framers intended.

The Court should have struck down the Ninth Section of the National Bank Act. Congress should not have had this means to destroy state banks or compel their mutation into national banks. The war was over, the national debt was stabilized, greenbacks were being retired, and national banking could have been encouraged by other means, such as less restrictions and regulations, which for both state and national banks were onerous, uneconomic, and harmful.[12]

According to a majority of Justices, however, the Ninth Section of the Act of Congress of the 13th of July, 1866, under which the tax on state bank notes was levied, was a "valid and constitutional law." Thus, the first step was taken in what would be the post-war vitiation of the Framers' Constitution. The decision was a critical element in the transition of states' powers to the federal government, and the legal tender decisions that followed completed what the *Veazie* decision had begun.

---

[12] For a summary list of bank regulations and restrictions, see, J. Huston McCulloch, "Bank Regulation and Deposit Insurance," *Journal of Business*, Jan. 1986, No. 59, pp. 79–85.

# TWELVE

## *Hepburn v. Griswold,* 1870: The Legal Tender Issue

Government expenditures declined precipitously after the Civil War, while tax revenues fell only gradually. With surplus fiscal balances, Treasury Secretary McCulloch was able to begin a policy of greenback retirement. When greenbacks came into the Treasury as fiscal revenues, he instructed the Comptroller of the Currency simply to destroy them instead of allowing them to be spent back into circulation. In December 1865, Congress supported his policy with a resounding resolution. "Contraction," as it was labeled, was supposed to undo the greenback expansion that occurred during the war by reversing the fiscal policy that created it.

By April 1866, four months later, Congress was having second thoughts on the matter. Taxing money out of the economy turned out to be much more painful than spending it into the economy. Reflecting popular pressure from its constituencies, Congress subjected McCulloch's "immediate and persistent contraction of the currency" to an intensive reappraisal "on account of those who had incurred pecuniary obligations in the expanded currency."[1] It then passed the "Contraction Act," which limited greenback retirement to $10 million in the succeeding six months, and to $4 million per month thereafter.[2] At this rate, the outstanding stock of greenbacks would have declined by $48 million per year after the initial withdrawal, and would have been completely retired in about 8 years. In the event, all types of government currency – greenbacks, demand notes, and Treasury

---

[1] Blaine, James M. *Twenty Years of Congress.* Norwich, Conn., Henry Bill Publishing Co., 1886, p. 320.

[2] Dunbar, Charles. *Laws of the United States Relating to Currency, Finance, and Banking from 1789 to 1896.* New York: Augustus Kelley, 1969 (Boston: Ginn and Co., 1891, revised ed., 1897), p. 200.

notes bearing interest – declined by $252 million during the next 3 years, 1865–1868, or by approximately 39 percent.[3]

Contraction even at this new rate was harsher medicine than the public would endure. Reflecting this sentiment, Congress, in February 1868, suspended altogether any further retirement of the greenbacks.[4] Outstanding greenbacks at the time of the freeze were $356 million.

Once Congress froze the total stock of greenbacks, they looked like a permanent fixture, which meant that any legal questions concerning greenbacks would not go away but would have to be resolved in the courts. The freeze also implied that resumption of gold payments for greenbacks at the pre-war parity was indefinitely postponed. Congressmen who had voted for the Legal Tender Acts were now retired, dead, defeated, or had changed their minds for "practical" reasons. From now on, the Treasury Department would manage the greenbacks, and the economy would live with them.

While the continued existence of the greenbacks as a government-issued paper currency seemed decided, the constitutionality of their full legal tender status was not. This question was already under scrutiny in state courts. In his book, *The Greenback Era,* Irwin Unger noted that the question of constitutionality came before state courts some sixteen times between 1863 and 1870. The decisions of these courts reflected a pronounced political bias: of the seventy state court justices who ruled on the cases, all but one Republican judge upheld the legal tender clause as constitutional, while all save two Democratic judges pronounced it unconstitutional.[5] If such decisions seem anomalous in view of the later Democratic penchant for easy money, it is because traditional Democratic monetary thinking still had the Jacksonian momentum of hard money running through it. Republican judges, on the other hand, not only had a national bank principle in their heritage, but also tended to support the Republican administration's wartime monetary policies.

Andrew Johnson, Lincoln's successor, had retained Hugh McCulloch as Secretary of the Treasury, but in 1869 the newly elected Ulysses S. Grant appointed George Boutwell to the post. Boutwell was a former Governor of Massachusetts and a prominent congressman who had also served as Director of Internal Revenue in the Treasury during the war. Whereas McCulloch had favored continuous retirement of the greenbacks and

---

[3]  Department of Commerce, *Historical Statistics of the United States*, pp. 648–649.

[4]  Dunbar, *Laws*, p. 201.

[5]  Unger, Irwin, *The Greenback Era*. Princeton: Princeton University Press, 1964, p. 175.

an early resumption of specie payments, both Boutwell and Grant were pragmatists, who supported a policy of "growing up to the money stock."[6] This idea had gained considerable favor. It called for maintaining the outstanding stock of government currency, primarily greenbacks and national bank notes (and later silver), approximately constant, and allowing the economy's natural growth in output gradually to reduce prices, including the prices of gold and silver, to the point at which the operational gold standard could be resumed at the pre-war parity.[7]

The Treasury, through the office of the Comptroller of the Currency, regulated the national banks. After 1867, the 10 percent tax on state bank notes had eliminated them from the monetary system, while national bank note issues were fixed by law at $300 million. The Comptroller of the Currency apportioned these notes "relative to population and current banking resources." Because a large measure of existing banking resources was located in northern states, most of the new national bank notes were allocated to banks there. To secure rights to issue notes, national banks pledged their holdings of government bonds as collateral for the notes, sending the bonds to Washington for deposit with the Comptroller, who then ordered packages of national bank notes sent to the conforming banks with their bank logos on them. Banks that issued the notes had to redeem them on demand in whatever was "lawful money." Greenbacks, gold, and silver were all lawful, but gold and silver were still too valuable on the market to be used at their monetary (par) values. Greenbacks, therefore, were the principal bank reserve medium, and the practical base of the monetary system.

About the time that Secretary of the Treasury Salmon P. Chase submitted his resignation to Lincoln in June, 1864, not expecting the President to accept it,[8] Chief Justice Roger B. Taney died. Possibly thinking that a man who was so inept in finance might be brilliant in law, Lincoln nominated Chase to be Chief Justice. More to the point, he thought from Chase's support of the Legal Tender Acts while he was Secretary of the Treasury that his

---

[6]  Hepburn, *History of Currency*, pp. 218–219.

[7]  Silver achieved parity status sooner than gold, simply because of the great silver discoveries in the West during the 1870s. The market value of silver fell, so that by 1875 it was near $1.29 per ounce, the legal mint price. The price of gold, however, stayed around 110 to 114 percent of the pre-war parity. Prospectors simply could not find enough gold, so the market system through price level reduction had to do its unpleasant job. Reducing the pre-war parity by twelve percent would have achieved a new parity, but nineteenth century polity would not accept that adjustment.

[8]  Mitchell, *History of the Greenbacks*, p. 126.

new Chief Justice would promote their constitutionality when the occasion arose.[9]

Chase's appointment created a situation on the Court unprecedented either before or since. Waiting in the wings were court cases challenging the constitutionality of the legal tender acts, and the man who would preside over their legitimacy was the very same person who aided and abetted their creation while he was Secretary of the Treasury! Looking further ahead, an even more bizarre event was in the offing, for Chase was to argue, successfully, the case *against* the constitutionality of the Legal Tender Acts!

The first Legal Tender case to reach the Court was *Hepburn v. Griswold* in January 1869.[10] The legal publication, Wall, described the case as follows:

On the 20th of June, 1860, a certain Mrs. Hepburn made a promissory note, by which she promised to pay to Henry Griswold on the 20th of February, 1862, eleven thousand two hundred and fifty "dollars." At the time the note was signed and at the time when it fell due, the only money in the country that could lawfully be tendered in payment of private debts was gold and silver coin.... Five days after the day when the note by its terms fell due – that is, on the 25th of February, 1862 – in an exigent crisis of the nation in which the government was engaged in putting down an armed rebellion of vast magnitude, Congress passed an act authorizing the issue of $150,000,000 of its own notes, [which declared] "And such notes, herein authorized, shall be receivable in payment of all taxes, internal duties, excises, debts, and demands of every kind due to the United States except duties on imports, and of all claims and demands against the United States of every kind whatsoever, except for interest upon bonds and notes, which shall be paid in coin, and shall also be lawful money and a legal tender in payment of all debts, public and private, within the United States, except duties on imports and interest as aforesaid."[11]

Because Mrs. Hepburn did not pay interest on the note, interest receivable accrued on it. In March, 1864, suit having been brought on the note in the Louisville Chancery Court, she tendered, in United States notes issued under the act mentioned, $12,720 – the principal of the note plus the interest accrued to the date of the tender, and a further sum to cover some costs, in satisfaction of the plaintiff's claim. The tender was refused. Hepburn then paid the greenbacks into court, and the chancellor, "resolving all doubts in favor of the Congress," declared the tender good and adjudged the debt, interest, and costs to be satisfied accordingly. Griswold then took the case to the Court of Errors of Kentucky, which reversed the chancellor's judgment,

[9]  Dunne, Gerald T. *Monetary Decisions of the Supreme Court.* (Rutgers University Press: New Brunswick, N.J., 1960), pp. 77–78.

[10] *Hepburn v. Griswold,* 75 U.S. (8 Wall.), 603.

[11] *Ibid.*, pp. 605–606.

remanding the case with instructions to enter a contrary judgment. Mrs. Hepburn, in turn, brought the case to the Supreme Court.[12]

The Court limited its arguments and decision to the question whether greenbacks were legal tender for debts incurred prior to the enactment of the legal tender laws, implying correctly that the question of the legality of the notes as legal tender for contracts negotiated *after* the law was passed was a separate question.

A complementary question was the legality of the notes as a wartime expedient.[13] The opinion noted:

The power to establish a standard of value by which all other values may be measured – or in other words, to determine what shall be lawful money and a legal tender – is in its nature, and of necessity, a governmental power. It is in all countries exercised by the government. In the United States, so far as it relates to the precious metals, it is vested in Congress by the grant of the power to coin money. But can a power to impart these qualities to [paper] notes, or promises to pay [paper] money, when offered in discharge of preexisting debts, be derived from the coinage power, or from any other power expressly given?[14]

The majority opinion of the Court, read by Chief Justice Chase, answered, "No," to this fundamental question. It reasoned as follows:

[The power to issue paper money] is certainly not the same power as the power to coin money. Nor is it in any reasonable or satisfactory sense an appropriate or plainly adapted means to the exercise of that power. Nor is there more reason for saying that it is implied in, or incidental to, the power to regulate the value of coined money of the United States, or of foreign coins. This power of regulation is a power to determine the weight, purity, form, impression, and denomination of the several coins and their relation to each other, and the relations of foreign coins to the monetary unit of the United States.[15]

The Court's opinion reflected accurately what Article 1, Section 8, of the Constitution had to mean by "coin Money, regulate the value thereof, and of foreign coin, and fix the Standard of Weights and Measures." The verb "regulate" could not have meant "determine the quantity of money," or "manipulate its value," or "issue paper money." Accepting a specie (bi-metallic) standard meant that its workings, not Congress, would determine the supply of money. For Congress to have this power would have contradicted a fundamental tenet of the Constitution.

---

[12] *Ibid.*, pp. 603–606.
[13] *Ibid.*, pp. 614–615.
[14] *Ibid.*, p. 616.
[15] *Ibid.*, p. 617.

In emphasizing this underlying principle, the Chase Court restored accurate meaning to a constitutional datum that many people misconstrued then, and that even more people misconstrue today. Any re-specification of either the gold dollar or the silver dollar would be occasional and marginally small. Both the power to "regulate the value thereof," and "to fix the value of weights and measures" were meant to specify values of measuring devices – money and yardsticks. Newtonian physics saw to it that the yardsticks stayed that way, but the gold and silver mines of the world just would not produce the two precious metals in quantities that would keep their market prices equal to their mint prices.

The question of constitutionality turned on the relationship of the implied powers Congress might assume relative to the express powers that the Constitution gave it. Clearly, the Constitution grants no express power to create paper money. Therefore, printing paper money is outside the law of the Constitution, unless Congress has some implied power to do so as provided for in the Necessary and Proper Clause of Article I, Section 8. That clause grants Congress the power:

To make all Laws which shall be necessary and proper for carrying into Execution [the Powers expressly granted to Congress or] vested by this Constitution in the Government ... or in any [of its] Departments or [officers].

Applied to the specific case at hand, the question the Court had to answer was whether the Acts that called for making issues of government paper money legal tender were "necessary and proper" for carrying out Congress's express power to wage war.[16] Only the greenbacks, which were full legal tender, were in question. The older limited tender Treasury notes and national bank notes, were tenders only for debts of and payments to the federal government, and were not a concern.

The decision noted, importantly, that neither the earlier Treasury notes nor the national bank notes had suffered any discount relative to the full legal tender greenbacks, concluding from this evidence that "all the useful purposes of the notes would have been fully answered without making them a legal tender for preexisting debts. It is denied ... by eminent writers that the quality of legal tender adds anything at all to the credit or usefulness of government notes. They insist, on the contrary, that [legal tender] impairs both." The "necessary and proper" argument, the majority opinion emphasized, "carries the doctrine of implied powers very far beyond any extent hitherto given it.... We are unable to persuade ourselves that an

[16] *Ibid.*, pp. 614–615.

expedient of this sort is an appropriate and plainly adapted means for the execution of the power to declare and carry on war."[17]

The opinion next considered the question of whether the legal tender provision impaired the sanctity of contracts and led to the deprivation of property. Contracts, the opinion noted, "almost invariably stipulate for the payment of money." Prior to the Legal Tender Acts, contracts to pay money "were contracts to pay the sums specified in gold and silver coin. And it is beyond doubt that the holders of these contracts were and are as fully entitled to the protection of this constitutional provision as the holders of any other description of property." Unfortunately using double negatives to make the point, the opinion added: "No one probably could be found to contend that an act enforcing the acceptance of fifty or seventy-five acres of land in satisfaction of a contract to convey a hundred would not come within the prohibition against the arbitrary privation of property." It concluded: "An act making mere promises to pay dollars a legal tender in payment of debts previously contracted, is not a means appropriate, plainly adapted, really calculated to carry into effect any express power vested in Congress. ... Such an act is inconsistent with the spirit of the Constitution, [and] is prohibited by the Constitution" – that is, by the Fifth Amendment.[18]

From a constitutional perspective, this decision appears just. "Dollars" may be labeled "dollars" whatever the means of payment – gold, silver, or paper. The label does not mean at all that the dollars of a later date are the same dollars that existed when a contract was made. An implication understood in any contract, which does not include the means of payment for settlement of the contract, is that payment must be made in the identical medium that was in force when the contract was drawn. Otherwise, what is the purpose of a contract? Why would parties to it sign it? Without a clear understanding that the money at the fulfillment of the contract is to be the same as it was at its initiation, the contract has any variable real value that random public policy may give it.

Justices of the time did not have a price index to measure the value of the greenback dollar in terms of its general purchasing power over time, but they had something else – the greenback price of gold on the gold exchange. When the *Hepburn* decision was handed down, the price of gold in greenbacks had risen to a high of 285 (in 1865) but had fallen back to about 120 by 1869. So the real loss to a creditor in 1869 for a payment in greenback

---

[17]  *Ibid.*, pp. 621–622.
[18]  *Ibid.*, p. 625. "No person shall ... be deprived of life, liberty, or property, without due process of law."

dollars to settle a contract drawn in early 1862, when the price of gold did not yet reflect wartime inflation, would have been about 20 percent.

The general principle of having the debtor pay the debt in whatever was legal tender at the time the contract was signed would answer the question of justice under virtually any circumstances, including the post-Civil War years. As it was, neither debtor nor creditor – Hepburn nor Griswold – could have known that dollars in circulation would depreciate significantly during the life of their contract. Under a specie standard, however, they did not need to know. They could presume, as they must have, that the purchasing power of the gold or silver dollar would remain relatively constant, and that the contract would have to be satisfied in those dollars. Before the Legal Tender Acts, no one even remotely imagined that anything except gold and silver coin would serve as money or as the redeeming medium for issues of bank notes.

Chief Justice Chase delivered the *Hepburn* opinion, the essence of which contradicted the views he had offered as Secretary of the Treasury in support of the Legal Tender Acts in 1862 and 1863. Near the end of his discourse, he offered what amounted to a personal *apologia* for having approved the acts 7 years earlier. "It is not surprising," he said contritely,

… that amid the tumult of the late civil war … different views, never before entertained by American statesmen or jurists, were adopted by many. The time was not favorable to considerate reflection upon the constitutional limits of legislative or executive authority.… Many who doubted yielded their doubts; many who did not doubt were silent. Some who were strongly averse to making government notes a legal tender felt themselves constrained to acquiesce in the views of the advocates of the measure. Not a few who then insisted upon its necessity, or acquiesced in that view, have, since the return of peace and under the influence of calmer time, reconsidered their conclusions, and now concur in those which we have just announced.[19]

The majority opinion, he concluded, has decided that "The defendant in error was not bound to receive from the plaintiff the currency tendered to him in payment of their note, made before the passage of the Act of February 25, 1862."[20] In sum, full legal tender greenbacks, tendered without adjustment for their altered gold value, were unconstitutional for payments of all debts incurred before the passage of the first Legal Tender Act.

Chase's change of view on the constitutionality of the greenbacks is entirely understandable, and commendable. He had had more than 7 years

---

[19]  *Ibid.*, p. 626.
[20]  *Ibid.*

to consider the matter since he was Secretary of the Treasury, and had observed both the greenbacks and the non-greenback currency generally used as money. His experience with the nonlegal tender Treasury notes and national bank notes after 1863 could easily have convinced him that making the greenbacks full legal tender was an unnecessary flourish and, therefore, unconstitutional. He now acknowledged that the greenbacks as legal tender for private debts did not fit the "necessary and proper" criterion for overruling the Tenth Amendment.

Chase was a Lincoln appointee to the Court. He had every political reason to support Lincoln's preferences, and now those of Grant who had become president. The fact that he did not do so, and that his opinion is constitutionally correct, is a tribute to his jurisprudence and integrity. Whatever his faults as Secretary of the Treasury, he more than made up for them with this decision as Chief Justice.

The controversy, however, was not over. At this time, the Court had eight members. Besides Chase, Lincoln had appointed four others: David Davis, Noah Swayne, Samuel Miller, and Stephen Field. The first three of these, reflecting the views of both the Lincoln Administration and post-war Republican policy, viewed the greenbacks as constitutional and wrote a dissenting opinion. Field, also a Lincoln appointee and a Democrat, agreed with Chase. The three other Justices had been appointed by former Democratic presidents – Samuel Nelson (John Tyler), Robert Grier (James Polk), and Nathan Clifford (James Buchanan). All three of the Democratic Justices agreed with Chase and Field. Grier, however, retired after the decision but before its announcement, so his vote was not recorded in the final vote of four-to-three that denied the constitutionality of the greenbacks for past debts.

The dissent, read by Justice Miller, took a wide view of the word "regulate," arguing that this verb bestowed on Congress the express power to make any note issues of the United States a lawful tender in payment of debt. Without this power, the opinion declared, "the nation would have been left divided, and the people impoverished. The national government would have perished, and with it the Constitution which we are now called upon to construe with such nice [sic] and critical accuracy. That the legal tender act prevented these disastrous results, and that the tender clause was necessary to prevent them, [we] entertain no doubt."[21] While the dissenters "had no doubt," they did not treat or defend the law's specific imposition of legal tender for private debts, except to parrot "necessity," the descriptive adjective initiated by Elbridge Spaulding, and thoroughly discredited by the

---

[21]  *Ibid.*, pp. 633–637.

government's long experience with millions of dollars of Treasury notes and national bank notes that were not full legal tender.

Nor did the dissenting Justices treat carefully and logically the word "regulate," as Chase had done in the majority opinion. They admitted that the legal tender law "undoubtedly impaired the obligation of contracts made before its passage." However, they argued that the Constitution forbade only the states, not Congress, from passing such laws. Moreover, they offered no evidence that the Constitution expressly authorized Congress to pass any such law. Consequently, their opinion, if upheld, would have gutted the whole purpose and logic of the Tenth Amendment.

The dissenters also compared the legal tender laws to bankruptcy law. "Congress is expressly authorized to establish a uniform system of bankruptcy," they argued, "the essence of which is to discharge debtors from the obligation of contracts … which in every instance operated on contracts made before [the law] was passed…. Such a law is now in force, yet its constitutionality has never been questioned." Violating the creditor's contract for the sake of the destitute debtor is much less crucial, they asserted, than violating a money contract "for the safety of the nation."[22]

This argument essentially changed the subject. Bankruptcy is a last-ditch solution where no other remedy is conceptually possible. It is not comparable to the Legal Tender Acts, which were first recourses. In any case, bankruptcy law says nothing about viable contracts and the payments that can satisfy them. The contracts scaled down under bankruptcy laws are already depreciated by the knowledge that bankruptcy is always available to the debtor, so the laws do not change anything not already altered by impersonal market forces. Furthermore, the power to violate the creditor's contract does not need to be inferred from the Necessary and Proper Clause. Rather it is inherent in the express power to establish bankruptcy law.[23] The "bankruptcy" argument of the dissenters was nothing more than a contrivance.

Finally, the dissenters entered an argument denying the propriety of "judicial review" – the same argument that Chief Justice Marshall had raised with regard to the Second Bank of the United States. "Where there is a choice of means [say, to obtain resources for waging a war]," their argument went, "the selection [of the means] is with Congress, not the court. If the act to be considered is in any sense essential to the execution of an acknowledged power, the degree of that necessity is for the legislature, and not for the court, to determine." To support this view, the dissenters cited

[22]  *Ibid.*, p. 639.
[23]  I am indebted to Roger Pilon for calling my attention to this argument.

*McCulloch v. Maryland*.[24] There, the opinion argued: "to inquire into the degree of [the] necessity [of a power] would be to pass the line which circumscribes the judicial department and to tread on legislative ground. This Court disclaims all pretences to such a power."[25]

That the Court did not want to encroach on legislative turf is commendable, but only the Court itself could decide the question of proper jurisdiction. Was the Congress of 1862–1863 any more sophisticated and objective in proposing and passing the Legal Tender Acts than the Supreme Court of 1869 in reviewing their validity? That particular Congress was in uncharted waters, groping around for expediencies, and coming up with some highly questionable "answers," as the debates on the Legal Tender Acts made clear. Subsequent events had proven the non-necessity of full legal tender, which the Supreme Court could now recognize and correct. No matter the level of wisdom that Congress applied in passing the Acts, the Court of 1869 was in a much fitter and more objective position to determine the question of "necessary and proper" than had been the Congress of 1862.

Making such judgments is the very reason-for-being of a Supreme Court. Certainly, the cerebral capacities of the Justices, no matter what their limits, were no less than the monetary wisdom of congressmen. The argument denying the Court's review seemed to be nothing more than a second strategy to maintain the greenbacks' constitutionality after the notes full legal tender aspect was seen to be unnecessary. Though this dissenting opinion did not prevail, it provided a new strategy that would appear when new Legal Tender cases surfaced again a few months later.

Summing up, the majority opinion decided three things:

1. Public acceptance of the greenbacks did not require that they be made full legal tender in the mode of gold and silver coins. Monetary experience both before and after the Civil War verified this judgment.
2. The government's war power, requiring large expenditures of money, no more necessitated the issue of full legal tender notes than any other governmental power to spend money. The magnitude of the government's "necessities" could never be an excuse for constitutionality.
3. Congress had no power to emit fully legal tender "bills of credit," first, because the Constitution offered no express power to do so, and, second, because the full legal tender power could not be justified as "Necessary and Proper."

---

[24] *Ibid.*, p. 316.
[25] *Ibid.* Also cited in Hepburn, *History*, p. 640.

# THIRTEEN

# *Knox v. Lee* and *Parker v. Davis:* Reversal of *Hepburn*

The Court heard the *Hepburn* case in 1869, but the 5–3 decision was not recorded until early 1870. By that time Justice Grier had retired, so the decision was recorded as 4–3. Nonetheless, the 5–3 decision was a full Court decision at that time, and should be treated as such for analytical purposes. Grier's retirement left the Court with two vacancies, since another vacancy had purposely been left open for political reasons.[1]

Irwin Unger, in his book *The Greenback Era*, noted that the *Hepburn* decision caused no appreciable distress in financial circles, and that its immediate effects were "modest." The price of gold did not respond either way – most importantly, it did not rise. Businessmen were surprisingly calm, because the decision "seemed to affect only pre-1862 debts, few of which were still outstanding."[2] Market thinking, however, was that the decision might not hold for long, and that the Court would have a different opinion on debts incurred after February 1862. Because of these later debts, a second decision *had* to be rendered. The public waited for the other shoe to drop, but did not expect that it would reverberate.

A momentous financial change had occurred in the U.S. economy since 1860: the federal government had become a very large debtor to households, business firms, and other institutions. In its role as debtor, would the government's monetary policies reflect a debtor's interests or the interests of the creditor-citizens who held its debt? Moreover, what was to be done with the greenbacks still outstanding that were also debts of the government? Would they be retired completely or would they be managed conservatively

---

[1] The Republican Congress did not want to allow an appointee to the Court by President Andrew Johnson. Therefore, when he made an appointment, Congress took no action, leaving the seat open.

[2] Unger, *Greenback Era*, pp. 175–177.

until they resumed their pre-war gold value? Would they remain full legal tender, or would Congress see to their conversion into the old form of limited tender Treasury notes?

The Grant Administration was not sanguine about the *Hepburn* decision. In fact, it was both irritated and alarmed. Administration officials felt that the Court ruling somehow threatened to destabilize the monetary status quo. It seemed as well to be a contrived Democratic attempt to repudiate the Republican Party's war policies. Since the five votes favoring the decision were all from (more or less) Democratic Justices, the *Hepburn* decision, politically, was five Democrats against three Republicans.

This disparity was easy for Grant to fix because of two Court vacancies waiting to be filled. Grant's two new appointments to the Court were William Strong from Pennsylvania and Joseph Bradley from New Jersey. From their decisions as state court judges on legal tender cases, their views were well known. Both were very much pro-greenback.[3] The erstwhile minority on the Court thereupon became a majority, with five pro-greenback Republican Justices and the four remaining Democrat traditionalists.

Immediately following the new appointments, Grant's Attorney General asked the reformed Court to consider two pending cases, *Knox v. Lee* and *Parker v. Davis*. Both cases included payments for debts contracted both before and after February 1862. The new Court majority of Republicans agreed to do so, but the Democratic members disagreed since the *Hepburn* decision had already treated pre-1862 debts. This issue was already decided, Chase and the Democratic Justices claimed, unless new evidence was available. But the new majority, pushed by the Secretary of the Treasury George W. Boutwell and others in the Grant Administration, insisted that the issue be re-argued.

*Hepburn v. Griswold* was argued in late 1869 and decided February 7, 1870. *Knox v. Lee* and *Parker v. Davis* were argued in February and April 1871, and decided on May 1, 1871. The composite decision reversed the *Hepburn* decision, and ruled that the Legal Tender Acts were constitutional for debts incurred at any time – either before or after the Acts were passed. Justices Strong and Bradley, reflecting their positive beliefs in the revised decision, and gratitude for their appointments to the highest judicial office, read the new majority opinion.[4] Chief Justice Chase, and Justices Nathan Clifford and Stephen Field, read dissenting opinions.

[3]   Unger, *Greenback Era*, p. 177, and McCulloch, *Men and Measures of Half a Century*, p. 173.

[4]   According to Dunne (*Monetary Decisions of the Supreme Court*, p. 77), both Strong and Bradley had been "railroad lawyers." Both had adjudicated the Legal Tender Acts in state

## THE CASE FOR CONSTITUTIONALITY OF THE GREENBACKS

Justice Strong read the first majority opinion. "The controlling questions in these [two] cases," he observed, "are the following: Are the acts of Congress, known as the Legal Tender Acts, constitutional when applied to contracts made before their passage, and secondly, are they valid as applicable to debts contracted since their enactment?" He argued, incorrectly, that the first question was still open because the *Hepburn* decision had been made by a Court that did not have a full complement of Justices. The decision had been 5–3 against constitutionality. However, even if a ninth Justice had been present and had voted for constitutionality, the decision would have been 5–4 against. Ignoring this simple arithmetic, Strong presented the new majority decision: "The acts of Congress known as the Legal Tender are constitutional, when applied to contracts made before their passage, [and therefore] *Hepburn v. Griswold,* 8 Wall. 603, on this point [is] overruled.... They are also valid as applicable to contracts made since."[5]

The debts contracted since February 25, 1862, Strong continued, "... constitute by far the greatest portion of the indebtedness of the country. They have been contracted in view of the acts of Congress declaring Treasury notes [greenbacks] a legal tender, and in reliance upon that declaration."[6] He then made a completely unwarranted presumption, contrary to the facts of the case. If the Court's decision were to declare the legal tenders unconstitutional so that debts could be "discharged only by [gold and silver] coin – if, contrary to all expectations of all parties to these contracts, legal tender notes are rendered unavailable(?) [something that the previous decision had not implied], the government has become an instrument of the grossest injustice; all debtors are loaded with an obligation it was never contemplated they should assume; a large percentage is added to every debt, and such must become the demand for gold to satisfy contracts, that ruinous sacrifices, general distress, and bankruptcy may be expected."[7]

Strong's hyperbole had no basis in logic, practical politics, or fact. If the Legal Tender Acts were declared unconstitutional, the existing greenbacks would not become "unavailable"; they would not disappear. Nor, most

---

courts and judged them constitutional. Moreover, their background as railroad lawyers, according to Dunne, had an influence on their judicial attitudes. Since the railroads had heavy bonded indebtedness similar to the post-war federal government in the 1870s, their attorneys were conditioned to defend debtors.

[5]  U.S. Wall, p. 457.

[6]  *Ibid.*, p. 530.

[7]  *Ibid.*, pp. 530–531. (Emphasis added.)

importantly, would such a decision have implied that debts contracted after February 1862 could only be discharged by gold and silver coin. The only practical result of the ruling would have been to deprive the notes of their full legal tender status, leaving them legally receivable only for federal government dues and payments, but not for debts between private parties. Congress could have amended the Legal Tender Acts by a simple measure stating this fact in order to comply with the Court's ruling. Once this formal legal change occurred, greenbacks would have continued in their routine currency functions as before, on a par with old-style (nonlegal tender) Treasury notes and national bank notes. No one would have noticed, since no one had made any distinction in the acceptability of these three common currencies for the past 7 years. The public used them all indiscriminately. The majority argument here was alarmist, lacking both evidence and reason.

Strong continued, "And there is no well founded distinction to be made between the constitutional validity of an act of Congress declaring Treasury notes [greenbacks] a legal tender for the payment of debts contracted after its passage and that of an act making them a legal tender for the discharge of all debts, as well those incurred before as those made after its enactment."[8] However, he noted:

There may be a difference in the effects produced by the acts, and in the hardship of their operation, but in both cases, the fundamental question, that which tests the validity of the legislation, is can Congress constitutionally give to the Treasury notes the character and qualities of money? Can such notes be constituted a legitimate circulating medium having a defined legal value? If they can, then such notes must be available[9] to fulfill all contracts (not expressly excepted)[10] solvable in money, without reference to the time when the contracts were made. Hence it is not strange that those who hold the legal tender acts unconstitutional when applied to contracts made before February, 1862, find themselves compelled also to hold that the acts are invalid as to debts created after that time, and to hold that both classes of debts alike can be discharged only by gold and silver coin.[11]

Again, Strong made the nonsequitur that to rule the greenbacks unconstitutional for debts before the acts were passed forced those who so argued also to deny their constitutionality for debts incurred after the acts were passed. Nothing in either the *Hepburn* decision or current policy supported Strong's presumption. His allegation was nothing more than a straw man.

---

[8]  *Ibid.*, p. 530.
[9]  "Obligatory" not "available" is the correct word.
[10]  That is, for contracts that had an explicit "gold clause."
[11]  *Ibid.*, p. 531.

To repeat, a simple amendment to the original Legal Tender Acts would still have allowed *ex post* 1862 debts to be discharged with greenbacks, "old" Treasury notes, national bank notes, or whatever was declared in the contract. In accordance with *Hepburn*, creditors in contracts before 1862 could continue to require gold (or its current equivalent) in greenbacks.[12] The Court could have explicitly prescribed this amendment. Strong's further assertion that the time at which contracts were made had nothing to do with the question of the constitutionality of the money implied by the contract suggests that he and the Court majority did not understand the fundamental reasons for contracts in the first place.

Contractual norms on either side of the timeline, February 1862, were markedly different. Economic activity prior to February 1862 presupposed a bi-metallic standard that had been in place then for more than 70 years. Contracts and their signatories anticipated continuance of that same standard. Consequently, the Legal Tender Acts passed after that date changed the framework conditions under which earlier contracts had been drawn, so greenbacks were not a legitimate means for paying off the earlier debts. To rule that they could is a perfect example of *ex post facto* law. *Hepburn v. Griswold* had properly denied their constitutionality on this ground. Once the game changed after February 1862, all contracts had to adjust for the greenbacks' possible effects on prices and the real values of debt over time. Both debtors and creditors would sensibly have adjusted for the ongoing presence of the notes.[13] The terms of the contracts and their agreed-upon interest rates then would have reflected the public's understanding of the greenbacks' monetary implications, particularly their effect on prices.

Strong next repeated the argument of "necessity," claiming that even if the legal tender feature was not necessary – which he dismissed as "mere conjecture" but which the fiscal history of the war had thoroughly proven – the very fact that Congress had decided that the legal tender feature was necessary precluded the Court from denying it and offering a second opinion.[14] Contrary to this allegation, many congressmen after the fact had

---

[12]  It is clear that Strong understood the role of gold clauses from his parenthetical clause in the previous quotation. A "gold clause" brought the contract back into the environment of THE Gold Standard.

[13]  The terms "greenbacks," "U.S. notes," "legal tenders," and "Treasury notes" all refer to the same currency – the full legal tender paper currency that Congress authorized the federal government to *issue* in the Legal Tender Acts of April 1862 and July 1863. "Full legal tender" meant that the notes had to be accepted not only for government dues and payments, but also in any contracts between private parties. The adjective "full" was what the fuss was all about.

[14]  *Ibid.*, p. 542.

concluded that the legal tender feature was unnecessary. Consequently, Strong's argument became invalid in the period between the end of the war (1865) and this decision.

Strong elaborated upon the "necessity" argument for many pages, without ever observing the fact that the acts and the great bulk of legal tenders were issued before the huge fiscal deficits of 1863–1865, during which years no legal tenders at all were issued.[15] If the legal tender feature was unnecessary during the latter years of the war, how could it have been necessary earlier when fiscal problems were less demanding? Presumably, Strong had been apprised of these facts, because sitting on the bench next to him as Chief Justice was the man who had managed the Treasury Department during that period.

Strong next discussed the 6 percent gold-dollar devaluation of June 28, 1834, and the silver devaluations of fractional currency in the early 1850s, as evidence that Congress had discretion over the determination of what constituted money.[16] This devaluation was the only one that Congress passed during the 100 years that metallic standards were operational, except for minor changes in fractional silver coins during the 1850s.

Strong treated the 1834 devaluation as proof that Congress could unilaterally reduce the legal commodity value of coined money. Creditors, he observed, were entitled to six percent less gold the day after devaluation than they had been the day before. He then argued that, "The result was thus precisely what it is contended the legal tender acts worked. But was it ever imagined that this [1834 Act] was taking private property without compensation or without due process of law? ... It might be impolitic and unjust, but could its constitutionality be doubted? ... Certainly, it would be an anomaly for us to hold an act of Congress invalid merely because we might think its provisions harsh and unjust."[17]

Strong here ignored several differences between the devaluation of 1834 and the Legal Tender Acts. First, in devaluing the gold dollar, Congress had used an *express power* granted by Article 1, Section 8. Second, the change of 6.6 percent, while a little much for a devaluation, allowed for the possibility

---

[15] Very often Strong seemed to ignore or be unaware that it was the *legal tender* feature, and not just Treasury paper currency, that was under scrutiny. (See, p. 544.)

[16] See, Carothers, *Fractional Money*, pp. 91–95, for an expert account of this episode. According to Carothers, the ratio should have been 15.625 (15 5/8)-to-1. But politics wanted a little more money in the system. The net effect of the change was to enhance gold, and therefore degrade silver. For the next two decades, silver was "overvalued" and a reluctant coin.

[17] *Ibid.*, pp. 561–562.

of a one-time increase of 6.6 percent more gold dollars than had existed before. It did not create hundreds of millions of dollars of legal tender paper money, as well as drive all the gold and silver out of circulation, on the pretext of an implied power. In short, devaluation was a power that the Constitution explicitly vested in Congress in order to keep both gold and silver currency functioning in the monetary system. A creditor who received less gold for his money after the devaluation still received the same money that would buy the same amount of goods and services, except gold, the next day. The legal tender laws were not just differences in degree of Congress's power to "coin money." The magnitude of their effect was hundreds of times greater than the simple devaluation of 1834.[18]

The majority's most striking modification of the monetary Constitution came next. The passage in question contains four critical explications that require review. Strong argued:

> To assert, then, that the clause enabling Congress to coin money and regulate its value tacitly implies a denial of all other power over the currency of the nation, is an attempt to introduce a new rule of construction against the solemn decisions of this Court. So far from its containing a lurking prohibition, many have thought it was intended to confer upon Congress [1] that general power over the currency which has always been an acknowledged attribute of sovereignty [2] in every other civilized nation than our own, [3] especially when considered in connection with the other clause which denies to the states the power to coin money, emit bills of credit, or make anything but gold and silver coin a tender in payment of debts. We do not assert this now, but there are some considerations touching these clauses which tend to show that if any implications are to be deduced from them, they are of an enlarging rather than a restraining character. [4] The Constitution was intended to frame a government as distinguished from a league or compact.[19]

First, the clause that Strong refers to is not to "coin money and regulate *its* value," as he phrased it, but "to coin money and regulate *the* value thereof," which meant to regulate the gold and silver content of coined money in order to keep both metallic coins current. It had nothing to do with the monetary system other than what it said about coinage. Presumably (and properly) the monetary system would be self-regulating in the presence of such a provision, as historical experience had long verified. True, the attempt to institute a bi-metallic standard was practically flawed. It turned out to have operational problems that led ultimately to a world-wide mono-metallic

---

[18] See, J. Huston McCulloch, "*The Crime of 1834*," pp. 57–65, in *Money and Banking, The American Experience*, George Mason University Press, Fairfax VA., 1995.

[19] *Ibid.*, pp. 545–546. (Emphasis added.)

gold standard, with silver coin a subsidiary currency[20] kept current by its redemption into gold. Silver currency became similar in this respect to government issues of paper money, with gold as their basis.[21] If the Framers had intended to give Congress the complete control over money that Strong alleged, the phrase would have been written "coin money and regulate the *quantity* thereof," rather than "the value thereof." But since the variable used was "value," it meant only the statutory value of a gold dollar relative to the statutory value of a silver dollar.

It is indeed inconceivable that the Framers would have allowed any Congress at any time to control the value of the money-unit by some unspecified control over the quantity of money in the economy. They could not have "confer[red] upon Congress that general power over the currency which has always been an acknowledged attribute of sovereignty in every other civilized nation than our own." And here the opinion entered a new word – sovereignty – that had appeared briefly in the *Hepburn* dissent and occasionally in earlier references. Strong added the notion that state control over the currency is "civilized," an assertion that would have made any Framer squirm.[22]

The majority, recognizing the inadequacy of the "necessary and proper" argument to excuse legal tender, had to develop a new strategy, and so resorted to declaring that the Constitution granted "sovereign" powers to the federal government. Even though the power "to make any Thing but gold and silver Coin a Tender in Payments of Debts" had been denied the states, they ruled that Congress had the power because it was an aspect of sovereignty in other "civilized" nations.

Significantly, the Constitution says nothing about "sovereignty." Congress's power over the coinage of gold and silver is *express* and limited to just that. Congress has no other monetary powers, and certainly not "that general power over the currency," that Strong alleged. Allusion to the claim that "every other civilized nation" had "general powers over the currency" is, if anything, a caution for not allowing the government of the United States the same license. One could argue, to the contrary and more appropriately, that only countries that limited the central government's power over the currency were in any way "civilized." However, since other countries had

---

[20] "Subsidiary coin" means a coin that has a higher monetary value than the market value of the metal in it. All coin currency at the present time is *subsidiary*. The extreme example of *subsidiary* currency is paper currency.

[21] See, again, Carothers, *Fractional Money*, Ch. XXI, and "Conclusion."

[22] *Ibid.*, p. 559.

not tied their governments to a constitution, no reference to their monetary practices was relevant to monetary affairs in the United States.

Justice Bradley, the other new appointee, largely agreed with Strong's arguments. He added the inane observation that "currency is a national necessity"; that "state governments are prohibited making money or issuing bills [of credit]"; and the incorrect claim that "uniformity of money was one of the objects of the Constitution." He repeated Strong's assertion that, "The coinage of money and regulation of its value is conferred on the general government exclusively." He then concluded: "It follows as a matter of necessity as a consequence of these various provisions that it is specially the duty of the general [federal] government to provide a national currency."[23]

Reflecting his sentiments for the debtor class, Bradley next paid homage to "the debtor interest of the country": "[Debtors] represent [the country's] bone and sinew, and must be encouraged to pursue its avocations. If relief were not afforded [presumably, to debtors], universal bankruptcy would ensue, and industry would be stopped and government would be paralyzed in the paralysis of the people."[24] Continuing his concern for "the" debtor, he exclaimed sarcastically: "But the creditor interest will lose some of its gold! Is gold the one thing needful? Is it worse for the creditor to lose a little by depreciation than everything by the bankruptcy of his debtor? Nay, is it worse than to lose everything by the subversion of the government?"[25] Bradley offered no comparable concern for "the creditor," which is not surprising. His employer was the federal government, by far the largest debtor at the time, while the largest creditor was the public that held greenbacks and other government debt. From a debt of just a few million dollars in 1860, dollar claims against the U.S. Treasury had reached $2,843 million in 1865. By 1870, federal debt, in all its different forms was still $2,437 million, or about 3 years of national product. Although the government had reduced the debt since the war ended, it remained a debtor on a grand scale.

Bradley repeated Strong's reference to the gold devaluation of 1834, and its effect on the ex ante gold value of contracts. However, he took the argument a step backward. The power to coin money and regulate the value thereof, he reported, especially when it resulted in an alteration of the value of gold, was much discussed in England "in the great case of Mixed Moneys." The power used there, Bradley claimed, was "the King's ordinary prerogative over the coinage of money, without any sanction from Parliament... Whether [the

---

[23] *Ibid.*, pp. 562–63.
[24] *Ibid.*, pp. 564–65.
[25] *Ibid.* Neither Justice Chase nor Field responded to Bradley's polemic.

value of gold] shall be changed or not [by devaluation] is a matter of legislative discretion. And such is undoubtedly the public law of this country. Therefore, the mere fact that the value of notes [greenbacks] may be depreciated by legal tender laws, is not conclusive against their validity; for that is clearly the effect of other powers which may be exercised by Congress in its discretion."[26]

Bradley's general theme here was that the federal government has an absolute prerogative over the control of the monetary system.[27] His assertion that "such is undoubtedly the law in this country" was the major claim that the Legal Tender cases sought to challenge. Its truth was by no stretch of the imagination axiomatic.

Bradley then took a moment to put political economists in their place. "I deem it unnecessary," he remarked, "to enter into a minute criticism of all the sayings, wise or foolish, that have from time to time been uttered on this subject by statesmen, philosophers, or theorists. The writers on political economy are generally opposed to the exercise of the power [to make greenbacks legal tender]. The considerations they adduce are very proper to be urged upon the depositary of the power. The question whether the power exists in a national government is a great practical question relating to the national safety and independence, and statesmen are better judges of this question than economists can be."[28]

Bradley concluded with a nationalistic *apologia* for a strong central government with corresponding monetary powers:

It would be sad indeed if this great nation were now to be deprived of a power [to make U.S. notes legal tender] so necessary to enable it to protect its own existence and to cope with the other great powers of the world [?]. No doubt foreign powers would rejoice if we should deny the power. No doubt foreign creditors would rejoice. They have, from the first, taken a deep interest in the question. But no true friend to our government, to its stability and its power to sustain itself under all vicissitudes, can be indifferent to the great wrong which it would sustain by a denial of the power in question – a power to be seldom exercised, certainly, but one the possession of which is so essential and, as it seems to me, so undoubted.[29]

The Framers had explicitly provided for the government to sustain itself by issuing unlimited quantities of interest-bearing debt. Therefore, Bradley's

---

[26]  *Ibid.*, p. 567.
[27]  By this reference to the Case of the Mixed Monies, Bradley reached backward for support of a central government's discretion over the monetary system to English polity in the sixteenth century. This case is discussed in the following, Chapter 15, *Juilliard v. Greenman.*
[28]  *Ibid.*, p. 568. Which is a major reason why this book is written.
[29]  *Ibid.*, p. 569.

argument that it also had power to issue legal tender paper money "to protect its own existence" was an improper exaggeration.[30] Furthermore, the later fiscal experience of the North during the war also refuted Bradley's assertion, as did that of the Confederate government, which never passed a legal tender law.

## MINORITY DISSENT TO THE MAJORITY OPINION

Chief Justice Chase, now in the Court minority, read the first dissent. He reviewed at length the original arguments in *Hepburn*, and noted that no Justice in the then-majority of 5–3 had reversed his opinion.

Chase drew attention to the only question that was germane to the case, and one that the new majority had ignored. "The real question is," Chase began, **"W**as the making of [the notes] a legal tender a necessary means to the execution of the power to borrow money? If the notes would circulate as well without as with this quality, it is idle to urge the plea of such necessity. But," he continued, "the circulation of the notes was amply provided by making them receivable for all national taxes, all dues to the government, and all loans."[31] The "political economists" of the time, whom Bradley had summarily dismissed, had all agreed on this point.

No event or other experience following the issue of the greenbacks demonstrated that the full legal tender feature was in any way necessary to the notes' acceptance and continued circulation. On this empirical evidence alone, the new majority opinion was wrong and the minority opinion correct. The majority never treated this issue explicitly, always roughing over the legal tender property by pretending that the power to issue paper money had to include the full legal tender feature. They did not deign to notice that the older form of Treasury notes, some of which were still in circulation during the war, and the greenbacks and national bank notes were all equally acceptable. That is, none of the different currencies circulated at a discount to the greenbacks. Only gold commanded a premium relative to both greenbacks and other currencies.

Chase continued: "The [legal tender clause] acts directly upon the relations of debtor and creditor. It violates that fundamental principle of all just legislation ... It says that B., who has purchased a farm from A. for a certain price, may keep the farm without paying for it if he will only tender

---

[30] Senator Collamer made this same rejoinder to the same argument in the debate over the first Legal Tender Act in 1862.

[31] *Ibid.*, p. 578.

certain notes which may bear some proportion to the price, or be even worthless."[32]

Chase then briefly addressed the sovereignty issue that the majority had broached. "It is unnecessary to say that we [the minority] reject wholly the doctrine, advanced for the first time, we believe, in this court by the present majority, that the legislature has any 'powers under the Constitution which grow out of the aggregate of powers conferred upon the government or out of the sovereignty instituted by it.' If this proposition be admitted, and it also be admitted that the legislature is the sole judge of the necessity for the exercise of such powers, the government becomes practically absolute and unlimited."[33]

Chase's response to the "sovereignty" argument was the first rebuttal of that claim, but it would not be the last. Sovereignty was to become the new bludgeon to forge power for the federal government. "Necessary and proper" was a key for opening the door so that legislative action could bypass the doctrine of enumerated powers and the Tenth Amendment.[34] "Sovereignty" became a sledge hammer for breaking down the door.

Justice Nathan Clifford, an appointee of President James Buchanan, next entered his dissent. He also discussed at length the history of the Constitution and all the constraints written into it to preclude making any kind of paper money a legal tender. Clifford summarized the general doctrine that had been unquestionably accepted over the previous eighty-plus years. "Throughout that period," he reminded his brethren, parsing for them the Tenth Amendment,

the doctrine of the Court has been, and still is, unless the opinion of the Court just read constitutes an exception, that the government of the United States, as ordained and established by the Constitution, is a government of enumerated powers; that all the powers not delegated to the United States by the Constitution nor prohibited by it to the states are reserved to the states respectively or to the people; that every power vested in the federal government under the Constitution is in its nature sovereign, and that Congress may pass all laws necessary and proper to carry the same into execution.

The new "theory" of the present majority, Clifford continued, holds that Congress's power "to coin money and regulate the value thereof" also

---

[32]  *Ibid.*, p. 580.

[33]  *Ibid.*, p. 582.

[34]  The Necessary and Proper Clause grants the means, but only if they are necessary and proper. The Court must then decide whether Congress has abused its discretion, as it did in this case, since the legal tender feature was neither necessary nor proper. (I am indebted to Roger Pilon for this clarification.)

gives Congress by extension and because Congress, not "the people," has sovereignty, the general power to "coin" legal tender paper money. Clifford objected that the majority opinion had no evidence, and no precedents of any kind to support its case. "Unsupported as the theory is by any historical fact," he continued – with some sarcastic implications,

… it would seem that the advocates of the theory ought to be able to give it a fixed domicile in the Constitution or else be willing to abandon it as a theory without any solid constitutional foundation…. The period of eighty-five years which has elapsed since the Constitution was adopted is surely long enough to have enabled its advocates to discover [the theory's] locality and to be able to point out its home to those whose researches have been less successful and whose conscientious convictions lead them to the conclusion that, as applied to the Constitution, it is a myth without a habitation or a name.[35]

Justice Stephen Field, the final dissenter, also reviewed the history of the Constitution and likewise found no basis for making the greenbacks legal tender. He concurred with Clifford, that "the advocates of the measure do not agree as to the power in the Constitution to which it shall be referred, some placing it upon the power to borrow money, some on the coining power, and some on what is termed a resulting power from the general purposes of the government."[36]

Field, too, denied the necessity of the legal tender provision. "Without the legal tender provision," he emphasized,

the notes would have circulated equally well and answered all the purposes of government – the only direct benefit resulting from that provision arising, as already stated, from the ability it conferred upon unscrupulous debtors to discharge … previous obligations…. The notes issued by the national bank associations during the war, … which were never made a legal tender, circulated equally well with the notes of the United States. Neither their utility nor their circulation was diminished in any degree by the absence of the legal tender quality. They rose and fell in the market under the same influences and precisely to the same extent as the notes of the United States [greenbacks].[37]

---

[35]  *Ibid.*, p. 626. Clifford noted further that the power to make paper money legal tender, "if admitted to exist, would nullify the effect and operation of the express power to coin money, to regulate the value thereof and of foreign coin, as it would substitute a paper medium in the place of gold and silver coin, which in itself, as compared with coin, possesses no value, is not money, either in the constitutional or commercial sense, but only a promise to pay money, is never worth par, and often much less, even as domestic exchange … and is never acknowledged as a medium of exchange or as a standard of value in any foreign market known to American commerce."

[36]  *Ibid.*, p. 638.

[37]  *Ibid.*, p. 648. This argument needs some modification. The public generally regarded national bank notes on a par with greenbacks and the other currencies. However, national

Field next argued that acceptance of the legal tender provision impaired the obligation of contracts because it "relieves the parties from the moral duty of performing the original stipulations of the contract, and it prevents legal enforcement.... It is obvious" he continued, "that the act of 1862 changes the terms of contracts for the payment of money made previous to its passage in every essential particular. All such contracts had reference to metallic coins, struck or regulated by Congress, and composed principally of gold and silver, which constituted the legal money of the country."[38] He agreed that Congress, in passing bankruptcy laws, had some limited powers over contracts. The legal tender power, however, was open-ended: it might even have been used to print enough paper money to make all contracts worthless to their creditors.

Field returned to the Constitution's original meaning, reiterating Clifford's point: "The doctrine that where a power is not expressly forbidden, it may be exercised would change the whole character of our government. As I read the writings of the great commentators and the decisions of this Court, the true doctrine is the exact reverse – that if a power is not in terms granted and is not necessary and proper for the exercise of a power thus granted, it does not exist."[39]

Field next entered a practical reason for negating the legal tender provision. The U.S. government, he noted, "is at the present time seeking, in the markets of the world, a loan of several hundred millions of dollars in gold upon securities containing the promises of the United States to repay the money, principal and interest, in gold. Yet this Court, the highest tribunal of the country, this day declares by its solemn decision that should such loan be obtained, it is entirely competent for Congress to pay it off not in gold, but in notes of the United States themselves, payable at such time and in such measure as Congress may itself determine, and that legislation sanctioning such gross breach of faith would not be repugnant to the fundamental law of the land. What is this but declaring that repudiation by the government of the United States of its solemn obligations would be constitutional?"[40]

---

bank notes were redeemable at banks for greenbacks, which were the reserves of the national banks. Consequently, acceptability of the national bank notes was to a degree a reflection of the acceptability of greenbacks. Nevertheless, most people regarded the two as separate currencies, and accepted the bank notes without thinking that they could go to a national bank and redeem them.

[38] *Ibid.*, p. 662.
[39] *Ibid.*, p. 664.
[40] *Ibid.*, p. 674.

The arguments of the dissenters were historically correct, and legally accurate. They repeated that the only constitutional question at issue was the full legal tender feature of the U.S. notes (greenbacks). Since that feature was patently unnecessary, as the facts of recent history confirmed, it was also improper. Second, the power to make paper money legal tender violated the integrity of contracts, and especially of contracts drawn before Congress passed the Legal Tender Acts. The majority decision denied the whole reason for the existence of contracts, namely, their role for reducing uncertainty by defining ahead of time the precise means for settling a debt at the due date.

Perhaps unwittingly, the minority did not address the practical implications of the position they had defended. How would the legal tender character of the greenbacks be undone if the Court had ruled them unconstitutional? If debts incurred before February 1862 had to be repaid in gold or silver or its equivalent, what about debts due after that date? Could creditors have demanded payment in gold and silver for debts contracted when no gold and silver circulated, as the majority had portended? By carrying forward the logical principle of paying off debts in the medium at the time the contract was signed, the Court could have ruled that any Treasury notes or national bank notes tendered for debts after 1862 would be legally acceptable. All the government-controlled currencies had become commonly used by that time and their qualities were well understood. The dissenting minority did not offer suggestions to these issues, perhaps believing that their other arguments were sufficient. Nonetheless, their failure to suggest a practical plan for eliminating the legal tender element from the existing greenbacks was a strategic mistake.

The Court might have offered a few guidelines for Congress to address this issue, and it would have been an easy call. Congress could promptly have passed a law rescinding the full legal tender provision and amending it to "tender only for government dues and payments," as declared on the Treasury notes occasionally issued before the Civil War. Then, as the Treasury received the existing fully legal tender notes for tariffs or taxes, or if commercial banks turned the notes into the Treasury as they wore out and had to be replaced, the Treasury would have issued the revised limited tender Treasury notes. This transition could have been so perfunctory that it might not even have required a formal act of Congress; a simple Treasury order or congressional resolution might have been enough. To allege, as the majority opinion did, that debtors would have to pay post-1862 debts in gold and silver coin, was absurd hyperbole. It never could nor would have happened.

The 5–3 majority that decided the earlier case of *Hepburn vs. Griswold* had been a valid majority. Its decision should have been accepted, or subsequently overruled only on the grounds of new evidence that proved the original decision invalid. Nothing of the kind had occurred. The 5–4 decision in the two cases, *Parker v. Davis* and *Knox v. Lee,* presented nothing new, except that the new majority discovered "sovereignty" for the federal government where it had not previously existed.

The majority that rendered the *Hepburn* decision had had no political axe to grind. Those Justices received no material or political rewards for that decision. Their spokesman, Chief Justice Chase, had been Secretary of the Treasury at the time the Legal Tender Acts were passed, and he had every incentive to vindicate his previous office by legitimizing the greenbacks when he had the chance,. Rather, he acknowledged that he had been wrong to support the greenbacks as full legal tender, and now regarded the acts as unconstitutional.

The majority decision legitimizing the greenbacks violated what for eighty-plus years the general public had believed was an inviolable constant – the exclusive constitutionality of the gold-silver standard. It did so by a single vote of a nine-man Court. That such a momentous change should have appeared at all under such circumstances was bad law, a bad omen for the integrity of government, and a violation of public trust. A responsible judiciary would have recognized that the arguments and the paltry arithmetic of a 5–4 majority were inadequate for the magnitude of the issue's importance. It could then have called for further evidence and opinions, and re-argued the case later, or it could have suspended the decision and asked for a "clarification on the currency question" from Congress and the Grant Administration.

## OTHER COMMENTS ON THE LEGAL TENDER DECISION

Several congressmen, Treasury officials, and political economists commented on the Court's verdict at various times after the event. The present Secretary of the Treasury George Boutwell, who had been a Treasury official for many years and had an obvious axe to grind, very much favored the decision. He had used his influence in the Grant Administration to further the appointments of Strong and Bradley to the Court. In his book *Why I Am a Republican,* Boutwell dogmatically repeated the majority's arguments, adding, "Every contract is to be performed in the currency of the country at the time the contract is liquidated. The power to decide the quantity and quality of that currency is an essential incident of sovereignty."[41] He offered no evidence to support either of these opinions.

A few congressmen also commented on the decision. Roscoe Conkling, a prominent Republican congressman from New York, saw the Legal Tender Acts as unconstitutional because of their effect on the real value of contracts.[42] Many congressmen, undoubtedly a majority, had originally opposed the acts as unconstitutional, except for what they regarded as the acts' immediate wartime necessity. Elbridge Spaulding, the congressional water carrier for the acts, was one such.[43] Simon Newcomb, the astronomer and political economist raised similar objections,[44] as did Hugh McCulloch, who preceded Boutwell as Secretary of the Treasury.[45]

In his work, *Pieces of Eight,* Edwin Vieira offers a recent perspective:

> The opinions of Justices Strong and Bradley in *Knox v. Lee* radically departed, not only from the true monetary powers and disabilities of the Constitution, but also from the most fundamental principle of American constitutional law as a whole. According to them, Congress has power to do whatever it deems "necessary and proper" to "preserve the government," unless the Constitution explicitly prohibits such action in so many words.... [It] thus purported to transform the national government from one of delegated powers, limited by specific enumeration, to one of almost totalitarian power, qualified by specific prohibitions only.... Not withstanding its aberrance, *Knox* was to set the pattern of argument in all decisions of constitutional law on monetary affairs that followed it.[46]

No matter what critics, past and present, argued and continue to argue, the Supreme Court of 1871 had decided otherwise. Now the only hope was that a future Court would undo the damage on the same terms as the Strong–Bradley Court had initiated it. That did not happen. *Knox v. Lee* and *Parker v. Davis* were never challenged.

---

[41] Boutwell, George. *Why I Am a Republican.* (Philadelphia: W. S. Fortescue & Co., 1884, p. 71.) *Sovereignty* gets its proper place in Vieira's *Pieces of Eight.* "In America, only the people were 'sovereign' – and, therefore, the government's authority was non-existent in those areas no matter what branch attempted to act" (p. 83). He adds in a footnote, citing the opinion *Chisholm v. Georgia* 2 U.S. (2 Dall.) 419, 471–472 (1793) (opinion of Jay, C. J.): "The term *sovereign* has for its correlative, *subject.* In this sense, the term can receive no application; for it has no object in the constitution of the United States. Under that constitution, there are *citizens,* but no *subjects.*"(p. 84. emphasis in original).

[42] Spaulding, *History of Legal Tender Paper Money*, p. 65.

[43] *Ibid.*, pp. 202–203, and Appendix, pp. 24–25.

[44] Newcomb, Simon. *Examination of Our Financial Policy during the Southern Rebellion.* New York: Greenwood Press, 1969 (New York: D. Appleton Co., 1865), pp. 94 and 180.

[45] McCulloch, Hugh. *Men and Measures of Half a Century.* New York: Charles Scribner's Sons, 1900, p. 178.

[46] Vieira, *Pieces of Eight,* p. 227. It especially set the pattern for the Court decisions on the Gold Clauses. (See the following, Chapter 22.)

# FOURTEEN

# Monetary Affairs in the United States, 1871–1883

The immediate practical consequence of the Court decision of May 1, 1871 was close to nil. At the time, gold was a commodity that a purchaser bought in "The Gold Room" in New York to use for international payments, with U.S. notes (greenbacks), national bank notes, or acceptable bank checks. Its price fluctuated around 112–114 percent of "par," that is, around $23–$24 per ounce. Post-war Republican policy aimed at restoring the old parity without devaluing the gold dollar. To achieve this goal, either the outstanding stock of government currency, primarily greenbacks, had to be reduced by some means, or the economy had to produce more goods and services while the existing stock of money remained constant, or some combination of the two events had to occur. One other possibility was discoveries of new gold ore that could be exploited more cheaply than what was currently available, thereby reducing the relative market price of gold. This last possibility was realized in the late 1890s, as it had been in the 1850s, but too late to alter the actual course of gold resumption.

All the various forms of paper currency circulated with each other on an equal footing. Silver was at a slight market premium. Its market price had lifted away from its fixed legal tender price just as had gold's due to the greenback inflation, but its premium was never as great as that for gold.[1]

Resumption – exchange of gold for greenbacks at the pre-war parity – was the overriding *desideratum* of Republican policy. In 1868, Congress had statutorily fixed the stock of greenbacks at $356 million, only $44 million below the war-time total of $400 million. However, as the Panic of 1873 abated in the late fall of that year, the Secretary of the Treasury re-issued $26 million of the $44 million "retired" greenbacks to meet the government's

---

[1] Jastram, Roy W., *Silver the Restless Metal*. John Wiley and Sons: New York, 1981, p. 76, 204.

immediate fiscal needs.[2] This action raised arguments in Congress on both the desirability and propriety of such a policy. After much wrangling, Congress allowed the additional $26 million to stand, fixing the new total of greenbacks at $382 million. However, the new maximum was specifically barred from any further Treasury changes. Total national bank note issues were still fixed by the National Bank Act at $300 million.[3]

The Grant Administration operated on the expectation that greater production of goods and services over time would reduce the price level enough to lower the market price of gold to parity – $20.67 per ounce. However, this policy was proving tediously slow. Consequently, when the post-war Republican congressional majorities started to crumble in 1874, the party leaders felt they had to "do something" while they still had a congressional majority. So they cobbled together a Resumption Act in 1875 that included a means for reducing the outstanding stock of government-controlled paper currencies – both U.S. notes (greenbacks) and national bank notes.

The new act declared that resumption would occur on January 1, 1879. It also abolished the $300 million statutory limit on national bank note issues. Henceforth, national banks could issue notes without limit, so long as they met legal reserve requirements and pledged the appropriate amounts of government bonds as collateral. Future issues of national bank notes were to depend solely on the "needs of business," as reflected by demands for bank loans in financial markets. If a national bank wanted to increase its issue of notes, it had simply to send to the Comptroller of the Currency approved government securities, plus greenbacks equal to 20 percent of the new national bank notes issued.[4] The Secretary of the Treasury would then by fiscal means retire greenbacks amounting to 80 percent of the issues of new national bank notes. Since the greenback reserve that national banks had to maintain was at least 20 percent of new bank notes issued, the implication was that the total stock of currency outstanding would remain approximately constant: national bank notes would increase on the greenback base, while the total amount of greenbacks outstanding declined.

Some national banks, however, decided not to issue bank notes any longer, or just went out of the banking business altogether. When they did so, they sent their unused notes back to the Comptroller who dutifully retired them. To get a correct net accounting of greenbacks for retirement,

---

[2]  See, Timberlake, *Monetary Policy*, Chaps. 7 and 8, pp. 84–117.
[3]  *Ibid.*, pp. 104–108.
[4]  Total collateral for the notes was 110 percent – 20 percent greenbacks and 90 percent government securities.

the gross allowances for new national bank note issues of currently viable banks should have been adjusted downward for the notes voluntarily retired by the national banks before the calculated quantity of greenbacks was destroyed. It was here that the Secretaries of the Treasury (three of them) practiced some legerdemain. When accounting the number of greenbacks to be retired, they simply ignored the notes voluntarily retired by the national banks themselves. By calculating 80 percent of *gross* national bank notes issued, they could retire more greenbacks than were intended by the Resumption Act.

The net effect of this act, as interpreted by the Secretaries of the Treasury during the next 3 years, was to retire an additional $36 million in greenbacks. When the smoke cleared in 1878, gross issues of national bank notes had increased by $45 million, but net issues of bank notes had declined by $25 million. This arithmetic was inescapable; greenbacks and national bank notes were equally acceptable for all ordinary transactions, but greenbacks were the primary reserves of the national banks that issued national bank notes. With fewer greenbacks to serve as reserves, the national banks had to reduce their issues of notes. Presto! The total stock of paper currency declined.

These reductions dumbfounded many members of Congress who thought they had created a money-neutral law. Indeed, the workings of the act and the Secretaries' sleight-of-hand also puzzled many scholarly investigators in the decades that followed.[5] In any case, the stock of common money, based on the eroding stock of greenbacks, declined gradually during 1876–1878.[6] As it did so, the price level fell correspondingly. Perforce, one price that fell was the market price of gold. By mid-1878, it was down to within a few cents of the pre-war parity price, and looked as though it would be there by year's end – as indeed it was.

When Resumption seemed certain, Congress repealed the clause in the Resumption Act that had led to the slow attrition of the greenbacks, and froze the outstanding stock on May 31, 1878, at $346.7 million. There it remained "forever."

Meanwhile, silver had come again into the policy picture. Throughout most of history, gold has gradually appreciated in value relative to silver (or silver has depreciated relative to gold), even though for short periods the

---

[5]   It takes a very careful reading of both the Resumption Act, and the *Annual Reports of the Secretary of the Treasury* to understand clearly just how this contrived contraction worked. But work it did.

[6]   See Timberlake, *Monetary Policy*, pp. 110–113, for more details.

shift in relative values has gone the other way. In the mid-1870s, rich silver ore was discovered in the American West, and more silver began to appear in markets. In addition and partly in response to this trend, the monetary preferences of the world's governments turned to gold and away from silver. Silver was fine for fractional coinage, but gold was the standard of choice for the world's financial dealings. Reflecting these changes, and the practical difficulties with bi-metallism, the U.S. monetary system was on a *de facto* gold standard as early as the 1850s, and made *de jure* in effect by the Coinage Act of 1873.[7]

Despite gold's long-run stability and prestige, strong Western silver interests in Congress wanted "something done for silver." That "something" became a reality with the passage of the Bland-Allison Act on February 28, 1878.[8] This act was the political price paid to silver interests to compensate for Resumption of gold payments and the deflation leading to it. It decreed that the U.S. Treasury should buy between $2 million and $4 million of silver each month, and coin the silver into standard silver dollars. The Treasury would only need to spend these dollars, however, if its current fiscal revenues were insufficient for its routine needs. Silver dollars not spent would simply accumulate in the Treasury. In practice, the Secretaries of the Treasury bought only the minimum amount of $2 million per month the whole time the act was in force. So "something" was done for silver, but most of the dollars coined were stockpiled in the Treasury. A pocketful of silver dollars is not very comfortable, and people used other media for small exchanges. Nonetheless, silver had its foot in the door. From this time on, it became the "cheap money" of choice for those who objected to the monetary discipline of a gold standard.

Resumption of gold payments at the pre-Civil War parity occurred on schedule – January 1, 1879. It was a remarkable political achievement because its success required the federal government to tolerate and even encourage deflation. Its occurrence, however, brought along with it two undesirable pieces of baggage. One was the subsidization and issue of silver coin mandated by the Bland-Allison Act. From this time on, the federal government issued silver currency – coined dollars and, later, silver certificates that were redeemable in gold even though they "represented" deposited silver. The

---

[7] Jastram, *Silver*, pp. 67–68, and Dunbar, *Laws*, pp. 241–243.
[8] Dunbar, *Laws, etc.* pp. 246–248. Richard Bland was a Democratic Representative from Tennessee, and William Allison was a Republican Senator from Iowa. The act reflected bipartisan support for silver. It therefore became law in spite of the veto of President Rutherford B. Hayes.

monetary value of all silver currency thereafter appreciably exceeded its commodity value, and the silver standard was history.

Far more portentous was the Supreme Court's legitimization of paper money as full legal tender subject to the discretion of Congress. The irony of the Court's action is that it did not influence at all the monetary path to Resumption. Given the political and economic events as they happened, gold payments at the pre-war parity would have occurred no matter what the Supreme Court decided on the legal tender issue. However, the long-run results of the legal tender cases were momentous.

# FIFTEEN

# The Third Legal Tender Case:
## *Juilliard v. Greenman*, 1884

After Resumption of specie payments in 1879, the U.S. economy enjoyed a period of ongoing stability. United States notes – greenbacks – were frozen at $346.7 million; national banks and their issues of national bank notes were operating within the bounds of the gold standard; and the silver question seemed reasonably well settled with the passage of the Bland-Allison Act. Above all, the gold standard was working smoothly and according to tradition.

Although it did not violate the rules of the gold standard, the U.S. Treasury had become something of a central bank. It managed three fiat currencies – greenbacks, national bank notes, and silver coin and certificates – keeping them at par with gold by redeeming them when called upon to do so at the legal price for gold. In support of its currency liabilities, the Treasury held a gold balance of $100 million that Congress had established for this purpose. However, the Treasury could add to that amount if its fiscal operations were favorable – that is, if its revenues exceeded its expenditures.[1]

A minor business boom occurred in the early 1880s, followed by a minor recession, and an uneventful banking crisis in 1884. The main monetary event in that year, however, was the third legal tender decision, *Juilliard vs. Greenman*,[2] which concluded the case for legitimacy of full legal tender paper money in the United States.

The make-up of the Court continued to reflect the influence of Republican presidents, as would be expected. Where the Court had been five Republicans and four Democrats in 1871, by 1884 it was eight Republicans and one Democrat.

---

[1]  See, Timberlake, *Monetary Policy,* pp. 146–151.
[2]  *Juilliard vs. Greenman*, 110 U.S. 421, submitted January 22, decided March 3, 1884.

The issue in *Juilliard* was simple. A creditor, Juilliard, refused payment of $5,100 in U.S. notes (greenbacks) for a debt of just over $5,100 due him from Greenman. Juilliard wanted gold. When the circuit court ruled in favor of Greenman, Juilliard brought the case to the Supreme Court.

Justice Gray delivered the opinion of the Court. He first reviewed all the provisions in the various acts of Congress that applied to this decision, including the necessity for the re-issue of greenbacks as they came into the Treasury. The only crucial provision, however, was the one from the first Legal Tender Act in 1862, stating that the U.S. notes were "lawful money, and a tender in payment of all debts, public and private, within the United States, except for duties on imports and interest on the public debt." Because the law stated that the notes had to be re-issued perpetually, "the single question ... to be considered," Gray observed, "is whether the notes of the United States, issued in time of war, under acts of Congress declaring them to be a legal tender in payment of private debts, and afterwards in time of peace, redeemed and paid in gold coin at the Treasury, and then re-issued under the act of 1878, can, under the Constitution of the United States, be a legal tender in payment of such debts." The Court unanimously agreed, he continued, that this case was the same in principle as the previously decided legal tender cases, "... and all the judges except MR. JUSTICE FIELD, who adheres to the views expressed in his dissenting opinions in those cases, are of the opinion that they were rightly decided."[3]

In support of the decision, Justice Gray cited what had become the Court's favorite precedent: "the reasoning of Chief Justice Marshall in the great judgment in *McCulloch v. Maryland,* ... by which the power of Congress to incorporate a bank was demonstrated and affirmed, notwithstanding [the fact that] the Constitution does not enumerate among the powers granted, that of establishing a bank or creating a corporation." Gray then observed: "The people of the United States by the Constitution established a national government, with sovereign powers, legislative, executive, and judicial." He cited Marshall's opinion on the scope of Congress's enumerated powers, noting that the government, "... though limited in its powers is supreme within its sphere of action...."[4]

Nowhere in Marshall's decision, or in the Constitution, can one find the words "sovereign" or "sovereignty." Gray's assertion that "the people ... established a national government with sovereign powers" was correct only in the sense that the "people" ceded certain powers to the federal and

---

[3]   U.S. pp. 436–438.
[4]   *Ibid.*

state governments, and retained the rest. The national government's powers were strictly prescribed, albeit made somewhat elastic by the "necessary and proper" clause.

Gray continued the "sovereignty" argument, which had become the majority's principal theme. "A Constitution … creating a national sovereignty, and intended to endure for ages," Gray read, "is not to be interpreted with the strictness of a private contract. The Constitution … does not undertake … to specify all the means by which [the government's powers] may be carried into execution."[5]

With regard to issues of tax revenues, finance, and especially currency, Gray emphasized, the government's powers are preeminent. He cited these powers – to lay and collect taxes, to borrow money on the credit of the United States, and to coin money, regulate the value thereof and of foreign coin, and fix the standard of weights and measures. He next dwelt on "Necessary and Proper," including Marshall's view that "the only reasonable interpretation of this clause … [is that it is] not limited to such measures as are absolutely and indispensably necessary, without which the powers granted must fail of execution, but … includes all appropriate means which are conducive or adapted to the end to be accomplished, and which, in the judgment of Congress, will most advantageously effect it."[6]

Gray reviewed at length the history of the original debates on the Constitution, as well as past decisions concerning money and finances. He repeatedly cited Marshall's opinion in *McCulloch* as a precedent for Congress's unlimited power to issue bills of credit and make them legal tender for private debts, even though the *McCulloch* decision had neither treated nor implied any such power. The opinion concluded with the flagrant nonsequitur that even though states are prohibited from coining money and emitting bills of credit, "no intention can be inferred from this [prohibition] to deny Congress either of these powers. … Congress is expressly authorized to coin money." Then Gray read the conclusion for which he has become renowned:

It appears to us to follow as a logical and necessary consequence that Congress has the power to issue the obligations of the United States in such form, and to impress upon them such qualities as currency for the purchase of merchandise and the payment of debts, as accord with the usage of sovereign governments. The power, as incident to the power of borrowing money, and issuing bills or notes of the government for money borrowed, of impressing upon those bills or notes the quality

---

[5]  *Ibid.*, p. 439.
[6]  *Ibid.*, pp. 440–441.

of being a legal tender for the payment of private debts was a power universally understood to belong to sovereignty, in Europe and America at the time of the framing and adopting of the Constitution of the United States. The governments of Europe, acting through the monarch or the legislature, according to the distribution of powers under their respective constitutions [sic], had and have as sovereign a power of issuing paper money as of stamping coin.[7]

Congress's "coining money power," Gray insisted, referred to paper as well as to gold and silver metal:

Under the power to borrow money on the credit of the United States and to issue circulating notes for the money borrowed, [Congress's] power to define the quality and force of those notes as currency is as broad as the like power over a metallic currency under the power to coin money and to regulate the value thereof. Under the two powers, taken together, Congress is authorized to establish a national currency, either in coin or in paper, and to make that currency lawful money for all purposes, as regards the national government or private individuals. [8]

Gray finished by reading the majority's infamous judgment:

Congress, as the legislature of a sovereign nation, being expressly empowered by the Constitution "to lay and collect taxes, to pay the debts and provide for the common defense and general welfare of the United States," and "to borrow money on the credit of the United States," and "to coin money and regulate the value thereof and of foreign coin," and being clearly authorized, as incidental to the exercise of those great powers, to emit bills of credit, to charter national banks, and to provide a national currency for the whole people in the form of coin, Treasury notes, and national bank bills, and the power to make the notes of the government a legal tender in payment of private debts being one of the powers belonging to sovereignty in other civilized nations, and not expressly withheld from Congress by the Constitution; we are irresistibly impelled to the conclusion that the impressing upon the Treasury notes of the United States the quality of being a legal tender in payment of private debts is an appropriate means, conducive and plainly adapted to the execution of the undoubted powers of Congress, consistent with the letter and spirit of the Constitution, and therefore within the meaning of that instrument, "necessary and proper" for carrying into execution the powers vested by this Constitution in the government of the United States.

It follows that the Act of May 31, 1878, is constitutional and valid, and that the circuit court rightly held that the tender in Treasury notes [greenbacks], reissued and

---

[7]  *Ibid.*, p. 448. Gray did not elaborate further on the "respective constitutions" of European governments.

[8]  *Ibid.*, pp. 448–449. Included here was the statement: "A contract to pay a sum of money, without any stipulation as to the kind of money in which it shall be paid, may always be satisfied by payment of that sum in any currency which is lawful money at the place and time at which payment is to be made." Here again was the Boutwell notion that would vitiate one of the principal functions of contracts.

kept in circulation under that act, was a tender of lawful money in payment of the defendant's debt to the plaintiff.

Judgment affirmed.[9]

In plain language, the reasoning of the decision went as follows:

(1) The Constitution was written to establish and maintain a sovereign government ruled by a Congress. Included in the powers granted to that Congress is the power "to borrow money."

(2) Since it can "*borrow* money," Congress also has the power "to *issue* bills of credit" – legal tender paper currency that can in turn be used to pay back the "money" it has borrowed.

(3) Congress also has the power to coin metallic currency and declare the value thereof.

(4) Because Congress has both the power to issue circulating notes, which are currency, and the power to make gold or silver coin legal tender, it is "authorized to establish a national currency, either in coin or in paper, and to make that currency lawful money for all purposes."

The most unmistakably misused words here are "borrow" and "issue." If Congress, having borrowed "money" – meaning "real resources" – can then repay in legal tender paper currency that it issues, why should it bother to borrow "money" in the first place? No government that could issue paper money need ever inconvenience itself by borrowing at interest.[10] The opinion did not properly distinguish between *borrowing* by selling interest-bearing securities to the public, using the proceeds to buy necessary goods and services, and *issuing,* that is, printing and spending legal tender paper money into circulation in order to buy such goods and services.

If one "puts together" the two "money" clauses, as the opinion suggested, the result is: "Congress shall have the power to coin paper money on the credit of the United States and regulate the value thereof." Nothing in the written Constitution supports such a construction. No man who attended the Constitutional Convention in 1787 would have imagined it, or endorsed it for an instant, or even tolerated it as arguable.

---

[9] *Ibid.*, pp. 449–450. The opinion again denied that the Court could exercise "judicial review" of Congress's determination of "necessity."

[10] To keep the two operations separate, modern-day central banks were prohibited from buying government securities directly from the Treasury. For a central bank to do so is simply a devious means of outright money creation.

Justice Field also did not accept this view. He dissented yet again from the majority, as he had done in *Knox v. Lee* and *Parker v. Davis*, reiterating many of the arguments he and the previous majority had initiated in *Hepburn v. Griswold*. Now, however, his was the lone dissenting voice.

Field noted that the attempt to make paper money legal tender immediately altered the "condition of contracts between private parties and authorize[d] their payment or discharge in something different from that which the parties [to the contract] stipulated." The Framers of the Constitution, he declared, "intended to prohibit the issue of legal tender notes both by the general government and by the states, and thus prevent interference with the contracts of private parties."[11]

Field cited Chief Justice Marshall, who had argued that the Framers wished to prevent the issue of paper money by any means. "To restore public confidence completely," Marshall had written, "it was necessary not only to prohibit the use of particular means by which [paper money] might be effected, but to prohibit the use of any means by which the same mischief might be produced. The [constitutional] convention appears to have intended to establish [the] great principle that contracts should be inviolable." Field continued, "It would be difficult to believe, even in the absence of the historical evidence we have on the subject that the framers of the Constitution ... ever intended that the new government ... should possess the power of making its bills a legal tender, which [power] they were unwilling should remain with the states."[12]

Field then referred to the work of the historian George Bancroft, who was to play a significant role in the subsequent intellectual history of this case. (See Chapter 16.) Bancroft had written a 10-volume *History of the United States*. Field cited Volume 2, *History of the Formation of the Constitution*, in which Bancroft reported that the power to issue legal tender paper money was refused to the general government by a vote of nine states against two. "Whenever such paper has been employed," Field observed, quoting Bancroft, "it has in every case thrown upon its authors the burden of exculpation under the plea of pressing necessity." Moreover, Field continued, "When the convention came to the prohibition upon the states, [Bancroft] says that the clause, 'No state shall make anything but gold and silver a tender in payment of debts,' was accepted without a dissentient vote. 'So the adoption of the Constitution,' he [Bancroft] adds, 'is to be the end forever of

---

[11]  *Ibid.*, p. 452.
[12]  *Ibid.*, p. 454.

paper money, whether issued by the several states or by the United States, if the Constitution shall be rightly interpreted and honestly obeyed.'"[13]

For three-quarters of a century, Field noted, no jurist or statesman challenged this prohibition. "There is no recorded word of even one [person] in favor of [the government] possessing the power. All conceded, as an axiom of constitutional law, that the power did not exist."[14]

Field next reviewed the legislative history of the legal tender clause, noting its exceptional role as a "war measure," how Chief Justice Chase had reversed his opinion as Secretary of the Treasury, and, as Chief Justice, had cast the deciding vote against greenback constitutionality in the *Hepburn* decision. "War," Field noted, "merely increased the urgency for money; it did not add to the powers of the government; ... If the power existed, it might be equally exercised when a loan was made to meet ordinary expenses in time of peace. ... *The wants of the government could never be the measure of its powers.* Never before," Field continued, "was it contended by any jurist or commentator on the Constitution that the government, in full receipt of ample income, with a Treasury overflowing, with more money on hand than it knows what to do with, could issue paper money as a legal tender.... So it always happens that whenever a wrong principle of conduct, political or personal, is adopted on the plea of necessity, it will be afterwards followed on a plea of convenience."[15]

Field then treated the issue of *sovereignty* that the majority opinion had latterly introduced and made the keystone of their argument. Previously, Field noted, some Justices had based their arguments on the government's power to borrow money, some on the coining power, and others as a power incidental to the general powers of the government. In the present case, "it is placed by the Court upon the power to borrow money, and the alleged sovereignty of the United States over the currency.... And [the majority opinion] adds that 'The power ... of impressing upon those bills or notes the quality of being a legal tender for the payment of private debts, was a power universally understood to belong to sovereignty, in Europe and America at the time of the framing and adoption of the Constitution of the United States.'"[16]

Field then asked,

---

[13]  *Ibid.*, p. 455. Cited by Field: George Bancroft, *History of the Formation of the Constitution, Vol. 2*, pp. 134–137.

[14]  *Ibid.*, p. 455.

[15]  *Ibid.*, pp. 458–459. (Emphasis added.)

[16]  *Ibid.*, p. 459.

"Does the Court find any authority for giving to [the words, 'borrow money'] a different interpretation in the Constitution from what they receive when used in other instruments, as in the charters of municipal bodies or of private corporations, or in the contracts of individuals? They are not ambiguous; they have a well settled meaning in other instruments. If the Court may change that in the Constitution, so it may the meaning of all other clauses, and the powers which the government may exercise will be found declared not by plain words in the organic law, but by words of a new significance resting in the minds of the judges. Until some authority beyond the alleged claim and practice of the sovereign governments of Europe be produced, I must believe that the terms have the same meaning in all instruments, wherever they are used; that they mean a power only to contract for a loan of money upon considerations to be agreed between the parties."[17]

Arbitrarily adding the quality of "legal tender" to the notes, Field argued, would be no more appropriate a means of ensuring their acceptability than making them "tickets to places of amusement," or a variety of other privileges. The power authorizing contractual arrangements between the government and private parties, he continued, "is a very different one from a power to deal between parties to private contracts in which the government is not interested, and to compel the receipt of these promises to pay in place of the money for which the contracts [are] stipulated.... There is no legal connection between the two – between the power to borrow from those willing to lend and the power to interfere with the independent contracts of others. The possession of this latter power would justify the interference of the government with any rights of property of other parties."[18]

The power vested in Congress to coin money, Field noted, referred only to metallic coin, and only the various coins could be impressed with the stamp "indicating their value with reference to the unit of value established by law." Moreover, only the precious metals qualified as money, and the term "money" was always used in the context of the Constitution to mean "coin." Therefore, "the only money the value of which Congress can regulate is coined money.... Between the promises of the government, designated as its securities, and this [coined] money of the Constitution [is] a distinction which disappears in the [majority] opinion of the Court." In fact, Field warned, the majority opinion allows Congress to make virtually anything legal tender, a doctrine that "is put forth as in some way a justification of the legislation authorizing the tender of nominal [paper] money in place of real money for payment of debts."[19]

---

[17]  *Ibid.*, p. 460.
[18]  *Ibid.*, pp. 461–462.
[19]  *Ibid.*, pp. 464–466.

Field then emphasized the role of the Constitution as the primary means of restricting the powers of government. He recalled how the Constitution came before the conventions of the several states for adoption after the Constitutional Convention. The states' "apprehension ... that other powers than those designated might be claimed ... led to the first ten amendments," presented after the state conventions had urged that "in order to prevent misconception or abuse of [the national government's] powers, further declaratory and restrictive clauses should be added." The sentiment of the states, which had issued excessive quantities of paper money during the war with England, was to abolish any such legal-tender power for any government, whether state or national.

"Of what purpose is it then," Field asked, "to refer to the exercise of the [paper money] power by the absolute or the limited governments of Europe? ... Congress can exercise no power by virtue of any supposed inherent sovereignty in the general government.... There is no such thing as a power of inherent sovereignty in the government of the United States. It is a government of delegated powers, supreme within its prescribed sphere but powerless outside of it. In this country, sovereignty resides in the people, and Congress can exercise no power which [the people] have not, by their Constitution, entrusted to it; all else is withheld. It seems, however, to be supposed that as the power was taken from the states, it could not have been intended that it should disappear entirely, and therefore it must in some way adhere to the general government notwithstanding the Tenth Amendment and the nature of the Constitution."[20]

Field criticized the alteration of contracts that the legal tender provision had provoked and would ultimately encourage. Sometimes, he noted, the laws of the land unintentionally result in incidental harm to personal property. "But far different," he argued, "is the case when the impairment of the contract does not follow incidentally, but is directly and in terms allowed and enacted. Legislation operating directly upon a private contract ... is forbidden to the states, and no power to alter the stipulations of such contracts by direct legislation is conferred upon Congress. ... [T]he framers of the Constitution never intended that such a power be exercised. One of the great objects of the Constitution ... was to establish justice, and what was meant by that in its relation to contracts ... was not left to inference

---

[20] *Ibid.*, pp. 467–468. Field's discussion of "sovereignty" reflects the traditional understanding of that term. These three concluding sentences succinctly summarize the entire *ethos* of the Constitution. See also Barnett, *Restoring the Lost Constitution*, pp. 172–173, 213, and 354–357.

or conjecture. Yet this Court holds that a measure directly operating upon and necessarily impairing private contracts may be adopted in the execution of powers specifically granted for other purposes because it is not in terms prohibited, and that it is consistent with the letter and spirit of the Constitution.... I see only evil likely to follow." [21]

Field next reminded his brethren that "the possibility of ... depreciation will always attend paper money. This inborn infirmity no mere legislative declaration can cure. ... If Congress has the power to make the notes a legal tender and to pass as money," he concluded, "why should not a sufficient amount be issued to pay the bonds of the United States as they mature? Why pay interest on the millions of dollars of bonds now due when Congress can in one day make the money to pay the principal? And why should there be any restraint upon unlimited appropriations by the government for all imaginary schemes of public improvement if the printing press can furnish the money that is needed for them?"[22]

None of the eight majority Justices responded to Field's arguments. They presumably had no counter-arguments, because there were none.

---

[21] *Ibid.*, pp. 468–469.

[22] *Ibid.*, pp. 470–471. Change "millions" to "billions" and then "trillions," and Field's rhetorical question becomes particularly pertinent to political-financial conditions in the United States during the past half-century.

# SIXTEEN

# Commentaries on the Legal Tender Decisions:
## The Issue of Sovereignty

The third legal tender decision in 1884 came when the monetary system had largely stabilized following the Resumption of specie payments and the return of what seemed a permanent gold standard. Though the gold standard in operation then was not "pure," and had elements of government control overseeing it and interfering with it from time to time, it worked tolerably well. In light of the monetary calm at the time, the final legal tender decision that gave Congress absolute power to make paper money full legal tender under any circumstances was neither necessary nor proper, nor even expedient. In fact, it was hardly noticed.

Given the absence of serious monetary problems, what might the Supreme Court have decided in 1884 to maintain both the integrity of "original intent" in the Constitution and preserve the ongoing economic equilibrium?

First, the Court could have declared the greenbacks unconstitutional as a forced tender for private debts, but constitutional for all payments due to and from the national government. This same possibility had been open to the Court as a judgment in the Second Legal Tender Decision decided in 1870–1871, and to Congress when it passed the legal tender laws in 1862 and 1863. Unfortunately, the Court majorities in the legal tender cases did not suggest this option, even though the government had issued such Treasury notes since 1812, and the notes had always been accepted by private parties as well as the U.S. Treasury to clear debts. Whenever notes are a tender for debts due to and payable by a government, they are accepted universally as well by private parties.

Second, nothing in law or in the arguments presented in the three legal tender cases implied that a creditor could demand gold payments for debts incurred after specie payments had been suspended in early 1862. The Court could have ruled consistently that debts incurred after that date were payable in greenbacks, or whatever was agreed to in the contract. It could then have ordered Congress to re-issue all greenbacks coming into the Treasury as receivable only for government dues, and reconfirmed to Congress that it had no constitutional power to make the notes legal tender for private debts. Because all paper money – greenbacks, national bank notes, and other Treasury notes not full legal tender – consistently circulated at par with each other, such a judicial-legislative correction would have caused virtually no business or economic disturbance. It is doubtful that anyone, except perhaps a few "Supreme Court watchers," would have noticed. After Resumption in 1879, however, the issue became dulled: Any creditor who did not want the paper money tendered to him for payment of a debt-contract could redeem the paper currency for gold at the par price through a commercial bank or a sub-Treasury office.

The three legal tender decisions were not primarily dispassionate judicial expressions of objective legal minds, seeking to expound constitutional precepts. More realistically, they were partisan political reactions – an unfortunate consequence of a civil war that found one nation conquering the other, and then imposing legal-tender-paper-money laws it had fostered during the war on the reconstructed post-war economy. Ironically, by the time of the third legal tender decision that forever settled the controversy, a proper decision rigorously adhering to constitutional principles would have had little political or economic impact. Resumption of the working gold standard at the pre-war value for gold in 1879 had removed any public apprehension over greenback value or acceptability. Consequently, the final Court decision resulted in no political gains for the Republican administrations that were so eager to justify their war-time currency policies.

All of the eight Justices whose majority decision sanctioned the government's power to issue legal tender paper money were Republican appointees. Their presence on the Court reflected the fact that from 1860 to 1884 – 24 years – all U.S. Presidents, except Andrew Johnson, Lincoln's successor, were Republicans who appointed Republican jurists sympathetic to the objectives of Republican administrations, and particularly to the constitutionality of the greenbacks.

The majority Justices, however, had to find a path through the obvious constitutional constraints that denied the decision they sought. They began with "Necessary and Proper," the key that had initially opened the Treasury's door for the issue of paper money. But something more compelling had to be found to extend greenback constitutionality. The Justices discovered what they wanted in "*sovereignty*," the prerogative, they argued, that was an inherent feature of the federal government's powers. They first introduced this notion when they were a minority in the *Hepburn* case, and then expanded and reiterated the concept in the following decisions when they were a majority.

## JUDICIAL COMMENTARIES

Once the *Juilliard* decision was widely circulated, several prominent jurists, legal historians, and academicians discussed it in print. An eminent legal scholar, James Bradley Thayer, contributed an article to the *Harvard Law Review* (1887) in which he supplied every *apologia* imaginable for the majority decision. He repeated all the arguments and assumptions of the majority. He used the words of the Constitution referring to "money," such as, "borrow," "coin," and "regulate" in any sequence that would excuse the assumption of power that the decision had sanctioned. He "put together" the two money clauses. He wore out "necessary and proper." He did not distinguish between issues of Treasury notes that were a tender only for payments to and from the government, and the full legal tender greenbacks that had become tender for all private contracts. He claimed that only the states were prohibited from making anything except gold and silver coin a tender in payment of debt, failing to infer from the Ninth and Tenth Amendments that the federal government was likewise prohibited. He concluded that the Framers had given Congress a sovereign power – "complete control" – to furnish a legal tender paper currency, similar in extent to the "power which had frequently been exercised by those legislative bodies [Parliament] with which the framers of the instrument were most familiar." Because the Framers were familiar with the sovereignty of European states, he suggested, they must have intended to vest the new Congress with the same prerogative! Surely it is doubtful that the Delegates to the Convention of 1787 would have accepted any such "inference" as germane to the task before them.

Another legal authority who apologized for the Court's decision was Alva R. Hunt, the author of a comprehensive treatise on the legal aspects of money in courts of law. Hunt also accepted and supported the "sovereignty" argument. "The power to issue money and declare the extent to which it shall be current," he wrote, "is, from the necessity of having a stable and uniform standard, an attribute of sovereignty, a power assumed very early in the history of civilized government." He cited the renowned English jurist, William Blackstone, to the effect that giving money "authority" and making it "current" were a part of the "King's prerogative."[1]

Hunt also gave his blessing to the clearing of debts with whatever is legal tender at the time of payment, without defending this view, but continuing the cant of the Court majority and the Boutwell Republicans.[2] He cited numerous decisions from state courts between 1864 and 1867 on legal tender cases. Virtually all of them had allowed greenbacks to serve as surrogates for gold, without any reference to the real values of the debts contracted. One decision stated that only by virtue of law were either gold coins or greenbacks a legal tender – without noting that gold had value as a commodity long before it was made a legal money, but that paper money would be only scrap without the force of a legal tender law behind it. Therefore, the opinion concluded, both kinds of money *had* to be "exactly equivalent for the purpose of payment." The market premium on gold at this time (1866) was a value "men voluntarily choose to give for [it]," and therefore could have no bearing on the legality of the case.[3]

Hunt used this "analysis" to argue that in the *Hepburn* decision the Court "made its comparison between the wrong things. It compared the declared or nominal value of legal tender notes with the market value of the bullion in a coined dollar. The declared value the government controls, while the [market] value of bullion is controlled by the law of supply and demand. If declared values had been compared," Hunt continued, "(and it seems absurd to compare equals), it would have been found that … $1,400 in 1857 was equivalent to $1,400 in 1868."[4]

With this kind of judicial sophistication backing it, no government need ever have been bothered with taxation or a national debt or any other fiscal problems. Instead, it would, as Field had suggested, simply print legal tender paper money to pay off all of its debts.

## ADAM SMITH'S AND OTHERS' VIEWS OF SOVEREIGN POWER

The emergence of the "sovereignty" concept from the Court's Republican majorities marked a new and very questionable means for establishing constitutional norms, for the argument that included this notion presumed for its initiation a contradictory assumption. The Framers, the new majority

[1]   Hunt, Alva R. *A Treatise on the Law of Tender, and Bringing Money into Court.* St. Paul: Frank Dufresne, 1903, pp. 61–61.
[2]   *Ibid.*, p. 63.
[3]   *Ibid.*, p. 105. Hunt cited, *Brown v. Welch*, 26 Ind. 116.
[4]   *Ibid.*, p. 114.

declared, knew they were setting up a government for all time, and that this government had sovereign control over the monetary system. "Sovereign" control meant that the government could do anything it wished with respect to money, as the final Legal Tender decision had ruled. However, the Framers were also well aware that to entrust a sovereign with the prerogative of discretion over the monetary system would offer a temptation few sovereigns have ever resisted. Such a privilege implies the power to debase the currency and to tax the public by means of unlimited seigniorage.[5] Understanding this danger, the Framers never would have allowed Congress to impose a discretionary monetary system that would have enabled the federal government to avoid the political rigors of taxation and borrowing at term.

One eminent scholar, Adam Smith, whose work the Justices might profitably have read, examined the responsibilities and powers of the sovereign as they applied to the English monarchy. In his treatise *The Wealth of Nations*,[6] Smith discussed at length economic principles, polity, law, and other subjects. He devoted two full chapters to the functions of the sovereign and his legitimate means for obtaining revenues due the state.

According to Smith, the sovereign had three functions: "First, the duty of protecting the society from the violence and invasion of other independent societies; secondly, the duty of establishing an exact administration of justice; and thirdly, the duty of erecting and maintaining certain public works and … institutions, which it can never be for the interest of any individual or small number of individuals, to erect and maintain." He included here such constructions as roads, bridges, canals, and harbors.[7]

While these "necessary" governmental functions reflect an English point-of-view for the later eighteenth century, they are a tolerable argument.

Smith next discussed the legitimate means that the sovereign had to acquire revenues. He could impose various kinds of taxes, Smith suggested, and he could obtain rents from public lands, as well as fees for operating post offices. In time of war the sovereign's immediate need for resources was an excuse only to borrow in lieu of taxes, and not any reason at all to tamper

---

[5]  *Seigniorage* is the excess revenue a unit of money returns to the issuer over the cost of producing that unit. For example, a silver dollar that cost the Treasury fifty cents for the silver and, say, ten cents for other costs, returns forty cents of seigniorage to the Treasury when it spends the newly coined dollar for ordinary goods and services.

[6]  Adam Smith, *The Wealth of Nations*. New York: Random House, 1937 [1776, Fifth edition, 1789].

[7]  Smith, *Wealth of Nations*, pp. 651 and 682.

with the coinage or currency. Coinage devaluations and debasements, Smith declared, cause "a general and most pernicious subversion of the fortunes of private people: ... enriching the idle and profuse debtor at the expense of the industrious and frugal creditor...." Depreciation of the currency, he concluded, was a "treacherous fraud."[8] In 168 pages of text, Adam Smith found no license for the sovereign to debase or devalue the coinage, or to issue legal tender paper money. The sovereign had prerogatives and rights, but none to tamper with the currency.

In another section in which he discussed the gold and silver contents of guineas and shillings, Smith observed that the government's role was only that of "reforming" the coinage to adjust for the wear and tear on the coin – the housekeeping function that every government issuing metallic coins had occasionally to face. Gold had in practice become the single standard. Silver had become currency only for small-sum transactions.[9]

This change caused no reduction in the metallic content of the pound sterling. Indeed, the gold value of the pound at the English mint was almost constant from 1665 to 1914.[10] The U.S. Supreme Court's alleged "Prerogative of the sovereign over the coinage" had been anything but an unlimited power in England since the time of Elizabeth.[11]

James Madison, probably the principal Framer of the Constitution and fourth president of the United States, explained in *The Federalist* (No. 44) just what the Framers had in mind when they fashioned the "money" clauses. "The extension of the prohibition to bills of credit," he wrote,

must give pleasure to every citizen in proportion to his love of justice.... The loss which America has sustained since the peace [after the Revolution] from the pestilent effects of paper money ... constitutes an enormous debt against the states chargeable with this unadvised measure, which must long remain unsatisfied: or rather an accumulation of guilt, which can be expiated no otherwise than by a voluntary sacrifice on the altar of justice of the power which has been the instrument of it.[12]

In the light of such an authoritative denial from one of the principal Framers, is it even conceivable, much less arguable, that the Constitution "clearly authorized [Congress] to emit bills of credit and provide a national currency ... and make the notes of the government a legal tender in payment

---

[8]  *Ibid.*, pp. 883–885.
[9]  *Ibid.*, pp. 40–46. Parliament made the transition to a monometallic gold standard *de jure* in 1816. Silver was a subsidiary currency in practice long before this Act of Parliament.
[10]  Jastram, *Silver, the Restless Metal*, 1981, p. 9.
[11]  Parliament had allowed a few minor changes after Elizabeth's death in 1603.
[12]  Madison, James, Alexander Hamilton, and John Jay, *The Federalist*. Everyman's edition. London: J. M. Dent and Sons, 1971. (Madison, No. 44, p. 227. Emphasis added.)

of private debts," as the *Juilliard* decision claimed? Nothing in the history of its creation, or in the document itself, suggests anything that remotely resembles this presumption.

Nor did the Framers construct what they hoped was impregnable armor only to make it vulnerable to a "Necessary and Proper" lance. This phrase was a key for allowing an implied power to assume the vestige of an express power, but it was not an open door. Nor could the Framers have denied the states the power to emit bills of credit[13] and then granted the power to a federal government that they trusted even less. As William Brough, a monetary historian of the late nineteenth century, stated the case in *The Natural Law of Money*: "Had a paper circulation been contemplated [during the Constitutional Convention], discussion upon the point, followed by the embodiment of specific rules for its regulation, would have been inevitable."[14]

### GEORGE BANCROFT'S "PLEA FOR THE CONSTITUTION OF THE UNITED STATES"

The most comprehensive and critical assessment of the *Juilliard* decision came from a distinguished historian of the era, George Bancroft, who was 84 years old when the Court wrote the *Juilliard* decision. During his long and productive life, Bancroft wrote a ten-volume history of North America,[15] and was recognized throughout the era as an eminent constitutional scholar.

When Bancroft learned of the *Juilliard* decision, he was both shocked and alarmed that a "Supreme" Court could have rendered it. His reaction stimulated him to write another book – a monograph of just ninety-five pages, in which he argued the case as if he had been on the High Court himself. The book's lengthy title, *A Plea for the Constitution of the United States, Wounded in the House of Its Guardians*, accurately describes what is between its covers.[16]

---

[13] The greenbacks issued during the Civil War were identical to the "bills of credit" issued by the state governments during the Revolutionary War. Both were *issued* and were full legal tender for all debts public and private. The earlier "bills of credit" were issued by state governments because the new federal government did not yet have such comprehensive power. Even though labeled "bills," the bills of credit were a paper currency.

[14] Brough, William, *The Natural Law of Money*, 1896, p. 131.

[15] George Bancroft, *History of the United States of America from the Discovery of the Continent*. Harper's: New York, 1886.

[16] Bancroft, George. *A Plea for the Constitution of the United States, Wounded in the House of Its Guardians*. New York: Harper and Brothers, Franklin Square, 1886.

In his Introduction, Bancroft quotes the infamous "sovereignty" opinion of the majority, which, he noted, the Court had pronounced before a crowd of listeners: "The power to make the notes of the government a legal tender in payment of private debts … [etc.] is an appropriate means, conducive and plainly adapted to the execution of the undoubted powers of congress." If this opinion should be accepted as law, Bancroft predicted, it "would be a death blow to the constitution; … It not only gives a sanction to irredeemable paper money, but clothes the government with powers that have no defined limit.…" The lone dissenter, Justice Stephen Field, Bancroft noted, had at his side "invincible vouchers for the rightness of his dissent.…"[17] Those "vouchers" were James Wilson, Oliver Ellsworth, and William Paterson, whom President Washington had "selected from among [the Constitution's] framers to be its earliest judicial interpreters." They were members of the first Supreme Court. "With them," Bancroft declared, "are to be counted a cloud of witnesses, among whom are the master-builders of the constitution."[18]

Bancroft first reviewed the history of paper moneys in the American colonies to their abolition in the mid-eighteenth century. "The experience of the war of the revolution," Bancroft notes, "completed the instruction of our fathers on the wastefulness and injustice of attempting to conduct affairs on the basis of paper promises, indefinite as to their time of payment." After the peace, most of the then-existing state governments began the difficult process of managing their outstanding paper bills of credit. "From end to end of the whole country," Bancroft wrote, "its best men were seeking remedies for what [James] Madison called 'the epidemic malady' of paper money." Bancroft cited William Paterson's opinion that, "An increase of paper money, especially if it be a tender, will destroy what little credit is left, will bewilder conscience in the mazes of dishonest speculations, will allure some and constrain others into the perpetuation of knavish acts, will turn vice into legal virtue, and sanctify iniquity by law.… Why give legislative sanction to positive acts of iniquity?"[19]

Part II of Bancroft's book describes in detail how the constitutional convention of May–September, 1787, "barred the doors against paper money." Here, Bancroft quoted "a lawyer [Representative Roscoe Conkling of New

---

[17] Field's dissent, treated above, cited as his source Bancroft's earlier work on the Constitution.

[18] *Ibid.*, pp. 6–7.

[19] *Ibid.*, pp. 29–34. Bancroft footnoted this quotation: "From Paterson's manuscript, in his own handwriting."

York] who, but for his own refusal, would twelve years ago [1874] have become chief justice … in the line of succession from Ellsworth [the third Chief Justice]: 'No suggestion … of a power to make paper a legal tender can be found in the legislative history of the country. Had such a power lurked in the constitution, we should find it so recorded.… It is hardly too much to say, therefore, that the uniform and universal judgment of statesmen, jurists, and lawyers has denied the constitutional right of congress to make paper a legal tender for debts to any extent whatever.'"[20]

Bancroft then proceeded to analyze the majority decision in detail, observing that Great Britain between 1688 and 1788 – between the establishment of the British constitution and its American counterpart – never "impressed" upon bills of its government the quality of legal tender, never claimed the right to do so, and never acted in any way that would imply such a claim.

The court therefore falls into "… a stupendous error," Bancroft continued, "when it asserts that the power of impressing upon notes the quality of being a legal tender for the payment of private debts was universally understood to belong to sovereignty in Europe and America at the time of the framing and adoption of the constitution of the United States." Both the statute books and the opinions of all men in business before the French Revolution "… did not suffer even the rising of a thought for the issue of paper money as legal tender by the state or by its authority." Even in France the same attitude prevailed "until the Revolution unleashed the assignats and the Terror."[21]

Bancroft next examined the notion of "sovereignty" that the majority decision had made the center point of its case. The majority argument, he noted, constitutes a "new interpretation.… It assumes that apart from the [explicit] grants by the constitution [to the central government], the United States has powers of a sovereign government; but this is the language of revolution." If the president, vice president, and cabinet "were to agree together to exercise powers as inherent in themselves because the United States are a sovereign government, they would be guilty of a conspiracy." True, "our union in its foreign relations presents itself with all its states and territories as one indivisible; a garment without a seam; but at home we are states in a union. Within the limits of the states, the [federal] government

---

[20] *Ibid.*, p. 52. Conkling, Roscoe, *Congressional Globe*, Part I, Second Session, XXXVII. Congress, 1861–1862, pp. 634–635.
[21] *Ibid.*, pp. 57–60.

has no powers but those that have been delegated to it; some powers are distributed, some of them going alone to the United States, some to each several state, and some equally to both."[22]

Bancroft cited several notable Framers in support of this view: James Wilson of Pennsylvania, who became one of the first Court Justices; Roger Sherman of Connecticut, Alexander Hamilton of New York, and Oliver Ellsworth, "who framed the law for organizing the supreme court." According to Ellsworth, "The additional powers vested in congress extend only to matters respecting the common interests of the Union, and are specifically defined; the particular states retain their sovereignty in all other matters." Ellsworth's opinion was shared by Hamilton, who informed the public through the press that since the convention aimed at only "a partial union or consolidation, the state governments would clearly retain all the rights of sovereignty which they before had, and which were not, by that act, exclusively delegated to the United States."[23]

Bancroft was able to cite many other prominent jurists in support of his claim that the Tenth Amendment was to be taken literally. He noted how Chief Justice Marshall had said as much in 1819 in *McCulloch v. Maryland*. Chief Justice Chase had likewise declared: "No department of the government has any other powers than those delegated to it by the people.... All these powers ... arise from the constitution, and are limited by its terms."[24] In the October term of 1882, Bancroft continued, when "the Court was composed identically man for man, of the very same nine men that constitute it now, it referred to the opinion of Marshall ... and adopted it without reserve as its own.... For itself it added: 'The government of the United States is one of delegated, limited, and enumerated powers. Therefore, every valid act of congress must find in the Constitution some warrant for its passage.'"[25]

Finally, Bancroft quoted Hamilton Fish, who was a member of Grant's cabinet and the man Grant wanted to appoint as Chief Justice after Chase's death in 1873. Fish offered his view of sovereignty in a personal memo to Bancroft. The Constitution, Fish observed, gave the general government sovereign powers, "but *only* in its dealing with foreign governments.... In [its] internal relations, the [central] government ... is far, very far, removed from the powers of a sovereign state."[26]

---

[22]  *Ibid.*, pp. 60–61.
[23]  *Ibid.*, p. 63. Alexander Hamilton, *The Federalist*, No. XXXII. (Emphasis added.)
[24]  *Ibid.*, pp. 65–67.
[25]  *Ibid.*, p. 67.
[26]  *Ibid.*, p. 69. (His emphasis.)

Bancroft concluded his indictment of the majority's "understanding" of "sovereignty" by noting that "The voice of the imitative civilized world, watching our career [of the United States with a constitution] has followed our example, and kingdom after kingdom has like ourselves established written forms of government, in order to define and establish lines within which every public authority should move, [and] every delegated political power should confine its action. Are these sublime evidences of the advance of civilization to be thrown out of sight? ... The court ... has set itself in conflict, not with the constitution and the people of the United States alone, but with the voice of all the nations which have successfully aspired after free institutions and well defined governments throughout the world.... Like the heralds at the Olympic races," Bancroft declared, "all these states lift up their voices to call the court back within the limits of their path of duty that the very life of constitutional government may not perish among men."[27] Then, despairingly, he asked, "What is to be done?"

Bancroft's final chapter treats this question, arguing that the Court majority (eight of nine men) had no "right to change the constitution.... The constitution contains within itself the enumeration of the methods by which it may be amended; and in the process the votes of the nine justices of the supreme court weigh no more than those of any nine private citizens.... That is to say, that the constitution is a law of laws, ... and unchangeable by any act which either of the three branches of the government or all three together may be called upon to perform.... An interpretation of the constitution by the court, to be permanently valid, must not only be the opinion of the court at the moment, but must be in conformity to the constitution, and every time it is repeated must owe its validity to that conformity."[28] The current Court, Bancroft implied, had violated precedent. Had all the former members of the Court, back to its formation in 1789, been able to discuss and determine this case, their opinions would have overwhelmingly supported his.

No, the votes of the nine Justices ought not to have weighed more than the opinions of any other nine citizens. The Justices were only supposed to interpret where the Constitution does not establish sharp conclusions. However, on the creation of money, the Constitution was explicit – gold and silver had to be the monetary base. The *Juilliard* decision, therefore, violated all pertinent constitutional principles for constraining the creation of money.

---

[27]  *Ibid.*, p. 72.
[28]  *Ibid.*, pp. 74–75.

Court judgments had to be subject to judicial review. "The opinion in the present case," Bancroft wrote, "is a reversal of the first opinion [*Hepburn*] given on the subject by its predecessors.... When the court of last resort decides a case, the executive government accepts the decision on that case as final; but the constitution is the master of the court, which are bound ... to obey; to support, not to alter, nor ... to suffer to be altered. They must ever be as learners at the feet of those who made it; reverently searching after its true meaning; and in their sphere setting themselves against every tendency to the claim of an exclusive, absolute, and final power of interpretation."[29]

Despite the gravity of the decision it was making, Bancroft noted, "The court proceeded to its judgment on a case of which both sides were [argued] by one man, without even hearing or inviting a public argument." He called upon the Court to reexamine what it had done and the implications of its decision. Then, he hoped, "... the court will not persist in an erroneous reversal of the just judgment of its predecessors, when better investigation establishes the rightfulness of that first opinion.... An error becomes an immorality only when it is persisted in after it has been found to be an error.... [T]he court from its allegiance to the constitution must correct its own misinterpretation."[30]

Bancroft did not outline a procedure by which the Court might manage a correction, particularly on what legalistic grounds it might do so. Neither did he discuss any political problems that the Court faced. He simply exhorted the Justices as a group to think things through and correct the decision just pronounced.

Bancroft next entered arguments about the folly of a paper money system that this decision now made possible, all of which had been aired out many times in the past. He referred to Adam Smith in support of his argument that debtors favored paper money to lessen the real burden of their debts. "Let us then see," he added, "who in our republic are the capitalists and who the debtors of the country." Of course! "The greatest debtor of all is the United States [government] itself. Shall it discharge the money borrowed to save the life of the nation [during the Civil War] by the use of its own paper money?"[31]

To Bancroft this question was rhetorical, but nothing was more obvious; nothing made more political sense. The federal government was still the largest debtor in the country. Other debts – of banks, merchants engaged

[29]  *Ibid.*, pp. 76–77.
[30]  *Ibid.*, p. 77.
[31]  *Ibid.*, p. 81.

in foreign commerce, and the railroad and canal companies – all would become of uncertain value under a paper money system. "Shall these debtors," Bancroft asked, "be encouraged to escape from their obligations under the shelter of this new system of constitutional law?"[32]

"We have had every opportunity," Bancroft continued, "of making our money equal to that of the best in the world. Shall we throw it away? The moment of choice is less favorable than it was, but the choice is still before us. If we refuse to avail ourselves of our opportunity, it can hardly be recovered except after a series of calamities. How much better it would be to hold prosperity fast, while she asks to make with us her home!"[33]

Bancroft's assessment of the potentially inflationary consequences of the new decision was only too apt. Referring to the wording in Article 1, Section 8, of the Constitution, he compared a fluctuating currency with "... the use of varying scales and weights in the market.... Paper money," he emphasized, "is a corruption of the blood. Or paper money is the dry rot, which silently and unseen consumes the beams and joists which support the house and its floors."

Bancroft was pleading, he wrote, for "the welfare of society....What I have written is the fruit of many hours, employed in examining the laws of our period of colonial life, as well as the study of our own constitution and of the corresponding history and affairs of many lands. I may utter these last words of admonition as assurances of that love of country, of liberty, and of truth that has been the rule of my life, and still glows in a heart which so soon must cease to beat."[34] He died 5 years later in 1891 at the age of ninety-one.

Despite Bancroft's stature as a jurist and historian and the exhaustive analysis in his book, the Supreme Court of the day did not re-argue the case, nor did any faction of the Democratic Party seize on his arguments to excoriate the Republicans for perpetrating such an out-and-out violation of the Constitution. As it was, Bancroft had to publish his little monograph with his own resources. His book had very limited distribution when it was published in 1886, and no impact whatever on jurisprudence stemming from the *Juilliard* decision.[35]

---

[32] *Ibid.*, p. 82.

[33] *Ibid.*, p. 85.

[34] *Ibid.*, p. 88.

[35] It is only with difficulty that a researcher can locate an original copy of a *Plea for the Constitution*. In Bancroft's professional bibliography, *A Plea* is not even mentioned, although a small book he wrote one year later is.

## THE EVOLUTION OF THE SOVEREIGNTY CONCEPT

Frank van Dun, a legal theorist, has outlined recently the evolution of the logic and practice of sovereignty. His systematic account provides a rationale for the appearance of the concept in ancient times and its evolution to the present age. It applies particularly to the judicial actions that found the Legal Tender Acts constitutional.[36]

Before the first medieval sovereigns successfully imposed their dominions on unwitting subjects, money had appeared and been used for centuries, including the monetary debasements by the Romans. Even with the negative experiences of the Roman emperors in front of them, van Dun notes, medieval legal theorists built upon Roman Law, and "included coinage or minting among the traditional prerogatives of the king. They presented no specific arguments for this royal monopoly but merely recorded the existence of an old practice and sanctified it in the language of their discipline. The power of the 'logic of sovereignty' proved to be immense," van Dun emphasizes. "The state became sovereign as if it was some natural or corporate person, and sovereignty came to be seen as the union of the state and people."[37]

The modern view of sovereignty, van Dun continues, "is that states ... are sovereign persons.... If we take the state to be a sovereign person, state sovereignty, implies state absolutism: the omnicompetent state ... *an authority-based order* grounded in the sovereign right of the state to do with its own what it wills." This theory of sovereignty "provided a justification for any exercise of the sovereign power of the state. It completely undercut the legal case for any limitation of state power.... Over time the insistence on legal form – on the compliance with formal rules of procedure – grew stronger but so too did the insistence on implied powers, even in states with a formal constitution.[38]

The "doctrine of absolutism survived the demise of monarchical absolutism and the rise of the constitutional state. It fostered the idea that constitutional limitations on the government must be seen as auto-limitations imposed by the state itself. Even when the wisdom of a particular extension of government powers may be questioned, the notion that such an extension is never to be permitted should not be expected to survive in the regular

---

[36] Frank van Dun, "National Sovereignty and International Monetary Regimes," in *Money and the Nation State*, eds., Dowd and Timberlake, 1998, New Brunswick, N.J., Transaction Publishers for the Independent Institute., Chapter 2, pp. 47–76.

[37] *Ibid.*, p. 48.

[38] *Ibid.*, pp 56–57.

processes of constitutional change.... Legal grounds for an expansion of government authority can always be found, if not in specific constitutional texts or precedents, then in the reading of those texts as containing the constitution of a sovereign state. The appeal to the inherently absolutist notion of sovereignty imparts a systematic pro-government bias to constitutional interpretation." [39]

Even though the Framers thought they had foreclosed against any such warping of constitutional axioms, the pressures that the post-Civil War Republican administrations sensed in their attempts to restore fiscal and monetary stability were too much for the Founders' Constitution. The Supreme Court just would not allow greenbacks to be unconstitutional, and Congress just would not contradict Republican administrations that sought legal whitewash for war-time excesses.

---

[39] *Ibid.*

# SEVENTEEN

# Other Commentaries on the Legal Tender Cases

The four years between the Resumption Act of 1875 and actual Resumption on January 1, 1879 witnessed a great deal of political uncertainty on the question of whether Resumption would occur as scheduled. When it looked certain to occur, a combination of votes of both political parties in the House and Senate in May 1878 stopped the retirement of the greenbacks, freezing their stock forever at $346-plus million.[1]

Had the greenbacks been fully retired, as many congressmen and many public figures urged, the legal tender cases never would have appeared.[2] Issues of limited-tender government currency would have had the same inflationary effects on the economy as the full legal tender greenbacks, but government spokesmen and Supreme Court Justices would have had no occasion to argue the "necessity" of legal tender, and then to "discover" the monetary "sovereignty" of the national government. Subsequently, the law of contracts – the power of creditors and debtors to decide payment in whatever was current at the time the contract was written – would never have been violated.

## THE ANOMALOUS VIEWS OF A. BARTON HEPBURN ON THE LEGAL TENDER ACTS AND SOVEREIGNTY

A prominent banking scholar, journeyman economist, and one-time Comptroller of the Currency, A. Barton Hepburn, discussed the legal tender episode at length in what was certainly the best documented book on the

[1] Dunbar, *Laws*, p. 217.
[2] For a detailed account of this period, see, Friedman and Schwartz, *Monetary History*, Chapter 3, "Silver Politics and the Secular Decline in Prices," pp. 89–134, and Timberlake, *Monetary Policy*, pp. 146–165.

history of money and banking for its time. Hepburn was an experienced New York City banker, and active in organizations such as The Sound Money League and the Republican Party. He was appointed Comptroller of the Currency by President Benjamin Harrison in 1892, but resigned in 1893 when Grover Cleveland, a Democrat, took office. His book, *A History of Currency in the United States* went through three editions, 1903, 1915, and 1924.[3] Hepburn received honorary doctorates from five institutions of higher learning, and was a consultant in the writing of *The Federal Reserve Act*.[4] His treatment of money and banking issues during Reconstruction, particularly the legal tender cases, is that of a professional and highly successful banker. His book, therefore, reflects serious professional thinking of the time.

Hepburn, while chronicling the monetary path to Resumption, referred occasionally to the sentiments of legislators on the legal tender question. Although the greenbacks after Resumption were on a par with gold at the pre-war parity, their permanent legitimacy was a separate issue. A segment of strict constructionists still denied their legality, but many observers were willing to believe that with Resumption in place, the constitutional question did not much matter. After Resumption, a creditor who was paid in greenbacks but wanted gold could go to his bank and immediately redeem the greenbacks for gold coin.

Nonetheless, Congress had not sealed the cracks against further issues of greenbacks. It still offered no guarantee that it would never use its "sovereignty" to issue more of them. It might have gone a long way toward such a guarantee by seeing to their complete retirement and by providing for some other currency, such as silver, to replace the remainder still outstanding. It also had the authority to pass a law funding the greenbacks into interest-bearing debt, even though cheap-money advocates constantly scuttled this option. So legal possibilities for cleansing what was still a "mixed" monetary system were still within reach, as Bancroft's *Plea* suggested. None of them happened.

---

[3]  The first edition of his book, published in 1903, had the lengthy title, *A History of Coinage and Currency in the United States and the Perennial Contest for a Sound Money* (New York: Macmillan, 1903) and sounded a bit polemical. The title was shortened later to just *A History of Currency in the United States*. Though the text reflects Hepburn's monetary preferences, the book is scholarly and historically sound.

[4]  For a brief biography of Hepburn, see Benjamin Klebaner, "A. Barton Hepburn," in *Encyclopedia of American Business History and Biography: Banking and Finance to 1913*, ed. Larry Schweikart: Brucoli, Clark Layman, Inc., 1990, pp. 260–265.

Hepburn reported that after the momentous *Juilliard* decision of 1884, "amendments to the Constitution prohibiting … making aught but gold and silver legal tender were proposed but not acted upon." He cited Hugh McCulloch, who was again Secretary of the Treasury during 1883–1884. In his *Report of the Secretary of the Treasury, 1884*, just after the *Juilliard* decision was made public, McCulloch commented that to regard the greenbacks as money was a "delusion [that] will be proven whenever there is a large demand for gold for export. They are not money, but merely promises to pay it, and the government must be prepared to redeem all that may be presented, or forfeit its character for solvency."[5]

Grover Cleveland, a New York Democrat who favored the gold standard, won the presidential contest of 1884 and appointed Daniel Manning to be Secretary of the Treasury. [6] In his first *Report* as Secretary (1885), Manning was outspokenly critical of the Silver Purchase (Bland-Allison) Act and of the Act that stopped further retirement of the greenbacks in 1878. Still reflecting the hard-money legacy of the Democratic Party, he recommended repeal of both.

Again, in his *Report* for 1886, Manning argued that the power of making greenbacks legal tender could not have been exercised "in relation to any power to borrow money," as the Court majority had asserted. "Not until after 1861," he noted, "when a great danger had beclouded most men's perceptions of financial as well as constitutional law, was a legal tender money made out of the debts of the United States; not until this infection spread was it ever deliberately argued that any representative of the unit of value could justly be suffered to be made, or to abide, in permanent depreciation and disparity therewith." He persisted even more forcefully: "Every argument now forbade the continuance of the 'legalized injustice,' whether lawful according to the Supreme Court or not, to issue such notes twenty-one years after the exigency that called them into existence had passed." If Congress truly had the power under the Constitution to make paper money legal tender, he emphasized, it should be abrogated: "No executive and no legislature is fit to be trusted with the control [that such a power confers] over the earnings and savings of the people."[7] "How unfortunate Manning's recommendations were not adopted," commented Hepburn, the Republican

---

[5] Cited in Hepburn, *History*, pp. 241–242.

[6] Cleveland had two separate terms, 1884–1888, and 1892–1896. He was arguably more conservative than any of the post-war Republican presidents.

[7] Hepburn, *History*, p. 244. Manning presumably would have included a *central bank* in the list of those "not fit to be trusted," had he known of such an institution. But not even the Bank of England was a full-fledged central bank at the time.

banker who became Comptroller of the Currency, as he approvingly cited the text of the Democratic Secretary.

Hepburn offered yet another criticism of Congress's policy on the greenbacks: "The first and perhaps the greatest error committed in our financial legislation, after the issue of the legal tender notes," he commented, "was the repeal of the law permitting them to be funded into government bonds. This [Act] closed the door to their retirement and ... left them a permanent feature of our currency system." Even in 1886, Hepburn noted, the "surplus" gold and silver in the vaults of the Treasury was over $250 million, so, "no more fitting a time or desirable conditions for retiring the legal tender notes could be hoped for." Redeeming most of them with the Treasury's existing money balance, and funding the rest into interest-bearing bonds could have retired all of the frozen $346-plus million, but "cheap money" congressmen had closed the door on this option.[8]

Despite the magnitude of the legal tender decision, legislative attention in the late 1880s eased away from this issue to concerns about the size of the Treasury's cash balance, and how much silver currency should be issued relative to national bank notes and greenbacks. Because the outstanding stock of greenbacks was frozen, all quarters denied that they would ever be issued again. Consequently, the legal tender issue gradually lost its political immediacy.

Hepburn's next chapter (Chapter XIV, "Legal Tender Cases in the Supreme Court") directly examined the issue of greenback constitutionality. Similar to Bancroft, and citing Bancroft, Hepburn reviewed the substance of the cases, the characteristics of the successive Courts that made the decisions, and the arguments pro and con. He summarized the majority arguments, including the majority's introduction of "sovereignty" and Justice Field's refutation of it. Finally, he devoted a few paragraphs to Bancroft's argument that the federal government had no inherent sovereignty.

Hepburn's book was originally published in 1903, almost 20 years after the *Juilliard* decision, and 17 years after the appearance of Bancroft's monograph. While he seemed to find much more to criticize than to applaud in the Court's later decisions, Hepburn's final judgment of the Court's momentous ruling – affirmation of Congress's power to issue legal tender paper money – unaccountably concedes the issue as the Court had decided it. He observed that the "federal government was a compromise in which the states sought by united strength to command respect and achieve consequence in

---

[8]   *Ibid.*, p. 245. The Treasury's cash balance was $250 million greater than necessary to meet ongoing expenditures.

the sisterhood of nations, at the same time jealously guarding their local sovereignties in order to avoid the dangers which experience had taught them to apprehend from a strong central government." The states "naturally wished their local governments interfered with as little as possible." However, "the adoption of the federal Constitution gave to the people two sovereigns – a double allegiance. The question, which was to be paramount, state or nation," he continued, "was an active issue until settled by the sword and sealed in favor of the nation, by the surrender at Appomattox. A strengthening of the central government inevitably [sic] ensued. State sovereignty ceased to be an influence, and the courts were left free to discriminate between what the framers of the Constitution had done and what [the courts] thought [alleged] they had done." [9]

Until he discussed the creation of the "two sovereignties," Hepburn's analysis is objective and scholarly. Then, unaccountably, he presumes that one or the other sovereignties, state or federal, must be "paramount," ignoring that the states' powers were what the Constitution did not deny them, while the central government's powers were only what the Constitution granted it. The Constitution did not state, or even imply, that one or the other set of powers was "paramount": they were two different sets of powers under two separate sovereignties. Hepburn then concludes that the issue "was settled by the sword, and sealed in favor of the [federal government] by the surrender at Appomattox." That is, the issue was not discussed dispassionately in Congress, academia, and courts of law through rational argument and an appeal to the given conditions that inspired the Founders. Instead it was settled by force of arms as had been done throughout history until the U.S. Constitution was written. The federal government became dominant, as the weight of its military forces overwhelmed state sovereignties. Then, a Supreme Court re-interpreted the Constitution, "discriminating between what the Framers of the Constitution had done and what [the Courts] thought they had done," which turned out to be the political preferences of the Executive branch throughout the post-bellum period.

Hepburn's final paragraph displays his conventional Republican orthodoxy. Above all other considerations, he contended, the "framers intended to create a perpetual government, and when the life of the government was at issue the technical reading of the Constitution yielded perforce to broader lines [?], gauged by the civic and economic changes which a century had wrought. The law of self-preservation [as interpreted by the courts in the

---

[9]　*Ibid.*, pp. 266–267.

legal tender cases] construed the Constitution broadly as to the power of Congress over currency, in the interest of preserving the government."[10]

Here, sheer misinterpretation masquerades as "practical" analysis. This concluding argument violates virtually all of the substance of Bancroft's work that Hepburn had quoted so approvingly, and most of Hepburn's stated principles as well. Of first importance is the fact that the Constitution was not written to *preserve* government; it was written to authorize, institute, empower, and *constrain* the government so created – the central government relative to state governments, and all governments relative to "the people." The Founders wrote the Constitution as a contract in perpetuity, with adequate machinery for its amendment, as Bancroft had observed. Moreover, by 1884 any danger to the federal government's existence as a union was long past; so the excuse that the continued presence of the notes was "to preserve the government" was empty rhetoric.

Hepburn's *apologia* was a product of his Republican mindset, rather than a reasoned restatement of constitutional principles. His style suggests that he was distinctly uncomfortable with his conclusions, but was not about to try to gainsay a Supreme Court decision that by this time was accepted polity. His conversion to the Court's opinion is a commentary on what concern for political expediency can do to an otherwise scholarly observer.

## WILLIAM BROUGH ON "LEGAL TENDER"

Another able critic of monetary affairs at the time, William Brough (mentioned in the preceding chapter), published a small but important book in 1896, *The Natural Law of Money*.[11] Brough did not treat the legal tender decisions directly. He began by noting that money "was not planned and brought into existence with an intelligent prevision of its nature and workings." Rather, primitive money "possessed inherent properties which fitted it for certain services. . . ." When such monetary services were needed, men developed money spontaneously – "without any concert of action." Money was circulating "everywhere in the world before men even thought of making laws for its regulation."[12]

Brough then treated the question of "legal tender," which he regarded as the primary affront to his Natural Law of Money. "No power which can be

---

[10] *Ibid.*, p. 267.
[11] William Brough, *The Natural Law of Money.* (Originally published by G. P. Putnam's Sons: New York, 1896.) Greenwood Press: New York, 1969. I cannot find any biographical material on Brough.
[12] *Ibid.*, p. 1.

exercised by a community [that is, "the people"] should be delegated to the general government," he postulated, and banking was especially such an activity. All the restrictive laws on money passed during the Civil War interfered with the Natural Law of Money. Especially harmful were the Legal Tender Acts and the section in the National Bank Act taxing state-bank notes out of existence.[13]

The Constitution withheld from Congress the right to issue paper money. "No act of the Fathers of the Republic," Brough stated, "marks more decisively their high standard of political virtue than the withholding from Congress the right to issue [legal tender paper] money."[14]

Brough especially criticized the belief that the "state" could impart value to money. "That this delusive doctrine should have been accepted in an age when it was believed that the king's touch would cure disease, is not remarkable; but that it should have a host of supporters in this age of steam, of electricity, and of practical common-sense, is strange indeed. Why we of the United States, who deny that divinity doth hedge a king, and who aim to restore sovereignty to its true source – the people – should still cherish this worn shred of monarchical prerogative which has no possible application or usefulness is difficult to explain."[15]

### "LEGAL TENDER" BY S. P. BRECKINRIDGE

Another important scholarly work, *Legal Tender* by S[ophonisba]. P. Breckinridge, explored the prerogatives of sovereignty in Europe and England from their beginnings in 1066 to the end of the nineteenth century.[16] In her "Introduction," Breckinridge asked three questions that she then purported to answer "as fully as may be [possible] with respect to English and American experience: (1) What organ of the state has exercised the power of bestowing upon money the quality of being a legal tender? (2) With respect to what forms of money or substitutes for money has the power been exercised? [And] (3) What have been the reasons for such exercise?"

---

[13] *Ibid.*, pp. 72–73, 129.

[14] *Ibid.*, p. 133.

[15] *Ibid.*, p. 134.

[16] S. P. Breckinridge was born in Kentucky in 1866, the great-granddaughter of Thomas Jefferson's attorney general John Breckinridge. Though she studied political science at the University of Chicago, her major professor was J. Laurence Laughlin, head of the Economics Department. Her doctoral thesis was published as a book, *Legal Tender*, in 1903 by The University of Chicago Press, and re-published by Greenwood Press in 1969. She dedicated her book to Laughlin. (Webpage: *Women's Intellectual Contributions to the Study of Mind and Society*.)

To set the stage properly for her investigation, she stated: "Legal-tender money will ... signify [in this book] such money as carries with its possession the right to use it in any lawful transaction, whether that transaction be a cash or time transaction; a transaction between private individuals or between an individual and the government to which he is subject."[17]

Breckinridge reviewed the development of the English law of tender from 1066. The power over the coinage, she noted, was a royal prerogative. The earliest important case concerning the legitimacy of a "tender" came in 1601, 2 years before Elizabeth's death, when an Irish woman named Elizabeth Brett paid for a shipment of merchandise with certain "mix't monies" that Elizabeth, the queen, had "proclaimed by stamp and inscription and declared by proclamation" to be lawful and current money in Ireland. Breckinridge quoted the details in this case: " '*Brett* tendered £100 in this mix't money, and resolved that the tender was good, the place of payment being in *Ireland*; ... that altho this were not in truth *Sterling*, but of a baser alloy, nor a money current in *England* by the proclamation, yet the payment being made in *Ireland*, it was, as to that purpose, current money of *England*.' Thus the question was squarely raised whether the money with which a contract should be fulfilled was that current at the time of making the agreement or that current at the time of payment, and the law was settled in favor of the latter."[18] The ruling also implied that, henceforth, the form of money to repay a debt would have to be written into the contract. Otherwise, the proclamation would simply allow debtors to expropriate the wealth of creditors.

Throughout the centuries when gold and silver made up the coins of the realm, Breckinridge observed, the various kings of England took advantage of their coinage prerogative to procure seigniorage tax revenue. This kind of tax, "was an avowed right claimed by the sovereigns of Europe." Regencies deducted it by various means from the coinage of both gold and silver. Only with the reign of Henry VIII was this royal prerogative seriously abused, but many of Henry's abuses were corrected during the reign of Elizabeth.[19]

Breckinridge's summary of English experience concluded, first, that to the crown belonged the power over the coinage, particularly the legal-tender quality that gold and silver coins had at specified (mint) values. Generally, Parliament and even some kings tried "to do the right and honest thing and

---

[17] Breckenridge, *Legal Tender*, pp. 1–3.

[18] *Ibid.*, p. 25. (Her emphasis.) Breckinridge added in a footnote, p. 24: "This case [of the mix't monies] is cited in the dissenting opinion in Griswold v. Hepburn, 2 Duval (Ky.), 71." (See above, pp. 136–137.)

[19] *Ibid.*, p. 34. Seigniorage was eventually abolished.

to meet the needs of the people in this vital matter of the money with which the ordinary transactions of life were performed."[20]

Nevertheless, the seigniorage tax obtained through partial debasement of the coinage was sometimes exacted. A re-coinage of the metals that left the king with two or three percent seigniorage of the total was only slightly different in degree from a re-coinage that corrected marginally – a few percent – for small shifts in real market values of the two metals. However, Henry had gone too far. "The law of tender was formulated by the courts ... immediately subsequent to the abuses of Henry" and the parliamentary subservience that permitted his mischief. From the time of Elizabeth's death in 1603 until 1816, no significant change occurred in the gold content of the pound sterling.[21]

The judicial precedents in English law carried over, as one would expect, into the Constitution of the United States. Breckinridge compared the English experience with American policy as structured by the Constitution:

While the [U.S.] government set up by the constitution was said to be sovereign within its proper sphere, the doctrine [of the Founders] was that the sovereignty, in the sense in which it had inhered in the English kings had passed to the people, not to the government of the United States. So much of the right of English monarchs as had been derived from the doctrine of unlimited and prerogative power was wholly without [that is, outside, or, withheld from] the sphere of federal power. The abuses of the coinage which had been justified by the courts on the basis of this power were limited to the reign of Henry VIII, and his immediate successors. For over two centuries they had ceased on the part of the English government. Until the time of the construction of the Legal-Tender Acts it would have seemed absurd to argue that such a power was included in those granted to the federal Congress by the constitution of the United States.[22]

Breckinridge, reflecting the interest in bi-metallism of her academic mentor, J. Laurence Laughlin, who wrote three books on the subject, then traced the authorizations and specific values of gold and silver coins in the United States from 1789 to the Civil War. She examined the recent bi-metallic controversy culminating in The Gold Currency Act of 1900 making gold the only standard, and then compared the earlier issues of Treasury notes before the Civil War with the full legal tender notes issued in 1862.

The Treasury had first issued Treasury notes at the close of the second war with England (1814), she observed, "when all other resources had seemed exhausted...." But in 1862, "at the beginning of another war, before

---

[20] *Ibid.*, pp. 46–47.
[21] *Ibid.*, p. 48.
[22] *Ibid.* p. 91.

any other resources had been tried, resort was had to non-interest-bearing notes wholly adapted to use as a medium of exchange.... No precedent for such notes could be found during the life of the United States under the constitution." She discussed the list of options noted earlier, citing the "absolute necessity" argument of Congressman Spaulding. In response to "necessity," she quoted the conclusions of an economist, Don C. Barrett, who published a comprehensive article on the episode. Barrett's four major conclusions were that: (1) the temporary deposits and certificates of indebtedness, and not the legal tender issue, tided the government over in early 1862; (2) the legal tenders covered only a small and unimportant portion of total war expenditures; (3) Secretary Chase and Congress made "grave mistakes" in their tax policies and bond sales. Otherwise, these traditional methods would have been sufficient without the legal tenders; and (4) alternative plans by bankers and a minority of the Ways and Means Committee were proposed and urged upon the government, to no avail.[23]

Breckinridge next explained how "necessity" had taken constitutionality through the gate of "implied powers," and how the Court had merged that concept into the absolute power of "national sovereignty." She quoted the words of Congressman Bingham, who proclaimed in 1862, "By that sovereignty, which is known by the name of 'We the people of the United States,' the government of the United States has been invested with the attribute of sovereignty, which is inseparable from every sovereignty beneath the sun – the power to determine what shall be money – that is to say, what shall be the standard of value, what shall be the medium of exchange for the purpose of regulating exchange and facilitating all commercial transactions of the country and among the people."[24] While Bingham was correct that "We the people" are sovereign and delegate certain powers to the government, he did not allow that those delegated powers were limited by the Tenth Amendment. Rather, he mistakenly extended express powers to include complete control over the monetary system.

Breckinridge criticized the Court's abrupt reversal of *Hepburn v. Griswold*, in 1871, noting that "considerations of a political and material character ... demanded its reconsideration." She condemned it: "The fact of such a change under such circumstances must be universally regarded as a deplorable incident in the history of the United States judiciary."[25] She cited Justice

[23] *Ibid.*, pp. 114–116. Don C. Barrett, "The Supposed Necessity of the Legal Tender Paper," *Quarterly Journal of Economics*, May, 1902, pp. 330–336.

[24] *Ibid.*, p. 117. Bingham's speech appeared in *Congressional Globe*, 37th Cong., 2nd sess., p. 636.

[25] *Ibid.*, p. 132.

Field's dissent in *Juilliard v. Greenman*, 1884, and commented that Field's objection to the decision "gains force when it is realized that for an analogous act on the part of the English government, from which American ideas of sovereign power are drawn, we should have to go back to the reign of Henry VIII."[26] In granting full legal tender status to the greenbacks, she concluded:

> ... the private individual, the creditor, was by a compulsory act of government, through the agency of the courts [which were] established to work justice between man and man, forced to share with the government, or bear for it, the cost of the conflict being waged. By an extraordinary departure from both legislative and judicial precedents an act as tyrannical as any act of Henry VIII in dealing with his coins found legislative and executive support and judicial sanction. It was fitting that the law based on the doctrine of the prerogative prevailing in the time of the Tudors should be invoked to sustain such legislation.[27]

If the "sovereignty" argument is valid, "necessary and proper" is superfluous. It has no utility in defining the limits to any powers in the Constitution. "Sovereignty" trumps every other consideration. So, why would the Framers ever have bothered with "necessary and proper"?

## JAMES MONROE ON "SOVEREIGNTY"

James Monroe, the last president of the United States from the Founding generation, wrote a book near the end of his life, *The People, The Sovereigns*,[28] in which he addressed the concept of "Sovereignty" as it was treated by him and the Framers. Monroe first examined the fundamental principles that distinguished the political culture of the United States from those of other republics. He argued that both national and state governments were independent of each other, "and sovereign to the extent, and within the limit, of specified powers.... Both [state and federal] governments rest on the same basis, the sovereignty of the people.... The terms Sovereignty and Government have generally been considered as synonymous." However, to Monroe and the Framers, separating the two concepts was essential to securing an enduring democracy. Only "by the institution of a government by compact to which all the people are parties," Monroe claimed, could the

---

[26]  *Ibid.*, p. 136.

[27]  *Ibid.*, p. 155.

[28]  Monroe, James. *The People The Sovereigns*, edited by Samuel L. Gouverneur (grandson of Monroe) with an Introduction by Russell Kirk. Cumberland Virginia: James River Press, 1987. [Philadelphia: J. B. Lippincott and Co., 1867]. Monroe wrote the text in the mid-1830s.

sovereignty of the people be kept separate from the limited sovereignty of the government. "Thus," he concluded, "the Constitution becomes the paramount law, and every act of the government, and of every department in it, repugnant thereto, void."[29]

Monroe's primary concern was the preservation of a government by compact. In order to guard against temptations that would destroy such a government, he prescribed "two great principles [that are] fundamental and invariable, in regard to governments over which the people hold sovereignty – first, that the government be separated from sovereignty; second, that it be divided into three separate branches, legislative, executive and judicial, that each be endowed with its appropriate powers, and be made independent of the others." It is by a "faithful observance of these principles, and a wise execution of them," he wrote, "that tyranny may be prevented; the government be made efficient for all its purposes; and the power of the people be preserved over it, in all its operations.... Concentrate all power in one body, although it be representative," he warned, "and the result, if not prompt, will, nevertheless, be equally fatal."[30] In a later section he repeated the principle of "Sovereignty of the people," and again stressed the tripartite division of powers, "legislative, executive and judiciary, under a wise arrangement" that would vest in each "the powers competent to its objects." The specification of powers to each of three branches of government, and the possession of sovereignty in the people, he asserted, are fundamental to a free society.[31]

Monroe denied that the People can exercise their Sovereignty merely by voting for other people to represent their arbitrary whims through governmental institutions. The People vote to allow Representatives and Senators to exercise only those powers explicitly granted to state and federal governments, and can take care of everything else with all of their unspecified residual powers. Sovereignty, he emphasized, "is distinct from the government, because the people who hold the one are distinct from their representatives who hold and perform the duties of the other."[32]

---

[29]  *Ibid.*, pp. 3–8.

[30]  *Ibid.*, p. 13.

[31]  *Ibid.*, p. 32.

[32]  *Ibid.*, p. 8. Edwin Vieira notes that the "*federal* government of the United States consists of five parts [sovereignties]: Congress, the President, the Supreme Court, the States, and the people. Each of these branches of government has the legal right and power, *and the duty,* to support and defend the Constitution ... because the Constitution requires them to take an 'Oath or Affirmation' to that effect, and the people, because they are responsible for 'ordaining and establishing' the Constitution in the first place" *Pieces of Eight*, pp. 380–381. (His emphasis.)

# EIGHTEEN

# The [Gold] Currency Act of 1900 and Monetary Affairs in the United States before 1914

In the early 1890s, the U.S. Treasury experienced a common problem of institutions that issued redeemable currencies based on fractional (gold) reserves. During the 5 years from March 1887 to March 1892, total Treasury currency in circulation increased by 29 percent, or slightly more than 5 percent per year.[1] (See Table 18.1.) Much of the increase was a result of the passage of the Sherman Silver Purchase Act that authorized issues of Treasury notes of 1890, a paper currency based on Treasury silver purchases. The notes, despite their silver "backing," had ultimately to be redeemed in gold.[2] This increase, modest though it was, caused U.S. prices to increase relative to "world" prices, and triggered a gold outflow. Gold exports from the United States began during 1892 and continued for the next 4 years, accompanied by much hand-wringing and complaining on the part of Treasury officials and commercial bank managers.

To maintain the value of its fiat currencies, the Treasury sold U.S. government securities, an open-market selling operation, to acquire the gold necessary to maintain redemption of the non-gold currencies at their par values.[3] This policy also tended to increase interest rates, but it provided

---

[1] This currency was what would be labeled the *monetary base*, or "high-powered money" in present-day accounts.

[2] Greenbacks were 100 percent fiat – they had no redeemable commodity value – while silver certificates and the notes of 1890 were 10 to 60 percent fiat, because their silver base was worth 90 to 40 percent of their monetary value. But both kinds of money were *legal tender*. Consequently, their *monetary* values were 100 percent of their *fiat* values: A commodity value of zero percent or a commodity value of 99 percent makes no difference if the *legal tender* value is 100 percent. Gold, being the standard, was by this time the only full-bodied currency, meaning that a 20-dollar gold piece, a double Eagle, contained 20 dollars worth of marketable gold.

[3] Hepburn, *History of Currency*, pp. 348–360, and Friedman and Schwartz, *Monetary History*, pp. 104–112. Grover Cleveland, a gold standard Democrat, stubbornly insisted on the maintenance of gold payments. He and his Administration realized that to retain

Table 18.1  *Total gold and silver coin and bullion in U.S. Treasury, total Treasury currency outstanding, and ratios of the former to the latter, 1880–1900*

| Year | Treasury Gold and Silver (Gold) $ millions | Total Treasury Currency Issues $ millions | Ratio (%) (Gold %) |
|------|------|------|------|
| 1880 | 204 (139) | 690 | 30 (20) |
| 1885 | 410 (247) | 854 | 48 (29) |
| 1890 | 569 (311) | 959 | 59 (32) |
| 1895 | 412 (126) | 999 | 41 (13) |
| 1900 | 703 (435) | 1317 | 53 (33) |

*Note: Figures in parentheses are Treasury gold and its percentage of total Treasury currency in circulationSource*: Reports of the Treasurer, 1895–1901. "Treasury gold and silver" includes the Treasury's silver bullion at market prices. Data are for June 30.

the Treasury with enough gold to meet all demands for redemption of its paper currencies. The Treasury's gold reserve-to-currency ratio, which had reached 36 percent in 1888 and was 32 percent in 1890, fell to 13 percent by 1895. (In Table 18.1, the gold values are in parentheses.) Similarly, the dollar value of gold coin and bullion in the Treasury, which was $311 million in 1890, declined to $126 million by June 1895 – a decrease of 60 percent. It reached its lowest value of $42 million in February 1895.[4]

Treasury policies at this time emphasized that the Treasury's role, as the official manager of fiat currencies, was its guardianship of the gold standard. When disequilibrium occurred, such as the conditions of 1892–1896, the Secretary did not declare a "moratorium" on Treasury gold to stop it from going out into the world to make the adjustments that had to occur in the rest of the world's monetary systems. Neither did he or Congress suggest issuing additional Treasury notes as sanctioned by the Supreme Court decisions in the legal tender cases. In fact, the Treasury at the time was

---

the gold standard, the ongoing monetization of silver had to cease. Acting in his Executive capacity, Cleveland and his Democratic Party affiliates in Congress were able to repeal the Sherman Silver Purchase Act in its entirety by November 1893. The political struggle was extremely bitter, and cost the Democrats control of Congress and the Presidency in the 1896 election (Timberlake, *Monetary Policy*, pp. 166–179). By the terms of the Repeal Act of 1893, the Treasury retired the Notes of 1890 when they came into Treasury offices as payment for taxes or tariffs.

[4]  Hepburn, *History*, p. 358.

retiring the silver-backed Treasury notes of 1890 in accordance with the Act of 1893 that authorized their redemption.[5]

Capital and commodity markets saw to the gold movements that generated the necessary adjustments in prices. During the recession of 1893–1896, U.S. prices fell roughly 10 percent.[6] In time, the general decline in U.S. and world prices that had been occurring also increased the real value of gold, stimulating world gold production. The Treasury's gold balance, which had fallen so alarmingly through early 1895, recovered steadily to $435 million by 1900, an increase of 346 percent from its value in 1896.[7]

The Currency Act of (March 14) 1900, sometimes labeled, "The Gold Standard Act," formally declared the monetary system of the United States to be based solely on gold. An earlier act, the Coinage Act of 1873, also labeled the "Crime of '73," had already provided for a monometallic gold standard simply by not legalizing the coinage of silver dollars. However, Western silver interests and other cheap-money advocates caught on to silver as a cheap-money improvement over greenbacks. They saw to passage of the Bland-Allison Act of 1878 and the Treasury Note Act of 1890.

The Currency Act of 1900 re-affirmed the gold standard, and provided explicitly for the redemption of all government-issued currencies, especially greenbacks and silver, in gold. The Act also formally authorized a $150 million gold reserve fund in the Treasury to carry out necessary redemptions. If the gold reserve were depleted, the Treasury was to sell government securities to get enough gold to replenish it. The Treasury Department had already been redeeming its outstanding currencies – greenbacks and silver certificates and coins – for gold since 1879 anyway. Now, however, a substantial reserve of gold was formally established to redeem the two subsidiary legal tender currencies on demand.[8]

The Court's Legal Tender decisions allowed Congress to issue any kind of money it felt was necessary and proper for the government's uses. According to those decisions, Congress's monetary powers had no limit. But Congress, by the Currency Act of March 14, 1900, determined that a gold base to the monetary system was now necessary and proper, and specified that only gold was the base of the monetary system. "Thus," wrote Horace White,

---

[5]  Timberlake, *Monetary Policy*, Ch. 11, "The Fall of Silver," pp. 166–182.
[6]  Friedman and Schwartz, *Monetary History*, p. 134.
[7]  Hepburn, *History*, p. 360.
[8]  White, Horace, *Money and Banking*, New Edition, revised and enlarged by Charles Tippetts and Lewis Froman. Ginn and Co: New York, 1935. See, Chapter XI, pp. 267–284, for an excellent account of these events.

"the act of 1900 did much to maintain the gold standard which had been established by law twenty-seven years earlier [that is, by the Act of 1873]."[9]

The Act of 1900 and the legal tender decisions that preceded it in 1871 and 1884 were incompatible. By the Act of 1900 Congress denied itself the unlimited monetary powers the Court decisions of 1871 and 1884 had allowed it, and implied that its money powers in the Constitution still had to qualify as "necessary and proper." Fine, but which canon would prevail at the next emergency? How would the three branches of the federal government view the monetary powers of the federal government when some real or imagined monetary problem resulted in the next "crisis"?

Meanwhile, monetary concerns had shifted to institutional problems. Throughout the later nineteenth century and into the twentieth, congressmen, government officials, economists, and bankers repeatedly decried the commercial banks' apparent inability to furnish an "elastic" currency – one that would gear issues of money to the production of goods and services, as well as provide liquidity for business and banking firms in a panic. This perceived inflexibility in the banking system was largely traceable to policies that fixed the stock of greenbacks and tied the issue of national bank notes to the relatively fixed quantities of government securities. Other contributing factors were bank reserve requirements, prohibitions of branch and interstate banking, prohibition of bank-issued post-notes and due bills, and the 10 percent tax on state bank notes.[10]

To compensate for these institutional rigidities particularly when a bank panic threatened, bankers devised their own lender-of-last-resort by extending the operations of their clearing-house associations from a daily tallying of debits and credits from and due each bank, to providers of high-denominational credit-currency. Beginning with the Clearinghouse Association of New York City in the Panic of 1857, clearing-houses issued Clearing-House Loan Certificates (CHLC) that served as surrogate bank reserves during currency stringencies accompanying bank panics. When excess demands for currency appeared, clearing-houses issued CHLC in high denominations, secured by interest-bearing loans that the clearing-house managers obtained from solvent banks that still had excess reserves. Clearing-House Loan Certificates then served as quasi-legal tender bank reserves until the panic abated, and then went out of existence when the banks paid off their clearing-house loans. As the practice spread,

---

[9] White, *ibid.*, pp. 264–265.

[10] McCulloch, J. Huston, "Bank Regulation and Deposit Insurance," *Journal of Business*, January, 1986, No. 59, pp. 79–85.

the clearing-house associations issued diverse forms of currency, many in the lowest denominations. No losses of any significance ever occurred from the clearing-house issues, and no bank panic ever became an out-of-control depression while the informal clearing-house system functioned as a lender-of-last-resort.[11] The clearing-house associations became an effective, privately managed "central bank."

The success of the clearing-house system in blunting bank panics emphasized the primary restriction on banks that allowed panics to develop – the largely unusable, legally required reserves in the central reserve city banks of New York and Chicago. Banks in the smaller reserve cities – St. Louis, San Francisco, Atlanta, Boston, and others – faced a similar problem.[12] Reserve requirement laws, which applied to all national banks and to most state banks, prescribed minimum reserve ratio requirements on banks' reserves regardless of circumstances. Consequently, a bank facing the statutory minimum that the banking laws prescribed lost its credit flexibility. Allowing the reserves to fall below the minimum resulted in costly penalties from bank regulators, and harmful adverse publicity from the media. Banks' reserves below the minimum, therefore, were virtually unusable. Reserves that should have been a cushion and allowed to vary in dollar quantity with credit conditions became a line in the sand. Consequently, banks felt obliged to keep higher-than-required reserves simply because of the undesirable side effects they would suffer in the event their actual reserves fell, even temporarily and for whatever reason, below the legal minima.[13] The paradoxical effect was that legal reserve requirements largely immobilized bank reserves and thereby exacerbated bank panics. They were a major

---

[11]  Timberlake, *Monetary Policy*, pp. 198–212. Clearing-house currency was at first employed only as bank reserves in super-high denominations – $1,000 and up. When it was issued in lower denominations, illegality was avoided by the issuers inscribing on the notes: "Not intended to circulate as money," or some similar disclaimer. Since the existence of the clearing-house currency was always short term – a few months to a year – no one had any interest in pursuing its illegality.

[12]  See, Sprague, O. M. W. *History of Crises under the National Banking System*. Government Printing Office: Washington, 1910, pp. 278–280. See also, A. Piatt Andrew, "Substitutes for Cash in the Panic of 1907," *The Quarterly Journal of Economics*, August 1908, pp. 111–115.

[13]  Deane Carson observed in an article written in 1964: "Bankers ... consider *legally required reserve* balances as the most illiquid segment of their asset portfolios, useful over long periods only at a penalty rate of interest.... Without legal ratios it would appear that the 'liquidity cushion' aspect of cash reserves would be enhanced." Carson 1964, as republished in: Ritter, Lawrence, *Money and Economic Activity*, Third Edition. Houghton Mifflin Co.: Boston, 1967, p. 250. (His emphasis.)

impediment to bank reserve adjustments that would have provided much needed elasticity to bank credit.

Instead of finding a way to allow banks under pressure to use their existing reserves, however, the popular answer in the pre-World War I era was to incorporate some new institution that would sequester reserves for the banks and mete them out by regulatory discretion when and where they were needed. As O. M. W. Sprague, a well-known Harvard economist, stated the case, "Somewhere in the banking system of a country there should be a reserve of lending power in the central money market."[14] Of course, all banks, and especially those in New York City, already had such "a reserve of lending power" but could not use it because of legal reserve requirements.

By 1910, three institutions had entered the picture as possible lenders of last resort for the banking system: First, the major national banks in New York and Chicago, which had plenty of reserves but were precluded from using them because of legal reserve requirements; second, bank clearing-house associations, which had devised an informal but effective "emergency currency" procedure; and, third, the U.S. Treasury Department, which occasionally had surplus reserves of gold and other legal tender that it could make available to banks during seasonal stringencies. Following the Panic of 1907, both professional economists and government officials found much fault with the improvised policies of both the clearing-house system and the Treasury's manipulation of its balances in the national bank depositories. Like Sprague, most observers thought that some "independent" reserve-holding agency was needed.[15]

The national banking system, despite its inflexibilities, was still the center of attention for "reform." In the view of many bankers and economists, the system's problems resulted from risk-prone banks that loaned speculatively or on long-term securities and mortgages. Seemingly oblivious to the excessive legal restrictions that handicapped all the banks, both state and national, current opinion had it that banks suffered suspensions because they did not pay adequate heed to the commercial credit theory of banking – what came to be labeled in later years the "Real Bills Doctrine" (RBD). This guide to bank operations was paramount in the minds of a large segment of economists, financial analysts, bankers, and legislators. It was a popular concept that had to be built into any institution supplying "credit" or reserves to troubled banking institutions, and it played a particularly important role in the formation of the Federal Reserve System.

[14]  Sprague, *History of Crises*, pp. 319–320.
[15]  Timberlake, *Monetary Policy*, pp. 183–213.

NINETEEN

## The Federal Reserve System, 1914–1929

The Federal Reserve System, like the Bank of England and the Banks of the United States, was *not* designed to be a central bank. To the newly elected Democratic Congress and President Wilson in 1912, a *central* bank was politically unacceptable. Bad enough that it was a bank, a central bank was also "monopolistic," and would operate only to further the interests of bankers. Instead, the ruling Democratic majority devised a system that complemented the regional structure of national banking with a new system of reserve-holding, super-commercial banks. The three central reserve cities of the National Banking System – New York, Chicago, and St. Louis – plus nine other reserve cities became twelve Reserve Bank cities under the new Federal Reserve System (the Fed).[1]

Prior to the organization of the Fed, however, both the Senate and House of Representatives proposed "emergency currency" bills that called for voluntary grouping of banks into "Associations" that would issue temporary currency on the basis of approved city, county, and state securities, and commercial paper. The notes would have the same qualities as national bank notes, and would be issued "under the direction and control of the Secretary of the Treasury." This measure passed Congress as the Aldrich-Vreeland Act (A-V Act) in 1908. It was written and sponsored by Senator Nelson Aldrich (Republican, New Hampshire) and Representative Edward Vreeland (Republican, New York). It simply formalized under federal government control the informal system the private clearing-houses had already developed.[2]

Representative Carter Glass (Democrat, Virginia), who became the leading congressman in the construction of the Federal Reserve Act, opposed

---

[1]  *Ibid.*, pp. 220–221.
[2]  *Ibid.*, p. 215.

the A-V Act and the whole idea of an "emergency currency." What the country needs, he lectured, "is not a makeshift legislative deformity, but a wise reformation of the entire banking and currency system of the United States whereby panics may be prevented, or, if not prevented … the evils consequent greatly abated."[3]

The A-V Act, besides creating national-bank currency associations, also set up a National Monetary Commission to promote research on banking and monetary history, with the idea of using this information to create a central "Reserve Currency Association," which would be, in effect, a central bank. This Commission published twenty-four volumes on monetary and banking subjects. Senator Nelson Aldrich, the co-sponsor of the A-V Act, summarized the findings of the Commission, which reflected accurately the professional opinions of bankers and economists.

Any U.S. banking institution, Aldrich began, should not copy the central banking institutions of European countries. First, it should mobilize and centralize reserves. Then, it should use its discount rate to ration its gold reserves to needy banks. It should adhere to the Bagehot principle, he continued, by freely advancing its reserves to solvent banks on any "paper" that would ordinarily be "good." At the same time, it should keep its discount rate higher than market rates. By this means it would ration its reserves as well as attract gold from other places, in accordance with Bagehot's prescriptions.[4] The central Association should also have a monopoly of note issue, but its discretion should be limited by explicit laws.[5] The immediate result of the Commission's proposals was introduction of a bill in Congress in 1911 to create a National Reserve Association that would consolidate the banking associations already in existence under the A-V Act.

By this time, however, the political landscape had changed. In 1912, the Republicans lost control of both Congress and the Presidency for the first time in 52 years (except for the Cleveland presidencies) due to the splintering effect of the new Progressive Party. With a Democratic Congress now in power, the National Reserve Association had to be renamed, and

[3]   Timberlake, *Monetary Policy*, p. 214. Glass, *Congressional Record*, House of Representatives, May 27, 1908.

[4]   Walter Bagehot (1821–1873) was Editor of *The Economist* and a learned scholar on monetary economics. He proposed a rule for the Bank of England to treat money market panics: In a period of bank-credit crisis, 1) lend freely, (2) on "good" paper – the kind of paper that is normally high quality, (3) charge penalty rates of interest, (4) advertise the policy widely, and (5) pursue it until the Bank's gold runs out. (Bagehot, Walter, *Lombard Street,* Kegan Paul, etc., 1892, London.)

[5]   Aldrich, Nelson W., *The Work of the National Monetary Commission,* Sen. Doc. No. 406, 61st Cong., 2nd Sess., 1910, pp. 3–29.

its sponsors had to be Democrats. Furthermore, the institution could not have the name or appearance of a central bank. Democrats rejected that institution as "monopolistic," and argued that it would be controlled by opulent, privileged bankers to their own benefit. In lieu of such an offensive institution, the Federal Reserve System that Representative Carter Glass and the Democratic Congress proposed would be a group of regional, reserve-holding, super-commercial banks, with a "nonpolitical" Federal Reserve Board in Washington to act as an arbiter over the lending practices of the regional Federal Reserve Banks.

Several other concepts of the new System emerged in the congressional debates over the Federal Reserve bill. One was that the new System would promote a "scientific" management of money and credit. Other legislators saw the Fed as a "public utility," with the Fed Board as a "Supreme Court of Finance." Congressmen generally wanted an objective, scientific, nonpolitical institution that would have only an occasional and temporary role in banking activities. Some predicted that the institution would be a catalyst of inflation. But Senator John Williams of Mississippi argued that under the bill pending, the Fed Board would have "no power to initiate, to compel or to consummate any inflation whatsoever." He claimed that the "character" of appointees to the Fed Board would prevent the fiat issue of paper currency.[6]

Williams's benign image of the pending Fed Board was at best wishful thinking. Another senator, Frank Mondell of Wyoming, expressed a skeptical and prophetic view of the proposed institution. He warned, correctly as it turned out, that "the Federal Reserve Board under this bill is an organization of vastly wider power, authority, and control over currency than the reserve associations contemplated by the National Monetary Commission.... It is of a character which in practical operation would tend to increase and centralize [power].... In your frantic efforts to escape the bogeyman of a central bank, ... you have come perilously near establishing in the office of the Comptroller of the Currency, under the Secretary of the Treasury, the most powerful banking institution in the world."[7]

A central bank is fundamentally an institution that creates money, as does a gold mine under a gold standard. But if a gold standard depends on having a money stock regulated by growth in monetary gold, how can it co-exist with a central bank that features a discretionary board vested with money-creating powers? That question was sublimated until near the

---

[6]   *CR*, 63rd Cong. 1st sess., p. 903.
[7]   *CR*, 63rd Cong. 1st sess., pp. 4865 and 4691.

end of the debates, and even then was not explicitly addressed. When the bill finally passed as "The Federal Reserve Act" and was signed into law by President Wilson on December 23, 1913, it included an important disclaimer that stated: "Nothing in this act ... shall be considered to repeal the parity provisions contained in an act approved March 14, 1900," that is, the (Gold) Currency Act. The gold standard was still supposed to be the basic monetary law for the U.S. monetary system. [8]

A notable emphasis of the act's Democratic sponsors was that the new institution would *not* be a central bank! It was to be a regional system of reserve-holding, private, super-banks. The act's primary implication was that any Federal Reserve Bank interventions to provide liquidity would be gratuitous – at the behest of member banks, limited in duration to a few months, and only in the form of short-term discounts and advances for "eligible" commercial paper. This "paper" was loans that financed production of real goods and services in one form or another. When the loans matured, the goods and services that the loans financed would be sold in markets and the loans paid off – first to the banks that had made them, and then by the banks to the Federal Reserve Bank that had discounted their paper.

This idea is known as the Real Bills Doctrine (RBD), mentioned previously. It dominated the thinking of most academics and legislators of the era, especially Representative (and then Senator) Carter Glass, who was the guiding force behind the Fed Act. It derived its substance from the legitimate gold standard, but it was not an essential element in the gold standard, and it was not internally stable. Where the gold standard provided for the monetization of "real" gold at a fixed dollar price, the RBD anticipated the monetization of Real Bills. However, the money loaned on a Real Bill is not fixed by any statute or formula as is the gold standard, but is subject to the discretion of the bankers making the Real Bills loans. Consequently, a Real Bills system cannot provide a faultless equilibrium. If bankers are too optimistic, bank lending on Real Bills generates too much bank credit and money, and promotes inflation. If bankers are too pessimistic, the effect is deflation. As Thomas Humphrey states the case: "Because it ties the nominal money supply to a nominal magnitude that moves in step with prices [dollars of new money to dollars of new Real Bills], the RBD provides no effective constraint on money or prices."[9]

---

[8]   For a more complete discussion of the formation of the Fed, see, Timberlake, *Monetary Policy*, Chapter 15, "Advent of the Federal Reserve System," pp. 214–234.

[9]   Humphrey, Thomas, "The Real Bills Doctrine." *Economic Review,* Federal Reserve Bank of Richmond 68, no. 5, p. 5.

A gold standard, by way of contrast, is neither optimistic nor pessimistic; it does not depend on anyone's discretion. No one ever had to define "real gold" for monetization purposes. Under a gold standard, an owner of gold can get a given quantity of gold coined into dollars at a fixed, statutory, mint price for the gold. Gold becomes the basis of all common money.

The RBD looks something like a gold standard. Whereas gold is coined into money at a fixed price, Real Bills – bank loans that reflect the production and marketing of goods and services – also are "coined" into new money through the banking system. It is not surprising that the RBD had its intellectual hey-day during the period when the gold standard was the dominant monetary institution of the country, since both the RBD and the gold standard look to the creation of money on what seem to be comparable terms.

As long as a Real Bills banking system is operating within the framework of the gold standard, it is harmless. A genuine gold standard will not allow banks to generate too much or too little money for very long, no matter how much credence bankers place in the RBD. The stock and rate of increase in monetary gold dominate monetary activity by determining the stock of common money, the price level, and the trends in both. If monetization of real bills tends to generate too little money relative to what the gold standard allows, banks' reserves continue to be excessive, and banker pessimism moderates. If bankers allow too much bank credit, gold flows out of the monetary system to other countries and into the "arts," depleting bank reserves and bringing bank lending up short. The important principle here is that no matter how invalid the RBD is in its role of creating the "right" quantity of money, the monetary systems' higher commitment to a working gold standard overrides and prevents the instabilities of the RBD from doing any significant harm.[10] Some proponents of the RBD, however, thought that with the RBD in operation, the monetary system did not need a gold standard to provide a stable system – that the RBD would do it all. The Great Contraction of 1929–1933 (discussed in the following chapter) demonstrated the fallacy of this belief.

Nowhere in the congressional debates on the Federal Reserve bill, nor in the final act, did any reference appear reflecting Congress's new-found power to issue paper currency that the Supreme Court's legal tender decisions had sanctioned. Everyone acknowledged without argument that the

---

[10] A. Piatt Andrew, "Credit and the Value of Money," *Publications of the American Economic Association* 6 (3rd Series): 1905, pp. 114–115. Also, Joseph Schumpeter, *History*, 1954, pp. 721–22.

gold standard still governed the economy's monetary system, and the Federal Reserve Act seemed to confirm gold's primacy. The universally accepted gold standard, having functioned for 34 years (from 1879 to 1913) without suspension, and similarly for most of the 70 years before 1860, seemed to have rendered the Court's legal tender decisions unnecessary and if not forgotten, at least irrelevant.

The new Federal Reserve System took over the function of the Treasury as manager of the government's fiat currencies, as well as the role of the clearing-house system as a lender-of-last-resort during bank panics. It was to serve as a self-regulating adjunct to the self-regulating gold standard. It was to be a Gold Standard Central Bank, and to do occasionally what the gold standard did constantly – provide seasonal money as needed, commensurate with seasonal spikes in productions of commodities. It would also become a system-wide, check-clearing institution for the member banks, since it held their reserve-deposit balances. It was also expected to provide currency and "reserve bank credit" when member banks experienced a liquidity crisis. It was not created as a centralized manager of the monetary system with unlimited powers, as the legal tender cases had implied, but as a technical device to reduce occasional instabilities appearing in the commercial banking system.

Virtually all of the Fed's Democratic supporters in Congress swore that the Fed would be nonpolitical, but Fed policy during World War I contradicted this supposition. The temper of Congress, and the government's wartime fiscal needs, pressured the Fed to adapt its policies to the dictates of the Treasury.[11] The *Annual Report of the Federal Reserve Board* for 1918 began by stating: "The discount policy of the Board has necessarily [sic] been coordinated … with Treasury requirements and policies, which in turn have been governed by demands made on the Treasury for war purposes."[12] Throughout the war and early post-war period, the Reserve banks adhered to Treasury pressure by charging somewhat lower discount rates to member banks that used government securities as collateral for their loans. They also made other allowances to provide easy credit for the government, including an embargo on gold exports.[13] The predictable result was the post-war inflation of 1917–1920, which saw an increase in the price level of about 56 percent.

[11]  Since the Secretary of the Treasury and the Comptroller were Chairman and Vice-Chairman of the Fed Board, the Treasury's fiscal needs always received top priority. How could it have been otherwise?

[12]  Board of Governors of the Federal Reserve system, *Annual Report, 1918*, p. 4

[13]  Friedman and Schwartz, *Monetary History*, pp. 192–196,

The Board's *Annual Report* for 1920, however, blamed the current inflation, not on the dominance of the Treasury and its provocation of credit on behalf of the government, but on "an unprecedented orgy of extravagance … overextended business, and general demoralization of the agencies of production and distribution," all in the private sector.[14] To end this "orgy," the Fed Banks finally shook themselves free of Treasury dominance and raised their discount rates, provoking the sharp post-war contraction of 1920–1922.[15] The Fed Banks' earning assets had grown by $2.5 billion from 1917 to 1920, and were the primary cause of the post-war inflation. During 1921, the Fed Banks allowed these base assets to shrink to almost nothing, while Fed Banks' gold holdings increased substantially.[16] (See Table 20.1 in Chapter 20.)

The 1920s witnessed a Federal Reserve institution emerge that was far different from the one either anticipated or legislated by the Federal Reserve Act of 1913. That act had declared that Fed Banks were "to furnish an elastic currency," which meant that they would rediscount commercial paper of member banks with new Federal Reserve notes when the banks did not have adequate reserves to do so. They would also serve as lenders of last resort for solvent but illiquid banks in a financial crisis to help maintain the existing level of bank credit and deposits in order to prevent bank failures.[17] In accordance with these principles, Fed Banks were supposed to keep their rediscount rates higher than general market rates, so that they would become financially active only in a liquidity pinch.[18]

The policies and reports of the Fed Banks and the Board of Governors during the 1920s reflect anything but such a subdued role. Starting in 1922, the New York Fed and some other Reserve Banks began open market operations (purchases) in government securities to furnish themselves with some

[14]  Board of Governors, *Annual Report, 1920*, p. 1.
[15]  Friedman and Schwartz, *Monetary History*, pp. 231–239.
[16]  The Fed Banks' *earning assets* are under the discretion of Fed managers, while the Fed Banks' gold holdings, a nonearning asset, passively depend on what is deposited by member banks. When Fed Banks bought more loans and discounts, earning assets increased, along with the Fed's *monetary* liabilities – Federal Reserve notes outstanding and member bank reserves. In this way Fed Banks deliberately altered the economy's stock of money. When gold entered the monetary system and was accounted in Fed Banks as a *nonearning asset*, it increased the stock of money without any action by Fed managers. Fed policies cannot manufacture gold. To initiate any increase in the stock of money, the Fed, in the mode of any central bank, must *buy* – that is, *monetize* – something. Most often that "something" has been outstanding government securities. But it could be junked cars – "clunkers" – or any kind of waste product.
[17]  Timberlake, *Monetary Policy*, pp. 254–255.
[18]  Hepburn, *History of Currency*, 1924, pp. 531–534.

needed interest income. Soon thereafter, this policy, under the direction of the New York Fed, became a formalized and accepted means for manipulating the money stock.[19]

The use of open market operations reflected the fact that the main thrust of Federal Reserve policy practically ignored both the RBD and the Gold Standard. Fed Banks, particularly the Fed Bank of New York, were inundated with gold reserves. To prevent current gold monetization, gold inflation, and a subsequent deflation when the accumulated gold acquired during the war returned to European monetary systems, the New York Fed sterilized gold inflows by selling some of its other assets to prevent gold monetization – an action that private banks would never, and could never, have taken. By its dominant place in the System, the New York Fed instituted what was essentially a stable price level policy. This policy worked as intended. From 1922 to 1929, the Consumers' Price Index (CPI, 1947–1949 = 100) stayed virtually constant, "increasing" only from 71.6 to 73.3, a 2.3 percent increase over 7 years, or less than one-half of one percent per year. The Wholesale Price Index actually decreased by about the same amount. Prices and the real value of the dollar were as stable as they would ever get.[20]

---

[19]　Friedman and Schwartz, *Monetary History*, p. 251; Elmus Wicker, "Federal Reserve Monetary Policy, 1922–1933: A Reinterpretation," *Journal of Political Economy* 78, no. 4: pp. 325–327.

[20]　It is nothing short of astonishing that contemporary observers of several different theoretical persuasions look back at the 1920s and *presume* that because the economy was healthy and productive it was also going through an inflation, which they attribute entirely to Federal Reserve policy! All that one must do to correct this notion is to look at any price index for the 1920s, and observe total dollar assets in the Fed Banks' Consolidated Statement of Condition. Fed Banks' holding of earning assets actually declined, meaning that the Fed on net balance tended to *reduce* the money stock. (See Table 20.1, Column 8.) In fact, the Fed's stable price level policy prevented a temporary gold inflation. One school of thought refers to the event as a "profit inflation." It holds that firms' profits were artificially inflated by the New York Fed's stable price level policy.

# TWENTY

## The Great Contraction, 1929–1933

The principal driving force behind Federal Reserve policy in the 1920s was Benjamin Strong, Governor of the New York Fed. Besides his practical experience as a banker who had supported clearing-house operations in the Panic of 1907, he had the counsel of Professor Irving Fisher and some other economists who proposed that the Fed adopt a policy of price level stabilization through its control over the quantity of money.[1]

At the time, Strong felt that a law requiring stabilization was inappropriate: "Governor Strong believed that the government should not have the power to control the price level, and [that] the gold standard was the accepted means of keeping this power from the government."[2] The New York Fed's policies were largely based on its substantial influence over bank reserves and were in lieu of a gold standard.

By 1928, three operating systems and supporting arguments had appeared in discussions of Federal Reserve policy: (1) the gold standard, in remission but still the ultimate norm in official discourse; (2) price level stabilization by quantitative control of bank reserves through open-market operations, as the New York Fed had been doing; and (3) the real bills doctrine that argued for "credit control" under the discretion of the Board of Governors and the Reserve Banks, using the Fed Banks' discount rates as the controlling medium. When Strong died in October 1928, Real Bills proponents on the Fed Board moved to take control of the policy machinery.

Both the administrations of the twelve Reserve Banks and the Federal Reserve Board in Washington had policymaking powers. The Board, which

---

[1] Chandler, L. V. 1958. *Benjamin Strong, Central Banker*. Washington, D.C.: Brookings Institution, pp. 194–206. Robert Hetzel, "The Rules versus Discretion Debate Over Monetary Policy in the 1920s." *Economic Review*, Federal Reserve Bank of Richmond, 71, no. 6, pp. 7–8.

[2] Hetzel, "Rules versus Discretion," *ibid.* Also see, Chandler, *Benjamin Strong*, p. 199.

Table 20.1 *Money stock M1, and selected items in all Federal Reserve Banks, 1920–1933, with gold reserve ratios*
*($ billions, except ratios)*

| Year | M1 | Total Monetary Liabilities. | Gold and Other Reserves Total | Gold and Other Reserves Excess | Net Monetary Liabilities | Net Change Monetary Liabilities | Bills Bought | Gold Reserve Ratio (%) |
|------|-----|------|------|------|------|------|------|------|
| (1) | (2) | (3) | (4) | (5) | (6) | (7) | (8) | (9) |
| 1922 | 21.6 | 4.03 | 3.14 | 1.62 | 0.89 | – 2.10 | 0.98 | 77.8 |
| 1924 | 23.2 | 3.93 | 3.25 | 1.78 | 0.68 | – 0.21 | 0.86 | 82.5 |
| 1926 | 26.1 | 3.94 | 2.98 | 1.51 | 0.96 | 0.28 | 1.00 | 75.4 |
| 1929 | 26.2 | 4.04 | 3.10 | 1.51 | 0.94 | – 0.02 | 0.82 | 74.5 |
| 1931 | 23.9 | 4.14 | 3.50 | 1.96 | 0.64 | – 0.30 | 0.62 | 84.3 |
| 1932 | 20.5 | 4.80 | 2.80 | 0.99 | 2.00 | 1.36 | 0.25 | 58.4 |
| 1933 (March) | 19.1 | 6.14 | 3.15 | 0.80 | 2.99 | 0.99 | 0.12 | 51.3 |

*Sources*: Board of Governors of the Federal Reserve System. *Banking and Monetary Statistics, 1943*, Table 93, pp. 347–349, and Friedman and Schwartz, *Monetary History*, Tables B-3 and A-1, pp. 709–714 and pp. 801–804.

operated as a supervisory-and-review body, had veto power over discount rates set by Reserve Banks. It also made the final determination of the "character of paper eligible for discount" – whether the discounts the Banks made were Real Bills-ish enough – and it could set other regulations and limitations on discounting.[3]

Besides its proscriptive powers over Fed Bank discount rates and the eligibility of commercial paper, the Board also had extensive emergency powers that it could use actively in a panic. First, on the affirmative vote of five members, it could "require Federal Reserve banks to rediscount the discounted paper of other Federal Reserve banks at rates of interest to be fixed by the Board of Governors." With this power, the Board could move gold from one Fed Bank to another whenever the gold-needy Reserve Bank required and requested such help.[4] Additionally, the Board could order the suspension of "any [gold] reserve requirements specified in this Act" for a period of thirty days, and it could renew such suspensions every fifteen days thereafter for an indefinite period.[5] This clause gave the Board the power to let the Reserve Banks use up *all* of their gold reserves if necessary, just as commercial banks without a central bank would do when the situation demanded it, and as the U.S. Treasury had almost done to protect gold redemption of its currencies in the monetary shrinkage of 1893–1896.

The Fed Board in Washington (housed in the U.S. Treasury Building) successfully assumed policy control after Strong's death. The Secretary of the Treasury was Chairman, and the Comptroller of the Currency Vice-Chairman, of the eight-man Fed Board.

One notable member of the Board was Adolph C. Miller, a journeyman economist who had been instrumental in writing Real Bills norms into the Fed Act. Miller was appointed by Woodrow Wilson (Democrat) in 1914, and re-appointed by Calvin Coolidge (Republican) in 1924. In his earlier days, Miller had studied economics under Professor J. Laurence Laughlin, the most outspoken proponent of the Real Bills Doctrine in the economics profession. (Laughlin was also the major professor of Sophinsba P. Breckinridge at the University of Chicago, who authored the work on *Legal Tender* discussed previously).[6]

---

[3] Board of Governors of the Federal Reserve System, *The Federal Reserve Act as Amended Through October 1, 1961*. Washington: 1961, pp. 44–48.

[4] This section of the Fed Act was the one that persuaded A. Barton Hepburn to support passage of the Fed Act in 1913. He was particularly concerned that Fed Banks operate as a unified central bank in the event of a serious threat to gold reserves (Hepburn, 1924, preface, x–xi.).

[5] *Ibid.*, pp. 34–35.

[6] Both Miller and Professor H. Parker Willis, who taught at Columbia University in New York for many years, were closely associated throughout their professional lives with

Miller became the primary influence on Fed policy.[7] He was instrumental in writing the Board's *Tenth Annual Report* in 1923, which is virtually a handbook on Real Bills policy. That *Report* stresses the notion that goods create money through the banking system, and that central bankers, who are Real Bills agents, must be informed and skillful in applying the central bank's powers to "each specific credit situation at the particular moment of time when it has arisen or is developing." In the Congressional *Stabilization Hearings* of 1926–1928, Miller was the quintessential Real Bills advocate. His final observation in the *Hearings* was: "The total volume of money in circulation is determined by the community. The Federal Reserve system has no appreciable control over that and no disposition to interfere with it." Miller was particularly opposed to the price-level stabilization policies of Governor Strong, and was insultingly indiscreet when he labeled Strong one of those "amateur economists" who "constitute one of [the System's] dangerous elements."[8]

Besides stressing that banks and the central bank should grant "credit" only for Real Bills, the Real Bills Doctrine (RBD) also has an important negative proscription. It unequivocally condemns bank lending for long-term loans, such as mortgages, government bonds, and, especially, for speculative loans that support stock market and real estate "bubbles." These latter were particularly alien to the RBD because investment "bubbles" did not contribute to real production.

By 1929, an anti-speculation-in-the-stock-market fervor was prominent in the financial community. Miller and other members of the Fed Board recognized this sentiment, and adopted it as the new Fed policy. They were probably sincere enough in their own beliefs, but they also knew that an anti-speculation policy would have much popular support. Anti-speculation policy, especially when it chastises those speculators who

---

Professor Laughlin. Both, but particularly Willis, were close advisers to Carter Glass who was Chairman of the House Banking and Currency Committee when it wrote the Federal Reserve Act in 1913 (See, Alfred Bornemann, *Chapters in the Career of an Economist. Washington, D.C.*: American Council on Public Affairs, 1940, pp. 2, 3, 5, 27, 31, 45, 51, 53, 59). In Congress, Glass promoted their ideas into the Federal Reserve Act.

[7]   Several studies confirm Miller's successful assumption of policy control. In an article in the *JPE*, vol. XL, Sept. 1934, p. 391, Karl R. Bopp, who became President of the Fed Bank of Philadelphia, wrote: "Mr. A. C. Miller, who seems to be the dominant figure on the Board, has stated that he is opposed to open-market operations – the only effective method of stimulating revival from a severe recession.… Even through 1931 he was not of the opinion that such [an] operation was necessary."

[8]   Hetzel, "Rules versus Discretion," *Economic Review*, pp. 10–11. Miller made these remarks and others in the House of Representatives *Stabilization Hearings of 1926–28*. Contrary to Miller's stated opinion, Strong and the New York Fed did control the economy's quantity of money through 1928–1929.

have been successful, has always been popular. It can use words such as "greed," "exploit," and "the rich" in lieu of scientific analysis.

The shift in control from Strong, who died in October 1928, and the New York Fed to Miller and the Fed Board in February 1929 prompted an evangelical crusade to crush speculation in the stock market. The result was disastrous beyond measure. It was a prime example of what happens when some version of the RBD trumps the gold standard. Due to the precedent Strong and the New York Fed had initiated in promoting a stable price level policy without heed to the dormant gold standard, the Real Bills Fed Board that was now in control could proceed equally unconstrained. The gold standard remained where it had been – a star performer waiting in the wings for an opportune time to reappear.[9]

Fortunately for the historical record, Miller had the conceit to write an article for *The American Economic Review* in which he explained, defended, and lauded the Fed Board's single-minded, anti-speculation crusade.[10] He began by claiming that Strong's policy leadership of the New York Fed in the late 1920s "proved to be unequal to the [speculative] situation ... in this period of optimism gone wild and cupidity gone drunk." The Board's "anxiety," Miller continued, "reached a point where it felt it must [intervene] in the speculative situation menacing the welfare of the country." To carry out this merciful intervention, the Board, on February 2, 1929, sent a letter, largely penned by Miller, to all the Reserve Banks stating that the Board had the "duty ... to restrain the use of Federal Reserve credit facilities in aid of the growth of speculative credit. To that end, the Board ordered the Fed Banks to initiate a policy of 'direct pressure' that restricted borrowings from the [Fed Banks] by those member banks, which were increasingly disposed to lend funds for speculative purposes."[11]

"Direct pressure"[12] added a major obstacle to bank borrowing over and above the cost of the discount rate. It was not just "jaw-boning." "It put the

---

[9]  Friedman and Schwartz, in discussing the shift in control from the Fed Bank of New York to the Board of Governors, observe "that something more than the characteristics of the specific persons or official agencies that happened to be in power is required to explain such a major event as the financial catastrophe in the United States from 1929 to 1933" (*Monetary History*, p. 419). The "something more" that they look for, I suggest, was not only the laxity of policy but the shift in power to those who acted on the principles of the real bills doctrine. They refer to this belief several times, but provide no explicit link in their treatment between it and the subsequent policy of do-nothing that they document so thoroughly.

[10] Miller, A. C., "Responsibility for Federal Reserve Policies, 1927–1929," *American Economic Review*, 25, September, 1935, pp. 442–457.

[11] *Ibid.*, p. 454.

[12] "Direct pressure" in action meant to discourage by innuendo those banks that applied for loans. A bank seeking Fed Bank help had to endure a severe cross-examination,

member bank," Miller reported approvingly, "under pressure by obliging it to show that it [the bank] was entitled to accommodation.... It was a method of exercising discriminating control over the extension of federal reserve credit such as the purely technical and impartial method of bank rate could not do."[13]

Miller's resounding praise of "direct pressure" is itself damning. The very fact that a Board could "discriminate" its favors, in spite of the traditional non-discriminating, impartial discount rate, took the financial adjustment away from market forces and put it into the hands of Real Bills zealots. The formal discount rate became irrelevant. The true discount rate under "direct pressure" was whatever the Fed Board wanted it to be. To a bank with some kind of speculative "stain," the applicable discount rate was infinite: that bank could not get a Fed Bank discount no matter what the formal discount rate was.

The effect of the "direct pressure" policy on the banking and monetary system was catastrophic. Whether it was advisable or not, Congress had created the Fed System to support the member banks when they were short of reserves. Now, this new policy, with its emphasis on speculation, was denying them the emergency credit the Federal Reserve Act had promised, and at the very time that the promise was obligatory.[14]

Clark Warburton, an eminent monetary economist of the mid-twentieth century, noted that in support of the "direct pressure" policy, the Fed Banks "virtually stopped rediscounting or otherwise acquiring 'eligible paper'." Though the commercial banks had plenty of eligible paper, "direct pressure" from the Fed Board was "so strong as to amount to a virtual prohibition of rediscounting for banks which were making loans for security speculation, and a hard-boiled attitude towards banks in special need of rediscounts because of deposit withdrawals."[15]

Ordinarily, the operational gold standard would have overridden any "Real Bills" excesses or deficiencies, no matter the perspective of the central bankers who were in charge. However, *the* gold standard had to be operating in its traditional fashion for its stabilizing properties to function, and that was not happening, either before 1929 under Strong's leadership at the New York Fed, or from 1929 to 1933 under A. C. Miller and the anti-speculation

---

emphasizing its possible role in speculative financial activities with the intention of discouraging its application for assistance.

[13] *Ibid.*, pp. 455–456.

[14] Board of Governors of the Federal Reserve System, Legal Division, *The Federal Reserve Act as Amended, 1961*, pp. 33, 43 and passim.

[15] Warburton, Clark, *Depression, Inflation, and Monetary Policy, Selected Papers, 1945–1953.* Baltimore: Johns Hopkins Press, 1966, pp. 339–340.

majority of the Fed Board. Consequently, the disastrous "direct pressure" policy had no antidote.

Miller attempted to be modest about who was responsible for the new policy. The champions of anti-speculation, he reported, were the five-member majority of the Fed Board, one of whom was A. C. Miller. The other members of the Board, including the Secretary of the Treasury and the Comptroller of the Currency, plus the administrations of all twelve Fed Banks, the Federal Advisory Council, and many of the largest member banks opposed the policy. "Nonetheless," Miller exulted, "the Board [majority] adhered to its position."[16] Most notably, gold had again been left out of the policy picture. Nowhere in Miller's discussion of "speculation" and "direct pressure" is there any reference to gold, gold reserve ratios of Fed Banks, or the Gold Standard.

What began in 1929–1930 as an evangelical crusade against commercial banks, innocently lending to borrowers who might have had a stock market connection, ramified into an out-of-control bank rout during the next 2 years. Friedman and Schwartz identify three banking crises without significant recovery – in 1930, 1931, and 1933.[17] As banks infected with "speculation" were allowed to fail, depositors in still solvent banks panicked and moved to convert their demand deposits into currency. But the currencies the banks had to pay out to these depositors were the banks' *reserves*! Consequently, the bank contractions became episodes of dynamic disequilibrium. Moreover, since the Fed Banks had abandoned their role as lenders-of-last-resort in favor of stamping out speculation, no Fed Bank "credit" was available to help still solvent banks, and many of them failed. One bank crisis followed another. By the time the catastrophe ended in March 1933, approximately 9,000 banks, of the approximately 25,000 banks operating in 1929, had forever closed their doors. Unemployment was near 25 percent; real Gross National Product had declined 30 percent; money prices had declined by 25 percent; commercial bankers were shell-shocked; and the "people" were desperate.

But how could such a monetary debacle occur? The United States not only had a gold standard, it had plenty of gold and a central banking system created to prevent just such a catastrophe. Since the Federal Reserve Banks were overloaded with gold, why weren't they and the gold standard providing the needed bank reserves and currency? Why couldn't the system recover even with a Real Bills Federal Reserve System in control?

---

[16]  Miller, *A.E.R.*, p. 456.
[17]  *Monetary History*, Chapter 7, "The Great Contraction, 1929–1933," pp. 299–407.

# TWENTY ONE

# Gold! Where Did It Go? Why Didn't the Gold Standard Work?

A true gold standard is a complete commodity-money system. Once set up by law whereby a political authority specifies the dollar value of a given quantity and fineness of gold, it requires no management, and, indeed, *demands* no management. If a gold standard is managed by a Treasury Department or a central bank, it is no longer a gold standard.[1]

Under a true gold standard, the demand for and supply of gold for money, jewelry, dentistry, and security interact constantly through market prices for all goods, services, capital and the monetary metal, gold, to determine a given quantity of money. To put it forcefully, and to repeat an earlier section: a gold standard determines the community's quantity of money. If money prices tend to fall, say, because of an increased demand to hold common money, the value of monetary gold, being fixed in dollar terms, rises in real terms. Its purchasing power increases, stimulating increases in the production and importation of gold, and the supply of gold to the mints. Since gold is the necessary base for currency and bank deposits, the new monetary gold increases the quantity of common money ending the fall in general prices and establishing a new equilibrium. Alternatively, if prices are in equilibrium and production is increasing normally, additional gold entering the system from established gold-mining industries also tends to raise money prices. However, ordinary increases in the production and marketing of goods, services, and capital require new gold-generated money for their purchase and sale. In either case, successive approximations of greater goods-and-services production and greater gold-and-money production through the market system generate ongoing market equilibrium.[2]

---

[1]  Officer, L., "Gold Standard," *E. H. Net Encyclopedia*, edited by Robert Whaples, 2001.
[2]  See again, A. Piatt Andrew, *Publications of the American Economic Association,* Vol. VI (3rd Series, 1905), p. 115, for a description of the gold standard's operation.

If the world's monetary gold production is for a time greater (less) than the production of goods, services, and capital, a modest inflation (deflation) may occur. The U.S. economy from 1838 to 1845, when prices fell about 17 percent (2.5 percent per year), reflected a less rapid growth of gold and money; and from 1896 to 1910, when gold reserves were burgeoning, prices rose about 15 percent (1 percent per year). So, a gold standard is not a guarantee against a mild inflation or deflation; but, without other disturbances, such as government issues of fiat paper money, it is virtually a guarantee against *extraordinary* price level changes. Experience over the ages reveals a remarkable constancy in the value of gold with respect to the values of all other marketable goods and services.[3]

A gold standard provides a government and an economy with a set of rules prescribing the conditions for the supply of common money. The system works on the principle of Spontaneous Order: human beings make contracts, arrangements, deals, and bargains with myriads of other human beings, all acting in their own interests, within the framework of easily understood and commonly accepted principles. The result is a working quantity of common money that establishes prices and clears markets of goods and services demanded and supplied. Human design is limited to the framework for the standard. In the case of the United States, that design was the Constitution of the United States, Article 1, Sections 8 and 10, which specify gold and silver as the base of the monetary system.[4] Congress could determine what would be the legal prices of the two monetary metals, and it could marginally and occasionally "regulate the [monetary] value thereof," but that was all. The system was self-regulating in all important particulars.

The Federal Reserve Act in 1913, *possibly* still within the framework of the Constitution, allowed the new Federal Reserve Banks to hold the gold reserves of the member banks, giving them "Reserve Bank credit" in return. Fed Banks were also fractional reserve institutions. Their reserves were the gold that member banks deposited with them, and their liabilities were the above-noted reserve accounts of the member banks, plus issues of Federal Reserve notes to banks that needed currency instead of bank reserves.

While the banks could still access the deposited gold at any time, their practical reserves now were their reserve-deposit accounts at the Fed Banks plus their holdings of Fed notes. The gold was a reserve for Fed Banks, and,

---

[3] Jastram, Roy, *Silver: The Restless Metal*, New York: John Wiley and Sons, 1981, Chart 1, 9f.

[4] Yes, silver was also a constitutional money metal, so the United States had a gold-silver standard. I use "gold" only to keep the argument simpler.

at one remove, the reserve for member banks.[5] Thus, the gold accounted in the Fed Banks' assets was a base that supported an inverted pyramid of banking system liabilities – outstanding Federal Reserve note currency, member bank reserves with Fed Banks, and checkbook (demand) deposits of member banks. With this monetary structure in place, virtually no ordinary people ever saw any gold coins.[6] They used Federal Reserve notes and fractional coins produced by the Treasury for their hand-to-hand currency needs, and personal checks written against bank deposit balances for larger exchanges.[7]

During and after the Recession of 1920–1922, Fed Banks built up their excess gold reserves (Table 20.1, Column 5) by selling off the government securities and other assets they had acquired during World War I. Then, from 1922 to 1929, the New York Fed's stable price level policy under Governor Benjamin Strong postponed any significant role for the Fed's gold. Anyone could still convert other moneys into gold, but no one had much incentive to do so. More to the point, movements of gold no longer determined changes in hand-to-hand currency and bank reserves, and had not since 1914. The gold standard had become a façade; it was not functioning as an operating system.[8]

To the "Real Bills" Federal Reserve Board that ramped itself into policy-making prominence in 1929, a conventional gold standard was not good enough, because gold standard machinery did not punish "speculation" in the manner that the Real Bills crusaders of the period wanted. Indeed, a gold standard may reward "speculation," when the speculators bet the right way and in their greed realize a profit. In any case, this federal institution was no longer constitutional.[9]

---

[5]  Fractional reserve requirements for commercial banks ranged between ten and twenty-five percent of their outstanding deposits, while the Federal Reserve Act specified fractional gold reserve requirements for Fed Banks of 35 percent against member bank deposit-reserves, and 40 percent against outstanding Federal Reserve notes.

[6]  On this writer's ninth birthday in 1931, his doting grandfather pressed into his hand a five-dollar gold piece – a half Eagle! I remember that it was larger than a nickel, but smaller than a quarter. So I saw and handled a real gold coin for about one day in my life. Of course, I could not prodigally spend more than a small fraction of it. And before I even did that, the half Eagle was back in a piggy bank, and then back in a real bank, and then ... (see below).

[7]  A few other currencies were also in circulation – the residual of the greenbacks, silver certificates and silver coins, national bank notes, and fractional currency. The U.S. Treasury administered most of this currency.

[8]  Leland Yeager, *International Monetary Relations, History and Policy*, New York: Harper and Row, 1966, p. 290.

[9]  Governor Benjamin Strong's stable price level policy from 1922 to 1929 was also questionably constitutional. The New York Fed, not the gold standard, controlled the quantity

The new "Real Bills" Fed Board sterilized gold by allowing it to accumulate in Fed Banks. As Table 20.1 shows, gold and other reserves in the Fed Banks peaked at $3.5 billion in 1931 – 2 years into the Great Contraction – from $3.1 billion in 1929. [10] This quantity of gold was more than double the Fed Banks' statutory gold reserve requirement. Even at the nadir of the Contraction – February 1933 – the Fed Banks had $1.35 billion *excess* reserves of gold, which could have been accounted substantially more by simple bookkeeping changes. There was no shortage of gold at any time during this period.[11]

Why, then, did Federal Reserve officials make so much fuss about such a nonexistent "shortage," and why were they so reluctant to use even their excess reserves?

To begin with, under the Real Bills Fed Board, the crusade against "speculation" was the dominant policy from 1929 to 1931, no matter what the gold situation was. The Real Bills evangelists paid almost no attention to gold reserves while imposing their "direct pressure" policy.

Second, the Federal Reserve Act specified a double-minimum gold reserve for Fed Bank obligations – 40 percent against outstanding Federal Reserve note currency, and 35 percent against outstanding member bank reserve accounts. (See Table 20.1.) These statutory gold reserve requirements, as a practical matter, were "excess" to begin with. They were analogous to a car with a twenty-gallon gas tank, and a matching gas gauge for the driver on the dashboard. Ordinarily, the "*Reserve*" on the gas gauge, to warn the driver of an upcoming shortage, appears when the tank is nearly empty, say, at about the three-gallon mark. For the Fed Banks, however, the "gold" gas gauge reserve was set at about the three-quarter full mark, much more than would ever be needed if the Fed Banks' gold was subject to market determinants.

However, mortal men, not markets, were controlling monetary policy from Washington, and doing so according to their beliefs and prejudices without heed to the Gold Standard. Furthermore, they had to be, and were, politically motivated. Similar to ordinary bank managers facing reserve requirements, Fed Bank managers also regarded the statutory reserve

---

of money. However, Strong recognized the problematic nature of his policies, and promised a return to the Gold Standard when the trading world's current instability ended. Unfortunately, Strong and the world waited too long. Had the U.S. system been put back on the Gold Standard in 1929, no Great Contraction would have occurred.

[10] The Fed Banks-U.S. Treasury held about 40 percent of the world's monetary gold at this time (Friedman and Schwartz, *Monetary History*, p. 396).

[11] *Ibid.*

requirement numbers as a "line in the sand" that was tantamount to a prohibition. Therefore, even though the Fed's gold in the early 1930s was still well above the abnormally high *Reserve* reading, Fed managers virtually shut down the monetary "engine," complaining that they were almost "out of gas (gold)" and that the car would no longer run. They seemed oblivious, first, to the financial harm they were doing by their failure to help ailing banks in the spirit of the Federal Reserve Act; second, to the *Reserve* level of gold-gas they still had; and, third, to the statutory power they had under the Fed Act to breach reserve requirement minima indefinitely. Even if the Fed Banks had completely run out of reserves, an event that was virtually impossible under the circumstances, and the now market-determined price of gold rose above the mint price, the gold standard would have been only temporarily violated. It would still have been the law, and markets would have restored the conditions for its reappearance.[12]

Had the commercial banks controlled their own gold reserves, no gold problems could have arisen. As market-directed enterprises, they would have expanded bank credits and deposits in the 1920s – long before 1931. When they did, prices would have begun to levitate, business activity would have expanded, the price of gold would have reached the gold export point, and some of the gold would gradually have been exported back to the European financial systems that had lost it during World War I. That would have been the end of any bank contraction, and the beginning of a new era of international gold standard stabilization.

Gold, under Federal Reserve control, had become a symbol without a function. The Real Bills Fed Board, after cleaning out "speculation," pretended that it was trying to "protect the gold standard" by not allowing gold exports, and thereby building up the stock of monetary gold in Fed Banks. Gold could only be a standard, however, if its presence determined the system's quantity of money. Rather, Federal Reserve policy makers were unwittingly performing that function – with disastrous results – while they converted gold into a useless relic to be preserved deep in the ground under heavy guard.

The monetary system was now set for a massive intervention of political "solutions." National elections were at hand, and the results were bound to be momentous.

---

[12] Reserve requirements for national banks after the Civil War, and for many subsequent eras, had the same pernicious effects. (See above, pp. 234–235.)

# TWENTY TWO

## The Gold Clause Cases, 1934–1935

Under the Hoover Administration prior to the elections of 1932, several measures passed Congress that attempted to deal with the Fed-generated tumble of money, prices, incomes, and employment that no one understood. New legislation included: The Reconstruction Finance Corporation Act, January 29, 1932; The Glass-Steagall Act, February 24, 1932; The Federal Home Loan Bank Act, July 22, 1932; and The Glass-Borah Rider to the Home Loan Bank Act, July 22, 1932.[1] Most of the provisions in these acts aimed at treating the symptoms of the malady that Federal Reserve malpractice had recently imposed on the banking and monetary system.

By the time that President Franklin Roosevelt took office on March 4, 1933, the banking system was shell-shocked and the economy paralyzed. The sheer quantity of gold in the Fed Banks and U.S. Treasury, however, seemed to offer hope that something expansive using gold could be done. Consequently, in his first week in office, the President called Congress into special session and offered his program for "Recovery." It included an Emergency Banking Act that Congress passed on March 9.

This act gave the President extensive power to regulate the operations of all member banks of the Federal Reserve System, and all foreign exchange transactions and gold movements. It allowed the Secretary of the Treasury, at his discretion, to call into the U.S. Treasury all gold bullion, gold coin, and gold certificates owned domestically, so that the gold could be melted down and recast into ingots that would be unusable as coin-currency. Another provision authorized Fed Banks to make advances to member banks on

---

[1]  White, *Money and Banking*, pp. 696–706. The legislation of the period is full of references to Carter Glass, Senator from Virginia. His position as Chairman of the Senate Committee on Finance and his longevity in Congress, gave him more power on monetary policy than any other ten congressmen.

the security of any "acceptable" assets, that is, not just Real Bills.[2] It was abundantly clear from this act that Congress, the President, and everyone in the government recognized that the Fed Board and Banks had not lived up to their promise to be lenders-of-last-resort, as implied in the Federal Reserve Act. The economy was starving for money in the presence of a huge mass of monetary gold and an omnipotent central bank that seemed paralyzed.

Two months later, on May 12, 1933, Congress passed the "Inflation Bill," which was formally labeled the Thomas Amendment to the Agricultural Relief Act.[3] This Act encouraged the Fed Banks to purchase $3 billion additional government securities, and to pay out Federal Reserve notes to buy them, something the Fed Banks could have been doing anyway. In case the Fed Banks did not do so, the Amendment authorized the President to buy the securities and pay for them through the Treasury with United States notes, that is, greenbacks! Although the President did not use this power – probably because he and his advisers thought something more conventional might work – it reflected the tension in the government between the managers of the Fed, and Congress and the Administration. The act also allowed the President to reduce the gold content of the dollar (i.e., increase the mint price of gold) by as much as 50 percent. First, however, the government had to own the gold, so that it would realize the seigniorage revenue from such a gold-dollar devaluation.

To implement the gold take-over, the President on April 5, 1933, issued Executive Order 6102, which required U.S. citizens to deliver on or before May 1, 1933, all but a trivial amount of gold coin, gold bullion, and gold certificates. The people returned the gold through the banking system to Federal Reserve Banks, and were paid the current mint price of $20.67 per troy ounce.[4]

Next, Congress passed the Legal Tender Act, June 5, 1933, which declared that henceforth all government-issued currencies were full legal tender at their face values.[5] In conjunction with this act, Congress issued a Joint

---

[2]   White, *Money and Banking,* pp. 706–708.

[3]   *Ibid.*, pp. 709–710. Elmer Thomas was a Senator from Oklahoma, who understood the economy's need for money.

[4]   Executive Order 6102 specifically exempted "customary use in industry, profession or art," an exemption that covered artists, jewelers, dentists, and sign makers among others. The order further permitted any person to own up to $100 in gold coins (equivalent to $7,500 in 2011 if adjusted for the current price of gold). The same paragraph also exempted "gold coins having recognized special value to collectors of rare and unusual coins." This exception protected gold coin collections from legal seizure and likely melting.

[5]   White, *Money and Banking*, p. 712.

Resolution on the same date that expressly abrogated, that is, voided, the gold clauses in all public and private debts and contracts of any sort.[6]

The stage was now set for the federal government's comprehensive management of gold and the monetary system. By October, 1933, the Fed Banks and Treasury had much of the monetary gold. It was accounted in Fed Banks as an asset, "Gold Certificates," at the 100-year-old mint price of gold – $20.67 per fine ounce. Once the Fed-Treasury had all the gold, the Treasury Department, together with the Reconstruction Finance Corporation, began an additional gold-buying program in the gold market that, by January, 1934, raised the market price of gold to above $34 per ounce. Congress next passed the Gold Reserve Act on January 30, 1934, giving the President the power to devalue the gold dollar by as much as 60 percent. The President, not timid with his new authority, proclaimed an increase of 59.06 percent in the mint price of gold – that is, from $20.67 per fine ounce to $35 per fine ounce. This formal increase in price was accomplished technically by reducing the gold content of the official gold dollar in the same proportion – 59.06 percent. The President, therefore, used only 97.4 percent of the authority Congress had vested in him!

The appreciation in the mint price of gold gave the Treasury-Fed Bank complex that now owned the gold a profit of approximately $2.8 billion, a sum almost equal to the total revenue the federal government realized in 1934 ($3.1 billion). Two billion dollars of this profit was placed in a Treasury Trust Fund to be used to control foreign exchange rates, and was otherwise invested in government securities. The Secretary could buy or sell foreign currencies with the gold, subject to the approval of the President.[7]

Such a magnitude of devaluation was a major distortion of Congress's power to "regulate the value thereof." That clause, as analyzed earlier (see Chapter 5), was only to effect marginal changes in the prices of gold and silver, in order to keep both metallic currencies in circulation. It had nothing to do with regulating the general stock of money, and could not have had any such meaning. The gold standard, when allowed to operate as intended, did that. Full-bodied silver coin was now out of the monetary picture

---

[6]  *Ibid.*, pp. 712–713. As an example of what professional economists thought of this act, White cited an article by James W. Angell of Columbia University, "Gold, Banks, and the New Deal," *Political Science Quarterly*, Dec. 1934, p. 492. Angell wrote that both acts were "completely immoral . . . and a flagrant violation of the solemn provision made in the Gold Standard Act of 1900, and of the solemn contracts made in subsequent government bond issues – notably the Liberty and Victory loans [of 1918–1920]."

[7]  *Ibid.*, pp. 136–144, and 707–721.

anyway, since silver had been only a subsidiary currency since 1878. So the devaluation had nothing to do with denominational problems of precious metal coins.

One further excuse for gold devaluation occurs when monetary gold becomes scarce enough world-wide so that its real price is constantly increasing as all money prices constantly fall. The ongoing price level adjustment required for this kind of disequilibrium is at least a valid excuse for Congress to raise the mint price of gold enough to minimize further market disturbances. Usually, such a change would be just a few percent, that is, similar to the U.S. gold devaluation in 1834.

Indeed, manifold monetary changes were also happening in the 1930s – market prices were falling and the real price of gold had risen proportionally, but these changes were not the results of natural market forces. They were induced primarily by the Fed's Real Bills policy, followed by the Fed Banks' inordinate sequestering of gold reserves during 1931–1933. Fed Banks still had significant excess accounted gold reserves, plus high levels of required gold reserves, plus the statutory authority under The Federal Reserve Act to operate without any gold reserves.

Federal Reserve officials and others made the gold standard the scapegoat for the world depression and all other monetary problems of the era. Political majorities in every country also repudiated it. The massive U.S. devaluation of gold and accompanying abrogation of gold clauses in contracts reflected that mindset, while giving the federal government complete hands-on control of the gold stock. Gold was to be neutralized so that its occasional use in the private sector would not interfere with governmental monetary policy.[8] The irony was that the Fed-Treasury gold stockpile,[9] even with all the reserve requirements in place, was still large enough to generate nearly twice as much common money – hand-to-hand currency and bank deposits subject to check – as then existed. By August 1934, the value of

---

[8]  Section 5 stated: "No gold shall hereafter be coined, and no gold coin shall hereafter be paid out or delivered by the United States: Provided, however, That coinage may continue to be executed by the mints of the United States for foreign countries in accordance with the Act of January 29, 1874 (U.S.C., title 31, sec. 367). All gold coin of the United States shall be withdrawn from circulation, and, together with all other gold owned by the United States, shall be formed into bars of such weights and degrees of fineness as the Secretary of the Treasury may direct."

[9]  Gold was *accounted* in the Consolidated Statement of the 12 Fed Banks as an asset, "Gold Certificates." The Treasury Department had custody of the actual gold. Had the gold "profit" realized from the gold devaluation been returned to "the people," it would have paid all federal taxes for the year, thereby allowing the economy to recover substantially from the Depression.

Gold Certificates accounted in the Fed Banks' Consolidated Statement of Condition, now at $35 per ounce, was $5.2 billion.[10]

The unprecedented magnitude of the gold-dollar devaluation practically ensured that creditors who had bonds or contracts containing "gold clauses" would see a legal opportunity to profit from the appreciation in the mint price of gold. To prevent such opportunism, the government had to prohibit gold payments for all debts and contracts. Thus the Joint Resolution of June 5, 1933, proclaiming Abrogation of Gold Clauses, anticipated the coming devaluation. Otherwise, creditors would have demanded payment in the now-appreciated gold rather than common money, and their profits in doing so would have been substantial.

The devaluation itself, the origin of this new problem, was never challenged in court, probably because very few people in control knew what did and what did not constitute a legitimate devaluation. Also, very few understood what the Fed was doing – except that it was not doing enough of what it was supposed to do – and its policies were outside of anyone's control anyway. Government policy aimed, first, to get all the gold into the hands of the Fed-Treasury; second, to keep the gold there under heavy guard; third, to pass any bill that included more government spending; and, fourth, to demote the Fed to a handmaiden for the Treasury, a role it now seemed willing to accept.

The Gold Clause cases that questioned the constitutionality of banning gold payments for contractual debts containing gold clauses were referred to the Supreme Court in 1934, almost immediately following abrogation and devaluation of gold in January. However, the cases had a precedent. The first Gold Clause case, *Bronson vs. Rodes*, 74 US 7 Wall, 255, occurred in 1868 when a debtor, Rodes, tried to use greenbacks to pay off a debt incurred in 1857 that included a gold clause. There, the gold clause guaranteed that the creditor, Bronson, could require payment in gold or its cash equivalent as payment for the debt when due. In that case the Chase Supreme Court had ruled: "It seems to us clear beyond controversy … that express contracts to pay coined dollars can only be satisfied by the payment of coined dollars." Thus, the Court upheld the sanctity of the contract as it was written.[11]

The *Legal Tender Cases* decided in 1871 and 1884 then denied the necessity of gold payments or their equivalent in common money. Unlike the

---

[10]  Physically, the gold weighed approximately *5,000 tons.* If loaded into a convoy of 500 ten-ton trucks with 100 feet, net, between each truck, the convoy would have stretched almost ten miles.

[11]  See Chapter 10.

contract in the *Bronson* case, however, the contracts featured in the legal tender cases did not contain any explicit reference to gold. The implication from the decisions in those earlier cases was that contracts with clauses *specifying* payment in gold or its equivalent would have to be paid in the gold-value of the debt. Absent an explicit gold clause in the contract, however, the decision in the legal tender cases ruled that payment could be made in any money that was legal tender at the time of payment. That is where matters stood when the Gold Clause cases came before the Supreme Court in late 1934.

Four cases were included in the decision. They were argued on January 8, 9, and 10, 1935, and were decided on February 18, 1935. Two of them, No. 270, *Norman v. Baltimore & Ohio R. Co.*, and the *Missouri Pacific* case, dealt with private individuals who owned corporate obligations containing gold clauses. The other cases, No. 531, *Nortz v. United States, post*, p. 317 and No. 532, *Perry v. United States, post*. p. 330, were between the United States government and private citizens who held U.S. government obligations containing gold clauses.[12]

All four of the cases in dispute had a common feature. Bonds, issued by private corporations and the government, marketed at different times in the past two decades, had contained "gold clauses," stipulating that the creditor, or *obligee* – the buyer of the bond – at his option, could demand payment of interest and principal in either a quantity of gold coin, valued at the legal price of gold at the time of purchase, or in an equivalent sum of common money. Gold clauses were obviously intended to protect the creditor-lender from possible depreciation in the value of these fixed-dollar claims due to possible inflation during the time the contract was viable. The government bonds in the case were a part of the "Liberty" and "Victory" loans that the federal government marketed between 1918 and 1920 when Treasury-Fed inflation was prominent.

The problem with the currency, however, had turned out to be precisely the opposite of the inflation possibility so often correctly anticipated by creditors. In 1930, when the B&O Railroad bond was sold, the Consumers Price Index (CPI) was 71.4 (1947 – 49 = 100). By 1934, the CPI had fallen to 57.2. Consequently, the real value of the bond and its contractual interest payments had risen by almost twenty percent: dollars received in 1934 for

---

[12] Holzer, Henry Mark, *The Gold Clause*, edited and with an introduction and two chapters by Henry Mark Holzer. iUniverse.com, Inc., San Jose, 1980 and 2000, explains the cases and summarizes them properly. The cases are also available in Justia, U.S. Supreme Court Cases & Opinions, Volume 294: *Norman v. Baltimore & Ohio Railroad Co.*, 294 U. S. 240 (1935).

interest on the bond and for redemption when the bond matured would buy twenty percent more goods and services than they would have in 1930. Even the government bond sold in 1918 had appreciated ten percent due to the net decline in the price level since that date. Nothing in the bond contracts provided for such appreciation, and no one disputed the fact that the real value of gold had appreciated.

A still greater appreciation of gold occurred when Congress and the Administration devalued the gold dollar in January, 1934. By law, gold was now worth 59 percent more dollars than it had been in 1930. Gold-dollar devaluation, as far as gold clause contracts were concerned, meant that the creditor who was the beneficiary of a gold clause could technically demand his debtor to redeem the contract in gold, now worth 59 percent more than it had been in 1930, or its equivalent in other money. So the creditor-*obligee* was looking at a windfall gain of 20 percent for the fall in the price level, plus a 59 percent gain due to the statutory appreciation of gold.[13]

How would the Court handle this dilemma? Would it rule that Abrogation of Gold Clauses was against the Constitution's sanctity of contracts, allowing already well-to-do creditors to realize "undeserved enrichment," or would it uphold Abrogation to prevent creditors from getting unwarranted gains, although doing so would appear to violate the Fifth Amendment? Or, third, would it rule that the devaluation itself was an unconstitutional exercise of Congress's monetary powers, and require Congress to repeal or amend the law? This third option, while plausibly constitutional, was politically impossible, given the mindset of the Administration and Congress.

The fundamental cause of the entire insoluble controversy was the Federal Reserve policy over the past 5 years that had provoked such price level chaos and uncertainty in the first place. Inexplicably, however, the constitutionality of the Fed was never addressed in any Court case. As it is, the Gold Clause cases furnish a revealing picture of Supreme Court monetary thinking, while they emphasize how radically the monetary system had changed since the appearance of the greenbacks in 1862.

*Norman v. Baltimore & Ohio Railraod*, No. 270, was a dispute over payment of interest on a bond the B&O Railroad sold to a man named Norman. The bond bore interest of 4.5 percent per annum, and declared that the payment

---

[13]  The various obligations in the Gold Clause cases had originated at different times in the previous 20 years, so their real appreciation due to price level changes varied. But the devaluation premium would be 59 percent for all of them.

of interest and principal "will be made … in gold coin of the United States of America of or equal to the standard of weight and fineness existing on February 1, 1930." The coupon for interest that Norman, the plaintiff, tried to collect was for $22.50, payable on February 1, 1934. However, he tried to collect the payment in a quantity of gold (or its dollar equivalent) at gold's new price, $35.00 per ounce. "On presentation of the coupon," the brief for the case stated, "defendant [the B&O Railroad] refused to pay the amount of gold, or the equivalent of gold in legal tender of the United States, which was alleged to be …the sum of $38.10, and plaintiff demanded judgment for that amount."[14]

The same question arose with respect to an issue of bonds of the St. Louis, Iron Mountain & Southern Railway, payable May 1, 1933. The bonds provided for the payment of "'One Thousand Dollars gold coin of the United States of the present standard of weight and fineness,' with interest from date at the rate of four per cent. Per annum."[15] This case was adjudicated together with *Norman*. Chief Justice Charles Evans Hughes delivered the Court's majority opinion.

Congress's Joint Resolution of June 5, 1933, abrogating Gold Clauses, noted the opinion, anticipated the devaluation of gold. It declared that, "every provision contained in or made with respect to any obligation which purports to give the obligee a right to require payment in gold or a particular kind of coin or currency, or in an amount in money of the United States measured thereby… [is] … against public policy." Clauses for such purposes in obligations thereafter incurred, it continued, are prohibited. The resolution further mandated that, "Every obligation, heretofore or hereafter incurred, whether or not any such provision is contained therein or made with respect thereto, shall be discharged upon payment, dollar for dollar, in any coin or currency which at the time of payment is legal tender for public and private debts." That is, any future debtor could pay off any debt with any legal tender U.S. currency. It was not necessary to pay in gold or its equivalent.

The majority, Hughes continued, "… have not attempted to summarize all the provisions of these measures. We are not concerned with their wisdom. The question before the Court is one of power [of Congress], not of policy. And that question touches the validity of these measures at but a single point – that is, in relation to the Joint Resolution denying effect to 'gold clauses' in existing contracts. The resolution must, however, be considered

---

[14]  Holzer, *The Gold Clause*, Appendix, p. 293. $38.10 is 69.3 percent more than $22.50.
[15]  *Ibid.*, p. 294.

in its legislative setting and in the light of other measures *in pari materia [of equal importance]*."[16]

In both the *Norman* and *Southern Railway* cases, Hughes observed, the gold clauses were inserted to protect the bondholders from "depreciation of one kind of money as compared with another, as for example, paper money compared with gold, or silver compared with gold." The clause did not anticipate "the existence of conditions making it impossible and illegal to procure gold coin with which to meet the obligations." Since Congress had outlawed the use of gold as money, payment could not legally be made in gold, and even if it could, the gold would immediately be subject to Treasury purchase. So, the opinion argued, these cases coming at a time when gold was no longer legal for payments were different from previous cases, such as *Bronson v. Rodes*, when gold could be bought on an open market.[17]

The primary and all-important issue, the opinion stated, is: "... (1) the power of Congress to establish a monetary system and the necessary implications of that power." Related to the current case were two more questions: "(2) the power of the Congress to invalidate the provisions of existing contracts which interfere with the exercise of its constitutional authority; and (3) whether the clauses in question do constitute such an interference as to bring them within the range of that power."[18] If Congress had plenipotentiary power over the monetary system, no other questions needed to be answered.

Hughes reviewed all the previous cases discussed above – *Bronson v. Rodes*, the legal tender cases, including the final opinion in *Juilliard v. Greenman* – granting Congress the power to make United States notes (greenbacks) legal tender for all debts previously contracted, whether in time of war or peace. He next cited Congress's explicit constitutional money power under Article 1, Section 8, paragraph 5, "To coin money and regulate the value thereof, and of foreign coin" (but he did not include, "and fix the standard of weights and measures"). He concluded with the constitutionally impossible decision that the Court had rendered in the legal tender cases: "But the Court in the legal tender cases did not derive from that express grant alone [that is, "coin money and regulate the value thereof"] the full authority of the Congress in relation to the currency. The Court found the source of that authority in all the related powers conferred upon the Congress and appropriate to achieve 'the great objects for which the government was framed' – 'a national

---

[16]   *Ibid.*, p. 297.
[17]   *Ibid.*, p. 298.
[18]   *Ibid.*, p. 302.

government with sovereign powers.'"[19] To support this contention, Hughes reiterated all the infamous decisions discussed above: "The broad and comprehensive national authority over the subjects of revenue, finance and currency is derived from the aggregate of the powers granted to Congress." The Congress is empowered, he quoted from the *Juilliard* opinion, "'to issue the obligations of the United States in such form, and to impress upon them such qualities as currency for the payment of merchandise and the payment of debts, as accord with the usage of sovereign governments.'"[20] As observed earlier, nothing in the Constitution implies any such power, nor does any statement suggest a possible inference leading to such a conclusion. Yet the majority opinion treated these misinterpretations of the Legal Tender Acts as if they were quoted from the Constitution itself, without re-examining the validity of the earlier arguments.

Hughes next discussed whether "Congress had the power to invalidate the provisions of existing contracts [private or public] which interfere with the exercise of its constitutional authority." He cited Justice Bradley, the Grant appointee to the Court who had inserted in the *Knox v. Lee* opinion the argument that even contracts that included "payable in specie or its equivalent," were subject to congressional overrule. Otherwise, Bradley had argued, specie clauses could easily be written into every contract, and would "completely nullify the power claimed for the government" to endow with *legal tender* anything it considered "necessary and proper."[21]

Hughes noted that creditors, who had not included the option of gold payments in their contracts, might "suffer equal hardship or loss with creditors who have so stipulated.... The point is pressed," he continued, "... that their express stipulations for gold payments constitute property, and that creditors who have not such stipulations are without that property right. The contestants urge that the Congress is seeking not to regulate the currency, but to regulate contracts, and thus has stepped beyond the power conferred."[22]

Congress's authority over revenue, finance, and money, Hughes contended, is derived from the aggregate of powers granted to it – all the

---

[19]  *Ibid.,* p. 303
[20]  *Ibid.,* p. 304.
[21]  *Ibid.,* pp. 306–307. The opinion also included a footnote referring to Justice Samuel Miller, a supporter of the "sovereign power" of the government on the Chase Court. It was he who had stated that a contract for gold dollars was in no respect different, in legal effect, from a contract for dollars without the qualifying words, "specie" or "gold," and that "the legal tender statutes had, therefore, the same effect in both cases."
[22]  *Ibid.*

money powers, plus the "added express power 'to make all laws which shall be necessary and proper for carrying into execution' the other enumerated powers." Therefore, "When contracts deal with a subject matter which lies within the control of the Congress, they have a congenital infirmity. Parties cannot remove their transactions from the reach of dominant constitutional power by making contracts about them." The same reasoning applies, he added, whether it be interstate commerce, employers' liability, or the constitutional authority of the Congress " … 'to regulate the currency and to establish the monetary system of the country' [from the *Juilliard* opinion]. If the gold clauses now before us interfere with the policy of the Congress in the exercise of that authority they cannot stand." Therefore, the opinion concluded, all the discussions and arguments are necessarily brought to a single narrow point. "That point is whether the gold clauses constitute an actual interference with the monetary policy of Congress in the light of its broad power to determine that policy."[23]

The opinion thus pointedly contrasted the primacy of Congress's endowment of power, which the Court had derived for it from the earlier decisions, with the Constitution's monetary limitations based on gold and silver. The answer here, Hughes noted, "depends upon an appraisment [sic] of economic conditions and upon the determinations of questions of fact…. to which Congress is entitled to its own judgment…. If [congressional policy] is an appropriate means to [a legitimate end], the decision of the Congress as to the degree of necessity for the adoption of that means is final."[24]

In short, the opinion decreed: Without reference to the gold and silver constraints of the Constitution, (1) Congress had complete power over the monetary system; (2) no private contracts or institutions could interfere with that power; and (3) Congress's judgment over the conditions for its actions was absolute. Besides ignoring the Constitution's actual reference to gold and silver, the opinion again misrepresented the nature of Congress's power "to coin money and regulate the value thereof."

Hughes cited the words of the Joint Resolution to confirm the opinion. "These gold clauses," stated the Resolution, "render ineffective the power of the Government to create a currency and determine the value thereof…. In this country virtually all obligations, almost as a matter of routine, contain the gold clause…. Two phenomena which have developed during the present emergency make the enforcement of the gold clauses incompatible

---

[23]  *Ibid.*, pp. 308–311.

[24]  *Ibid.* Once again, the disclaimer by the Court that it could not review Congress's ignorance or mistakes.

with the public interest. The first is the tendency which has developed internally to hoard gold; the second is the tendency for capital [gold] to leave the country."[25]

The economics underlying these allegations merits comment. First, no one can properly define "hoarding." All gold, money, and virtually all forms of productive capital are "hoarded" incessantly in the sense that they are held by their owners for *some* length of time. To say that "gold was hoarded" suggests that the people who owned the gold were holding it for a longer time than they had previously, so that the velocity of money was declining. Indeed, the velocity of money had declined since 1929, largely as a result of the deflationary monetary policy that the government's central bank – the Fed – had promoted. Therefore, the opinion implied, the answer is to endow Congress with the power to abrogate contracts in addition to its absolute power over the monetary system.

On a simpler note, if people and institutions were "hoarding" gold, they must have been expecting a rise in its price. They could exhibit the same behavior with respect to land, corn, family homes, or any other item, especially one that had become a lightning rod for public policy. By this time, everyone knew that the government was "doing something" about gold, and simply anticipated the results.

Much more important to this issue, however, was the fact that the greatest gold hoarder in the world at that time (and since) was the Federal Reserve-U.S. Treasury. By 1934, as pointed out previously, the Fed-Treasury had stockpiled over 5,000 tons of gold, and was getting more every day, due to policies that the Fed Board had initiated in 1929 and continued. The second point of the Resolution – the tendency for gold to leave the country – was simply belied by the facts. Ordinarily, the price-specie-flow mechanism, which was fundamental to the operation of an international gold standard, would have caused such an outflow. However, gold was not leaving the country; Federal Reserve–Treasury policies had prevented that. It could not both leave the country and, simultaneously, accumulate in Treasury-Fed depositories.

Hughes finished the Court's argument by discussing the devaluation of the gold dollar. He did not refer to its unprecedented magnitude, but to its real effects on buyers and sellers. "In the [new devalued] currency," he observed, "States and municipalities must receive their taxes, railroads their rates and fares.... The income out of which they must meet their obligations

---

[25]  *Ibid.*, p. 312.

is determined by the new standard. Yet, according to the contentions [of Norman, etc.] before us, while that income is controlled by law, their indebtedness on the 'gold bonds' must be met by an amount of currency determined by the former gold standard. Their receipts, in this view, would be fixed on one basis; their interest charges, and the principal of their obligations, on another.... It requires no acute analysis or profound economic inquiry to disclose the dislocation of the domestic economy which would be caused by such a disparity of conditions in which ... those debtors under gold clauses should be required to pay one dollar and sixty-nine cents in currency while respectively receiving their taxes, rates, charges and prices on the basis of one dollar of that currency.... We are concerned with the constitutional power of Congress over the monetary system of the country and its attempted frustration.... We think that it is clearly shown that these clauses interfere with the exertion of the [monetary] power granted to the Congress."[26]

The opinion's economic reasoning is sound enough. But what does it suggest? – that Norman was "greedy" to try and get what the new law explicitly provided? – that Congress must have the authority to overrule contracts, such as Norman's that interfere with its "legitimate" monetary functions? – or that the magnitude of the gold-dollar devaluation was incompatible with the Constitution's grant of power "to regulate the value thereof" and should be rescinded? The plain history of monetary policy confirms the validity of the last alternative. However, the Court could not even admit such an option, since their opinion had already conceded that Congress had absolute power over the monetary system, so could devalue gold to any level. Moreover, it was politically out of the question. Congress and the Roosevelt Administration were determined to unleash the U.S. monetary system from the "golden fetters" that the British economist, Walter Bagehot, had emphasized in discussing Bank of England policies.[27]

But suppose they had considered it, and thereby thrown the ball back into Congress's province, and suppose that Congress had complied with the Court's opinion. Never, under a Gold Standard, would gold-silver-commodity values be so distorted that a devaluation (or revaluation) of more than a few percent be necessary. Let's suppose, however, that Congress did restore the price of the gold dollar to $20.67 per fine ounce. No contracts with gold clauses would then have been contested, so

[26]  *Ibid.*, pp. 315–316.
[27]  Bagehot, Walter. *Lombard Street*, p. 206.

the Court would not have been forced to choose between economic justice and constitutional propriety.[28]

Hughes read the decision of the majority: "The judgment and decree, severally under review, are affirmed." That is, the Court denied the plea of Norman to be paid an amount of money on the basis of the new value of gold. He could only collect the debt due him in any legal tender of the United States.[29]

The decision was the only just conclusion to the case based on a realistic appraisal of what Norman had done and why. He had not expected an increase in the legal price of gold, but had insisted on the gold clause to protect his investment from dollar depreciation due to price level inflation, just as had everyone else who used gold clauses in contracts. However, the price level had gone the other way. Consequently, as a creditor, Norman was going to get twenty percent more in real terms from price deflation than he had anticipated when he bought the B&O bond. His net return for 6 years of holding the bond would have been the 4.5 percent per year coupon rate of the bond, plus at least 3 percent per year for the decline in "all prices" during the period 1928–1934, during which he held the bond.

To make this reasonably fair economic judgment, however, the Court had to violate the sanctity of contracts, which it had already done by granting Congress absolute monetary powers that body did not constitutionally possess. Otherwise, Norman would have received the 4.5 percent from the face value of the bond, plus the 3 percent per year from the price level decline, plus almost 10 percent per year from the gold-dollar devaluation. That adds up to about 17 percent per year, where Norman had expected only 4.5 percent per year, and had purchased the bond with that rate in mind.

The case of *Perry v. United States* was also argued and decided at this time. *Norman* was a case between two private litigants, while Perry, another private person, had a bond of the United States for $10,000, purchased in 1917. It was a bond issued during the Fourth Liberty Loan Gold Bond drive, payable between 1933 and 1938, so the government was the debtor in the *Perry* case. The bond provided that: "The principal and interest hereof are payable in United States gold coin of the present standard of value." The Court of Claims stated the question as follows: "Is the claimant, being the holder and owner of a bond of the United States, of the principal amount of $10,000,

---

[28] Another possibility was to legislate a devaluation, but expressly exempt all current contracts from the terms of the new law. That same procedure could (and should) have been used in the 1834 devaluation, even though that act was well within the scope of devaluation that the Founders had sanctioned.

[29] *Ibid.*, p. 316.

issued in 1918 [and] 'payable in gold coin of the present standard of value,' entitled to receive from the United States an amount in legal tender currency in excess of the face amount of the bond?"[30]

Hughes began the Court opinion on *Perry* by observing that, "The '*present* standard of value' stood in contradistinction to a *lower* standard of value. The promise obviously was intended to afford protection against loss ... [that he might suffer] through depreciation in the medium of payment [monetary inflation]."[31] The Joint Resolution, however, had retracted payments in gold, including obligations of the United States, and the question here again was whether the provision in the Joint Resolution was constitutional.

The opinion repeated what the Court had declared in *Norman*, to wit, that, "There is no question as to the power of Congress to regulate the value of money, that is, to establish a monetary system and thus to determine the currency of the country. *The question is whether Congress can use that power so as to invalidate the terms of the obligations which the Government has theretofore issued in the exercise of the power to borrow money on the credit of the United States.*" Congress had routinely borrowed money in an earlier time – 1918. Could a later Congress, exercising a different but legitimate monetary power repudiate some terms of the earlier act – in this case, of course, the gold clause? The opinion candidly observed: "If the terms of the Government's bond as to the standard of payment can be repudiated, it inevitably follows that the obligation as to the amount to be paid may also be repudiated. The contention necessarily imports [implies] that the Congress can disregard the obligations of the Government at its discretion and that, when the Government borrows money, the credit of the United States is an illusory pledge."[32]

Hughes's logic here is sound. It repeats the same reasoning that Justice Stephen Field recorded in his dissent in the legal tender cases in 1871 and 1884, discussed earlier.

The Court in 1935 answered that the Constitution did not allow repudiation of any kind. Citing earlier cases, the opinion declared: "'The United States are as much bound by their contracts as are individuals. If they repudiate their obligations, it is as much repudiation ... as it would be if the repudiator had been a State or a municipality or a citizen.'"[33]

---

[30]  *Ibid.*, pp. 347–348.
[31]  *Ibid.*, pp. 348–349. (Emphasis in original.)
[32]  *Ibid.*, p. 350. (Emphasis in original.)
[33]  *Ibid.*, p. 351.

The opinion then repeated the "sovereign-power-of-government" argument it had aired in *Norman*, but added a new wrinkle "The right to make binding obligations is a competence attaching to sovereignty. In the United States, sovereignty resides in the people, who act through the organs [?] established by the Constitution. The Congress as the instrumentality of sovereignty is endowed with certain powers to be exerted on behalf of the people in the manner and with the effect the Constitution ordains. The Congress cannot invoke the sovereign power of the people to override their will as thus declared."[34] Both Congress and the "people" have sovereignty, this Court correctly declared, but the one sovereignty cannot "override" the other. "Having this power to authorize the issue of definite obligations for the payment of money borrowed, Congress has not been vested with authority to alter or destroy those obligations.... The contractual obligation ... exists and, despite infirmities of procedure, remains binding upon the conscience [sic] of the sovereign. We conclude that the Joint Resolution of June 5, 1933, in so far [sic] as it attempted to override the obligation created by the bond in suit, went beyond the congressional power."[35] If the dispute was between two private parties, for example, *Norman v. B&O Railroad*, discussed above, Congress could nullify the gold clause because it interfered with Congress's monetary powers. However, if the litigation was between a private party and the *United States*, and because the issue and sale of the bond were integral to U.S. fiscal policy, its terms had to be honored.

This answer, however, did not dispose of the question of damages, which the Court treated next. "Because the Government is not at liberty to alter or repudiate its obligations, it does not follow," the opinion continued, "that the claim advanced by the plaintiff should be sustained. The action is for breach of contract. As a remedy for breach, plaintiff can recover no more than the loss he has suffered.... He is not entitled to be enriched."[36]

The opinion then turned to the magnitude of the damages: "The question of actual loss cannot fairly be determined without considering the economic situation at the time the Government offered to pay him the $10,000, the face of the bond, in legal tender currency." All the gold had been withdrawn from circulation, so was no longer available as a means of payment. The opinion then asked "what damages, if any, the plaintiff has sustained by the alleged breach of his bond," and answered that "[he] has not shown, or attempted to show, that in relation to buying power he has sustained any

[34]  *Ibid.*, p. 353.
[35]  *Ibid.*, p. 354.
[36]  *Ibid.*, p. 354.

loss whatever." On the contrary, due to "adjustment of the internal economy [that is, the decline in the price level], the payment to the plaintiff of the amount which he demands would appear to constitute not a recoupment [sic] of loss in any proper sense but an unjustified enrichment....We think his position is untenable."[37] So, Perry could not receive an amount of legal tender currency in excess of the face amount of the bond.

The Court at this time – January 1935 – was a product of the five previous presidents. Agreeing to the majority opinion in this case were Chief Justice Charles Evans Hughes (Hoover), Justice Louis Brandeis (Wilson), Justice Harlan Stone (Coolidge), Justice Owen Roberts (Hoover), and Justice Benjamin Cardozo (Hoover). The opinion, therefore, included three Hoover appointees, and one each by Wilson and Coolidge. The minority consisted of: Justice Willis Van Devanter (Taft), Justice James McReynolds (Wilson), Justice George Sutherland (Harding), and Justice Pierce Butler (Harding). As a rough generalization, the majority included more recent appointees (Hooverites), and the minority earlier ones.

The Court, even if politically representative of the past five presidents, had an impossible dispute to reconcile no matter what the Justices' political ideologies. To render economic justice, the Court had to prevent gold clause creditors from realizing "unjustified enrichment" owing to the unprecedented increase in the legal price of gold following the devaluation a year earlier. On the other hand, such an economically correct decision would violate the Constitution's sanctity-of-contracts clause under the Fifth Amendment.

The majority found a rationale for its actual decision in Congress's absolute, "sovereign" power over the monetary system, but the minority rebelled. The dissenters, McReynolds, Van Devanter, Sutherland, and Butler, were shocked, outraged, and apoplectic. Their objections, written and read by Justice McReynolds, began with the flat statement that if the majority's decision were given effect, it would "bring about confiscation of property rights and repudiation of national obligations. [Our] acquiescence in the decisions just announced is impossible; the circumstances demand statement of our views."[38]

The majority had presumed that "Just men regard repudiation and spoliation of citizens by their sovereign with abhorrence; but we are asked to affirm that the Constitution has granted power to accomplish both. No definite delegation of such a power exists; and we cannot believe the farseeing

---

[37]  *Ibid.*, pp. 355–358.
[38]  *Ibid.*, p. 362.

framers, who labored with hope of establishing justice and securing the blessings of liberty, intended that the expected government should have authority to annihilate its own obligations and destroy the very rights which they were endeavoring to protect. Not only is there no permission for such actions; they are inhibited. And no plentitude of words can conform them to our charter."[39]

"By the so-called gold clause," the dissent continued, "… found in very many private and public obligations, the creditor agrees to accept and the debtor undertakes to return the thing loaned or its equivalent. Thereby each secures protection, one against decrease in the value of the currency, the other against an increase." McReynolds reviewed the pedigree of the gold clause in both the United States and foreign countries. Again he referred to the intention of the gold clause "… to protect against a depreciation of the currency and against the discharge of the obligation by payment of less than that prescribed." He noted the recent gold devaluation of 59-plus percent – the gold dollar from 25.8 grains to 15 5/21 grains – and added: "The calculation to determine the damages for failure to pay in [the new] gold would not be difficult" – that is, multiply the face value of the debt by 25.8/ 15 5/21, which translates into paying 1.69 times the dollar value of the bond![40]

Where the Hughes majority had done economic justice to the debtor-creditor relationship while violating contractual norms, the McReynolds minority would have appreciated the value of all the existing gold-clause debts by factoring their face values and interest obligations with the devaluation ratio. Bond-holder creditors, such as Norman and Perry, would get the new amount, profiting 69 percent because of the recent devaluation! Where the majority had openly violated contractual law but maintained economic justice, the minority would uphold contractual law while doing grave economic injustice to the debtor – one of whom, notably, was the U.S. government.

The dissent did not dispute the power of the government, especially its license to devalue the gold dollar by any amount. But the very magnitude of the devaluation was the cause of all the trouble. The dissent concurred with the majority: "There is no challenge here of the power of Congress to adopt such proper 'Monetary Policy' as it may deem necessary in order to provide for national obligations and furnish an adequate medium of exchange for

---

[39]  *Ibid.*, p. 362.

[40]  *Ibid.*, pp. 362–365. The arithmetic of the devaluation can be confusing. The gold dollar was devalued from 25.8 grains of gold to 15.24 grains, so the dollar was now worth in gold 59 percent of what it had been. Therefore, to pay an old debt in the new dollars would mean multiplying the dollar value of the debt by 1.69 (25.8/ 15.24).

public use. The plan under review in the Legal Tender Cases was declared within the limits of the Constitution, but not without a strong dissent. The conclusions there announced are not now questioned; and any abstract [sic] discussion of Congressional power over money would only tend to befog the real issue."[41]

But would it? Rather to the contrary! An explicit discussion of the legal tender cases by this Court far removed from the original pressures of the Greenback Era would have been the most appropriate means to treat this dilemma. It could not have done any harm, and might have established a worthwhile precedent for a permanent program of "Updating Justice."

McReynolds, however, did not pursue this line of action. He only asked rhetorically whether the recent statutes passed by Congress in respect of money were designed to attain a legitimate end, or whether "Congress has really inaugurated a plan primarily designed to destroy private obligations, repudiate national debts and drive into the Treasury all gold within the country, in exchange for inconvertible promises to pay of much less value." He answered: "We must conclude they show that the plan disclosed is of the latter description and its enforcement would deprive the parties before us of their rights under the Constitution."[42]

McReynolds had already stated that the minority did not deny or even question the results of the legal tender cases. Their argument went further. It agreed that the President and the Treasury had the authority to call in all the gold, and "prescribe weight for [devalue] the standard dollar.... Plainly, ... 'to coin money and regulate the value thereof' calls for legislative action."[43] The dissent then discussed the reasons that devaluation was linked to the "coin money" power in Article 1, Section 8. It correctly reviewed the devaluation of 1834, which it said "was to restore the use of gold as currency – not to force up prices or destroy obligations.... No injury was done to creditors.... See Hepburn on Currency," the opinion suggested. [44]

Immediately following this correct explanation of devaluation, McReynolds referred again to the legal tender cases, and how the "Court was careful to show that [the greenbacks] were issued to meet a great emergency in time of war, when the overthrow of the Government was threatened. Both the end in view and the means employed, the Court [in 1871] held were lawful." The legal tender currency issued, McReynolds observed,

---

[41]  *Ibid.*, p. 369.

[42]  *Ibid.*, pp. 369–370.

[43]  *Ibid.*, p. 370.

[44]  *Ibid.*, p. 371. The dissent refers here to A. Barton Hepburn's treatise, *History of* Currency, discussed in Chapter 17.

was a temporary expedient "until the United States could find it possible to meet their obligations in standard coin. This they accomplished [with Resumption] in 1879."[45]

What the dissenting opinion failed to discuss here was, first, the "strong dissent," McReynolds mentioned earlier, that had accompanied the majority decision in the legal tender cases, and, second, that despite Resumption of gold payments, the fully legal tender greenbacks were still legal tender for all debts public *and private*. Now, the dissent objected, Congress was requiring the holder of a bond to accept payment in devalued currency. "If this is permissible, then a gold dollar containing one grain of gold may become the standard, all contract rights fall, and huge profits appear on Treasury books, maybe enough to cancel the public debt."[46] McReynolds did not refer to Justice Stephen Field's dissent in the legal tender cases or to George Bancroft's *Plea for the Constitution* that had observed the same thing, but his observation repeated their views.

The dissent argued that Congress's power "to create legal tender obligations is derived from the power to borrow money" – a contention that is altogether incorrect and treated earlier.[47] The Joint Resolution of June 5th, McReynolds continued, was aimed directly at destroying the contracts evidenced by the gold clauses, and "... had no definite relation to the power to ... regulate the value of money. ... If reduction of 40% of all debts was within the power of Congress, and if as a necessary means to accomplish that end, Congress had power by resolution to destroy the gold clauses, the holders of these ... bonds are without remedy. ... If this power exists, Congress may readily destroy other obligations which present obstruction to the desired effect of further depletion. The destruction of all obligations by reducing the standard dollar to one grain of gold, or brass or nickel or copper or lead, will become an easy possibility ... Congress had no power to destroy the gold clauses in private obligations. The attempt to do this was plain usurpation, arbitrary and oppressive.... The [Joint] Resolution was

---

[45]  *Ibid.*

[46]  *Ibid.*, p. 372.

[47]  Creating "legal tender obligations (LTOs)," all of which are necessarily *money*, is a disingenuous play on words. Since these LTOs must be *spent* into existence – since no money issuer can "borrow" by spending new money into circulation – the LTOs cannot be a form of "borrowing money." When "money" is borrowed, the act of borrowing requires creation and issue of an interest-bearing obligation – a bond, note, or bill, which the borrower exchanges for the money borrowed. The exchange is a means to command resources for the purposes of the borrower, but the money he gets by selling the bond, note, or bill already exists. The two verbs *create* and *borrow* are completely different in meaning and cannot be used interchangeably.

not appropriate for carrying into effect any power entrusted to Congress. The gold clauses in no substantial way interfered with the power of coining money or regulating its value or providing a uniform currency. ... They did not prevent the exercise of any granted power."[48]

The bonds were contracts, McReynolds continued, and, "Valid contracts to repay money borrowed cannot be destroyed by exercising power under the coinage provision. ... Congress brought about the conditions in respect of gold which existed when the obligation matured. Having made payment in this metal impossible, the Government cannot defend [its case] by saying that if the obligation had been met the creditor could not have retained the gold. ... Obligations cannot be legally avoided by prohibiting the creditor from receiving the thing promised." Therefore, the dissent concluded, the government should pay off its creditors in the equivalent of the now appreciated gold! "There would be no serious difficulty in estimating the value of 25.8 grains of gold in the currency now in circulation.[49] ... For the Government to say, we have violated our contract but have escaped the consequences through our own statute, would be monstrous. In matters of contractual obligation, the Government cannot legislate so as to excuse itself."[50]

Finally, the dissent discussed the practical matter of paying for the would-be inflated gold obligations that they had countenanced as the government's constitutional responsibility. Counsel for the government and railway companies due to pay the calculated premiums, they observed, had "asserted with emphasis that incalculable financial disaster would follow" if the debts were paid off at the new gold price. McReynolds scoffed: "Their forecast is discredited by manifest exaggeration." However, he did not produce any estimates of the costs, either for private debts with gold clauses or for the gold-clause government bonds still outstanding.[51]

---

[48] *Ibid.*, pp. 373–376.
[49] *Ibid.*, p. 378.
[50] *Ibid.*, p. 379.
[51] In 1935, the interest-bearing government debt was approximately $27 billion. Annual interest charges on the debt were about $750 million. *If* all the debt had had gold clauses, the interest payments would have increased to about $1,200 million. In an article, *Outline of the Gold Clause Cases*, that appeared in the *North Carolina Law Review*, Vol. 15, 1937, pp. 249–254, Angus McLean estimated that about $80 billion of private obligations contained a gold clause, and about $20 billion of government debts. If all these debts were factored up by the devaluation premium of 1.69, the amount of new debt would be $69-plus billion, or approximately 14 years of the country's GDP at that time. McLean concluded: "This meant bankruptcy on a national scale" (Holtz, *Gold Clause Cases*, p. 62.) However, if the government were to pay for its gold clause debts with new greenbacks or Federal

The Court had an impossible puzzle to resolve. If their decision followed the arguments of the dissenting minority, both the government and private debtors would have had to pay off gold clause obligations at $1.69 on the dollar. Bondholders – creditors – would have received a windfall that was completely unexpected, and that had nothing to do with their economic decision to buy the bonds. At the same time, this payment would have been exactly what the bonds promised – payment in a certain quantity of gold, now worth sixty-nine percent more in dollars. To add fuel to the fire, these same gold clause "profiteers" were already realizing substantial premiums of various amounts, depending on when they bought the bonds, due to the ongoing decline in the price level that enhanced the buying power of the dollars due them.[52] To populist minds such unexpected windfalls going to "the rich" were anathema. Nonetheless, the minority decision approved them, and was outraged that the majority opinion had gone the other way. Their contention that their dissent conformed to constitutional principles, however, was precisely correct: the gold clauses were constitutionally binding.

The majority, whose decision prevailed, also faced unpleasant realities. If they allowed the gold clauses to remain at face value, they would come into conflict (already one unpleasant reality) with the Roosevelt Administration and a large majority of the Congress, who believed that their gold policies, resolutions, and edicts were the best means to lift the economy out of the current depression.

Political strategists knew the gold clauses were perfectly legitimate and should have been binding, but they had to find a "constitutional" path to justify their nullification. Their solution for private obligations was to allege that the gold clauses interfered with Congress's superior role of determining monetary policy. Congress, they smugly pointed out, had the "power to coin money and regulate the value thereof," and – reaching back to the 1871 and 1884 decisions in the legal tender cases – the power to create fully legal tender paper money in time of war or peace. Because of these earlier (questionable) decisions, both the majority and minority agreed, Congress had absolute power over the monetary system. So, even contracts, the most sacred of constitutional objects, could be nullified when they conflicted with Congress's absolute monetary powers.

---

Reserve notes, it would have ended the depression that, instead, lasted five more years. Furthermore, the debts, private and governmental, would not all have been redeemed at once.

[52] Prices had stayed constant from 1922 to 1929, and fallen 25.5 percent from 1929 to 1933. (CPI, 1947–1949 = 100).

However, their opinion for government debts with gold clauses denied that the government's "sovereignty" over the monetary system could justify abrogation, because the bonds in dispute had financed crucial government fiscal operations. The opinion then made a separate case for "damages" done to owners of gold clause bonds, and found that because of the fall in the price level, gold clause creditors had not suffered any losses, but had experienced "unjustified enrichment." Therefore, Congress's Abrogation of Gold Clauses only required recompense if the *obligee* could show "damages." Virtually no bond or contract owner suffered any real loss, or could have. It was a time of creditor "heaven" when the real values of all debts had appreciated due to the falling price level.[53]

So, what judgment on the Gold Clause cases would have preserved constitutional integrity and prevented unwarranted "enrichment" of debtors?

Both the minority and majority opinions referred many times to the monetary decisions in the late nineteenth century – *Knox v. Lee* and *Parker v. Davis* in 1871, and *Juilliard v. Greenman* in 1884 – to support their view of the government's power over money These decisions, they claimed, were written in stone. They conveniently ignored the *Hepburn v. Griswold* decision in 1870 that had denied debtors the right to pay off their debts in greenbacks for debts contracted before greenbacks were authorized. Had the Court responsibly observed that the substance of the *Hepburn* case had been re-argued and the decision reversed the next year, they would have had both a model for further argument in the Gold Clause cases, and a decision that did not rest on the horns of a dilemma. If a later Court in 1871 could reverse the arguments of the 1870 Court, and if the same issues were crucial to the present case, why not bring the earlier cases out of mothballs and re-examine their parameters? Perhaps Congress did *not* have the

[53] The analysis of Angus McLean, cited in note 51, also accepted the majority-minority consensus on the government's absolute power over the monetary system. The government's "main position was stronger," McLean claimed, than the inhibitions emphasized in Norman, Perry, et al. "We relied," McLean said, "on a broad interpretation of the power of Congress to coin money and regulate the value thereof, ... and gathered much support from the Legal Tender Cases, which in their day were as important as the Gold Clause Cases became sixty years later." He cited approvingly the Court judgment, "Whatever power there is over the currency is vested in Congress. If the power to declare what is money is not in Congress, it is annihilated." He also cited approvingly Justice Gray's opinion in the *Juilliard* decision, that "the Government's power in money matters was not only plenary, by virtue of the Constitution, but inherent....This led to the taking by us," McLean concluded, "of the advanced [sic] position that power over coinage and currency is an attribute of sovereignty, as much so in this country as any other" ("FDR's Supreme Court," *The Gold Clause*, p. 63–64.). Nowhere in his article did McLean challenge or justify this very mistaken notion.

Divine Right of Money Creation, so willingly granted to it by Justices on both sides of the Gold Clause cases.

The Supreme Court is the ultimate judicial authority for the determination of disputes over constitutional issues. It has been so described many times, and several Justices have pointed out this fact. Does its superior standing imply that the Court cannot make a mistake? The Justices are mortal men (and now women), subject to the push-and-pull of political pressures and earthly rewards. Being human, they are also imperfect. The question is: how can the Court manage itself to provide for imperfections in decisions if it is the final arbiter on constitutional questions? Analogously: what can cut a diamond if a diamond is the hardest substance in existence?

The proper answer to the diamond question is, as everyone knows, "another diamond." Similarly, the only way to amend one questionable Supreme Court decision is to allow a later Supreme Court to monitor and perhaps change the earlier one. The Court of 1871 set such a precedent. That Court, with new appointees and operating under political directives from the Grant Administration, did not delay reversing the 1870 *Hepburn* decision. Having established the precedent, that Court's decision should have been subject to the same challenge, especially in 1935. Using the same license, the Hughes Court of 1935 could (and should) have questioned and reviewed the 1871 decision. Had it done so, it might have realized that Congress did not have and does not have the absolute power over money that the Court, Congress, and the Executive presumed. Profound "judicial review" is the only way a "Supreme" body can be kept human like the rest of us. The very fact that Court decisions, often split 5–4, inevitably appear when the issues are politically sensitive is reason enough to welcome subsequent reviews and an occasional reversal when the occasion warrants.

# TWENTY THREE

## Gold and Monetary Affairs in the Twentieth Century

Gold clauses were anachronisms; ownership of monetary gold was prohibited, and the Constitution was conveniently compromised. Eventually, however, the very absurdity of prohibiting people from owning an ordinary commodity, such as gold, became apparent. Prohibiting gold ownership was no more logical or legitimate than prohibiting ownership of agricultural implements, or land, or books, or cars. (Yes, some government policies at times have trespassed on ownership of these articles as well.) The difference was that gold, besides being a valuable commodity, had also been money. Nevertheless, the economy still lived after 1935 under the pretense of a gold standard; so the outward appearance of the monetary system still had to conform to what was now a fiction about gold, in particular, the fiction that each dollar was still worth 1/35th ounce of gold. All U.S. gold that had had any monetary properties now belonged to the Fed-Treasury.[1] Furthermore, this quantity was constantly increasing as gold flowed into the country due to its appreciated dollar price after devaluation, and to escape the predations of totalitarian governments in Europe.

The mechanics of the gold inflow expanded commercial banks' balance sheets in the usual way, though at a rate based on the official rather than the market value of gold. As the owner of the new gold sold it to the Treasury and deposited his Treasury check paying for the gold in his bank account, the U.S. Treasury created a Gold Certificate for the dollar value of the monetized gold and deposited the Certificate in one of the Fed Banks.[2] The Fed Bank entered a "Treasury deposit" to the account of the U.S. Treasury, and that amount was, of course, just equal to the check the Treasury had written

---

[1] Although the U.S. Treasury held the physical gold, mainly at Ft. Knox in bulk form (ingots), the Fed Banks' balance sheets accounted the gold-dollar value in their "Asset" column.

[2] Much of this activity was done only on accounting paper.

to pay for the gold. Next, the Treasury check came to the Fed Bank from the commercial bank in which the gold seller had deposited the check, and the Fed Bank added this amount to its "Member Banks' Reserves" liability.

As gold kept coming in, reserves of member banks burgeoned. By early 1936, accounted bank reserves in Fed Banks were approximately double the amount of legal reserves required for the member banks' deposit liabilities. Conservative bankers, remembering what had happened a few years earlier when the Fed Board and Fed Banks denied them reserve accommodation, were not making new loans very rapidly. They had survived the Contraction ordeal of 1929–1933, and the experience had made them even more conservative in their lending operations. Consequently, they were keeping their reserve ratios at levels appropriate to their estimates of liquidity "needs" no matter what the Fed Board prescribed as "required."[3]

While the gold inflow continued, Congress passed the Banking Act of 1935. This new act reflected Congress's view of its monetary powers. It formalized the Federal Reserve Open Market Committee (FOMC) that had worked informally during the 1920s to control the quantity of bank credit and currency. The new FOMC included all seven members of the Board of Governors, plus five of the twelve Fed Bank Presidents, who would rotate on and off the FOMC. (The President of the Fed Bank of New York was a permanent member.) This new configuration meant that the Fed Board based in Washington had a majority on the FOMC, which met there three or four times a year to determine monetary policy.

The new Banking Act also continued the gold reserve requirement for Fed Banks – 35 percent against member bank reserve accounts and 40 percent against Federal Reserve notes outstanding – even though no one could get gold or use it legally for monetary purposes. Nonetheless, its presence provided a mathematical limit to the Fed Banks capacity to create money. Whereas, under a gold standard, gold had provided the dynamics for determining the domestic money stock, it was now a balance sheet datum: Treasury-Federal Reserve policies determined the economy's quantity of money.[4]

---

[3]  Reserve requirements for commercial members banks of the FRS at the time were 7, 10, and 13 percent, with the higher requirements for banks in the largest cities – New York and Chicago – and the lower percentages covering the banks in the smaller communities. The *size* of the bank was not the criterion, but the *size* of the community in which the bank operated.

[4]  The proper theory for outlining this institutional change had shifted from the Commodity Theory of Money, where the quantity of money was the determinate of the system's operations, to the Quantity Theory of Money. The quantity of money was now a function of human design, that is, a variable determined by positive human decisions. The Quantity

To sum up: (1) What had been the economy's monetary gold was now a mass of approximately 370,000 twenty-seven–pound ingots buried three floors deep in Fort Knox and other Treasury depositories under heavy guard. (2) The use of gold for monetary purposes was illegal; the Gold Rule of Law had ended. (3) However, the presence of the buried gold, accounted as "Gold Certificates" in Fed Banks' assets, officially determined the limits of monetary activity by the Fed Banks.

The new Banking Act also enlarged and made discretionary the statutory reserve requirements for member banks of the Fed System. Where the requirements had been fixed at 7, 10, and 13 percent, the new act provided a range of requirements double the existing values, that is, 7–14 percent for banks in the smaller cities and towns, 10–20 percent for banks in larger cities, and 13–26 percent for banks in Chicago and New York. The act vested the authority to set the exact requirements for each classification of banks with the Fed Board, not with the Fed Banks or the FOMC.

Most of the provisions of the Banking Act of 1935 enhanced and codified the role of the Federal Reserve System in determining monetary policy. Such immense power was nowhere to be found in the Constitution, but by virtue of the Court decisions already discussed, Congress now had that power. The Banking Act of 1935 simply provided additional details for congressional control of money, and the stage was set for the Rule of Men in the Federal Reserve System to supplant the Rule of the Gold Standard that the Constitution had initiated. A new monetary venture was in the offing – the Fed-Treasury's upcoming Reserve Requirement Experiment of 1936–1938 – that would provide a contrast between the two rules.

Strangely enough, policymakers in Congress, the administration, the financial profession, and the economics profession in this era seemed to have little idea of the force that monetary policy could exert. Conspicuously absent in the new Banking Act was any policy prescription of targets or goals for Federal Reserve policy. The recent catastrophic collapse of the monetary system and the economy had occurred, in everyone's view, in spite of a Fed Board that claimed it had done everything conceivable to prevent it. One of the favorite remarks at the time was that monetary policy was like a string: you could pull with it, say, to prevent inflation, but you could not push on it to encourage spending and economic recovery.

---

Theory presumes that some kind of monetary authority, such as a central bank, provides for variations in this quantity to control the price level, and, therefore, the value of the money-unit.

The new alternative to an ineffectual monetary policy was an activist fiscal policy, featuring government agencies dutifully spending money financed by Treasury borrowing.[5] While this policy violated the traditional norm of balanced budgets, no one seemed alarmed. If Big Spending would do the job, future prosperity would easily pay the bills with the new product generated by the current deficits.

The new Chairman of the reformed Fed Board was Marinner Eccles, a successful commercial banker from Utah. President Roosevelt appointed him in 1934 after Eccles had been an assistant for a year or so to Secretary of the Treasury Henry Morgenthau, and with Morgenthau's recommendation. Eccles stated openly that the Fed should "support expansionary fiscal policy through discretionary monetary policy."[6] He saw the Fed as a department of the Treasury, and committed the Fed to do whatever the Treasury demanded. The Banking Act had removed the Secretary of the Treasury and the Comptroller of the Currency from the Fed Board. However, since Eccles regarded monetary policy as nothing more than an arm of Treasury fiscal policy, the absence of the Secretary of the Treasury from the Board made no difference. Fiscal policy was dominant, and would remain so for the next 15 years.

Abrogation of gold clauses, devaluation of the gold dollar, the Gold Clause cases, the Banking Act of 1935 – the early 1930s were filled with governmental monetary activity. In slightly more than 20 years, the Fed that Congress created to complement and preserve the gold standard by helping solvent banks meet short-term liquidity problems had become an omnipotent monetary authority without policy guidelines, and the gold standard was in the dust bin of history. Under the gold standard, thousands of "people" took part in the market system that had determined the quantity of money and where it went, even though none of them knew what the others were doing. They all just followed the "rules of the gold standard game," constrained by the provisions on money in the Constitution. In 1913, Congress had voted for a far different institution than the one that now ruled the monetary system. However, never once in its emergence as an extra-constitutional institution did any law, controversial action, or policy incident test the Fed's

---

[5] See, Timberlake, *Monetary Policy*, pp. 282–286, for revealing statements about the Rule of Men in policy in contrast to the Rule of Law. Representative Henry Steagall of Alabama, for example, in a classic statement during debate on the Banking Act of 1935, stated: "We all know that it does not matter so much what we write into law as it does who administers the law" *Congressional Record* 79 (1935) part 13, p. 13706.

[6] Donald F. Kettl, *Leadership at the Fed* (New Haven: Yale University Press, 1986), pp. 48–53.

constitutionality. If it started out as legitimate in 1913, it surely was not so by 1935. Yet there it was, and what was it doing?

One of the first things it did was to use its newly acquired power to raise legal reserve requirements. Because of continuous gold inflows from Europe and elsewhere, Fed Banks' holdings of gold and the corresponding increase of reserves in commercial banks became embarrassingly large. By August, 1936, Fed Banks held $8.54 billion gold certificate assets, $3.97 billion of which was "excess," that is, not legally required to "back" Fed Bank issues of Fed notes and member bank reserves. In the same vein, commercial member banks by June 1936 had $31.3 billion in deposits. Their required reserves for these obligations were $3.58 billion, while their actual reserves were $6.17 billion. So they had excess legal reserves of $2.59 billion.

Since the Fed Board now had discretion over member banks' reserve requirements, the presence of significant excess *legal* reserves prompted discussion in the Fed-Treasury on the possible danger that these excess reserves posed to the economy. The "danger" imagined was inflation! Even though the economy was struggling uphill to get out of the Depression, with unemployment still at 17 percent and a distressed business environment, the talk in both governmental circles and in the financial press was "inflation." Benjamin Anderson, a conservative columnist of the period, noted that the large gold-inspired increases in bank reserves had had very little effect on interest rates. Therefore, "mopping up" excess bank reserves by raising reserve requirements would have little effect in reverse. At the same time, the excess reserves also gave rise (inconsistently) to a "dangerously high potential of credit expansion."[7] Inside the Fed, Marinner Eccles, the Fed Board's Chairman, observed similarly that the burgeoning reserves "could become the basis of a potential expansion of bank credit [and deposits] of such proportions that the Federal Reserve could lose all control or influence over the supply and cost of money."[8] He recommended an increase in member bank reserve requirements of 50 percent to prevent this new-found problem. Reserves would still be sufficient, he added, to "provide a more than adequate basis for legitimate credit expansion."[9] Arguments in the Treasury Department called for an even greater increase.[10]

---

[7]   Benjamin M. Anderson, *Economics and the Public Welfare: A Financial and Economic History of the United States, 1914–1946.* (New York: Van Nostrand Co., 1949; 2nd ed. Liberty Press, Indianapolis, 1979), p. 405.

[8]   Eccles, *Beckoning Frontiers,* p. 287. "Cost of money" meant *interest rates.*

[9]   *Ibid.,* p. 289.

[10]   Friedman and Schwartz, *Monetary History,* p. 510–534.

In the event, the Fed Board heeded Treasury Department opinion and raised all commercial bank reserve requirements by 100 percent – from 7, 10, and 13 percent to 14, 20 and 26 percent. It did so in three steps – by 50 percent in August, 1936, and then by 25 percent in March and 25 percent again in May of 1937. Doubling reserve requirements was the equivalent of a FOMC sale of government securities of a magnitude greater than the total existing stock of government securities in the Fed Banks' portfolios! That is, if the policy had been an open-market sale of government securities to get the same "credit" effect, it could not have been done. Fed Banks just did not have that many securities to sell.[11]

The attitude throughout the Fed-Treasury was that excess *legal* reserves "didn't matter," simply because the banks were not using them. Marinner Eccles observed that total bank deposits and currency were greater in 1936 than they had been in 1929, implying that the system's greater quantity of money was not needed. What he failed to note was that the economy's employable resources in 1936 were 17 percent greater than they had been in 1929. Moreover, the velocity of money had also fallen significantly due to the Fed-inspired decline in prices and bank lending.

Measuring the potential effects of increases in reserve requirements on the money stock and employment is a relatively simple exercise. First, however, the term "excess reserves" needs some explanation. "Excess" when applied to bank reserves simply means that banks' accounted reserves exceed the minimum legally required reserves. It does not say anything about how bankers in the real world regard the reserves – adequate, excess, or deficient. Bankers of that era, in fact, very much needed those "excess" legal reserves, no matter the label. They had little faith in the Fed as a supplier of their credit needs, as they had seen it shamelessly neglect them when they desperately sought reserve support just a few years earlier.[12]

How much money did the economy in fact need? Since the recent Banking Act of 1935 gave the Fed complete control over the economy's stock of money, the Fed had the technical means to provide any necessary quantity. To treat this issue, the appropriate policy model is, perforce, the Quantity Theory of Money, which presumes that some controlling agency – a central bank, such as the Fed – has discretionary control over the stock of money. It assumes that the agency can manipulate that stock to counteract

---

[11] For a detailed account of how the two bureaucracies – the Treasury and the Fed – orchestrated this disastrous policy, see Allan H. Meltzer, *A History of the Federal Reserve*, University of Chicago Press: Chicago, 2003, pp. 490–534.

[12] *Ibid*. Friedman and Schwartz's excellent work covers this period in much detail.

changes in the other two independent variables in the expression, V, the velocity of money – the rapidity with which each dollar is spent – and, R, the quantitative flow of finished goods and services. By routine operating procedures, the central bank can promote changes in M, the quantity of money, that keep P, the average of money prices, constant.[13]

The Quantity Theory implies that in an economy suffering significant unemployment, increases in the quantity of money, M, act through the multitude of markets to stimulate increases in real output, but that they may also initiate increases in prices for those goods and services that are already at or near a productive maximum. Some sectors become relatively fully employed before others because of the stickiness of prices and other factors. In those markets, prices may rise before all other markets have achieved some measure of "full" employment. Consequently, a central bank's control over the stock of money that allows it indirectly to stimulate employment and real output during a recession, cannot guide the money properly to each sector. Once resources are fully employed, however, further increases in the money stock can only increase prices, until time is allowed for additional factors of production to enter the picture.[14]

The economy in 1936, when the Fed-Treasury ordered the increase in reserve requirements, was still deep in the Depression. Unemployment in mid-1936 was 17 percent, and prices (CPI, 1947–1949 = 100) were at 59 relative to the "full employment" price level of 72 that had occurred in 1929. So prices were still 22 percent below the 1929 level. In fundamental terms, to reach "full employment," the money stock needed to be increased by 22 percent to restore prices, plus another 17 percent to provide for the new output from the re-employed resources. Thus, the total increase in the money stock would need to be about 39 percent before any true inflation would appear. That is, "full employment" would occur when the price level was back up to its 1929 level, and the percentage increases in the stock of money similarly matched the percentage increases in recovered output.[15]

---

[13] The assumption here is that an average of prices constant over time is the desideratum of policy. Constancy of prices is not necessarily optimal. Nonetheless, it is (1) harmless, and (2) the easiest policy for laymen to understand. Given that a central bank has this control over the quantity of money, a stable price level policy is the best that it can do, since it has no control over real factors.

[14] I am holding V, the velocity of money, constant in this exercise. Empirical studies all show that the velocity of money is a laggard variable, and only becomes "dynamic" when further price rises are anticipated – ordinarily because of excessive increases in the quantity of money over time.

[15] It is possible that "full employment" could occur through real declines in factor prices before the price level regained its 1929 level. That is, all prices might fall somewhat during the period of monetary stringency. If costs and prices had fallen, the new money spigot

The supply of member bank deposits in August 1936, as previously pointed out, was $31.3 billion, on a reserve base of $6.17 billion. Legally required reserves were $3.58 billion, so banks' excess reserves were $2.59 billion, meaning that, given existing reserve requirements, the banks could legally have expanded deposits by $22.6 billion if they had chosen to do so. Such an expansion would have made all their reserves "required," and would have inflated the money stock from its current level of $43.3 billion to $65.9 billion. At that time, the computed "full employment" money stock, according to data on employment and prices, was $62.4 billion. This difference, between $65.9 and $62.4 billion, implies that the last $3.5 billion increase could have been inflationary, increasing the price level by perhaps six percent – *if* the banks had expanded credit and deposits to the limits of their reserves, and *if* people would spend money at the same rate in 1936 that they did in 1929. All practical real probabilities considered, even this modest "inflation" was very unlikely, but at least tolerable.

The new Treasury-Fed policy, however, increased member bank reserve requirements by 50 percent in August of 1936. After this increase, the banks could no longer generate a "full employment" volume of money and bank credit. Had they increased their deposits to the maximum possible under this new requirement, the total money stock would have increased to only $57 billion, which would still have been 9 percent short of the computed "full employment" money stock. Of course, no inflation would have been anywhere in sight.

As if this brutal increase in reserve requirements was not enough, Treasury-Fed policy designers increased the requirements twice more, in March and May of 1937, bringing the percentage requirements up to the maximum that the 1935 Banking Act permitted. After these increases, no activity in the monetary system could possibly have promoted a full employment market economy in the United States, let alone any inflation. The potential increase in the money stock from bank credit expansion was now only $5 billion, while the economy still needed almost $20 billion.

The Treasury Department under Treasury Secretary Morgenthau was even more culpable than the Fed for this new calamity. In late 1936, the Treasury decided that it would "sterilize" the gold as it came into the Treasury, and before it became bank reserves, so that new gold would no longer add numbers to those already bloated reserves. Beginning in December 1936, after the first increase in reserve requirements, the Treasury put newly purchased gold into an "inactive" account. Instead of

could have been turned off sooner. However, extension of the model's empirical data verify that "full employment" returned (in 1942) at just about the 1929 price level.

issuing gold certificates and depositing them in Fed Banks in the former mode, the Treasury paid for the gold by selling government securities in financial markets – an open-market selling operation. By this means, the new gold was not accounted in any banks' balance sheets. Treasury and Fed polices were "coordinated." Morgenthau announced in a press release that he had decided on this policy after conferring with the Fed Board of Governors. By mid-1937 "inactive" gold in the Treasury was over $1 billion, or about 10 percent of the Treasury's gold stock.[16]

The Recession-in-a-Depression of 1937–1938 persuaded Morgenthau, Eccles, and other government policy makers that the danger of "inflation" had probably passed, and in April 1938, Morgenthau announced the end of the Treasury gold sterilization policy. Gold henceforth was monetized in the usual fashion, but the newly increased reserve requirements on member banks remained in place. Many economists approved of the monetary restrictions; Benjamin Anderson, cited earlier was one. Others chimed in with few exceptions, and with no attempt at scientific analysis of the monetary activities that had taken place to assess what was "needed" and what was "excess."[17]

Everyone denied that raising banks' reserve requirements had anything to do with the new recession. If banks had excess reserves and were not using them, financial pundits argued, taking away the legal excess would not make any difference. However, Friedman and Schwartz point out that as soon as the first increase in reserve requirements was announced, member banks scrambled to restore the reserves lost because of the new reserve requirement arithmetic. Their behavior patently denied that the accounted "excess" reserves were excess in fact.

Recovery, which had begun in earnest in 1935–1936, was abruptly ended by the massive increase in reserve requirements. With the economy's money stock paralyzed by central bank gold sterilization and bank-reserve-ratio increases, high levels of unemployment continued until 1941. By then rearmament and the accompanying fiscal-monetary expansion of the Fed-Treasury resulted in burgeoning money stocks that even high reserve ratios in banks and Fed Banks could not retard.

The entire contraction-depression-recession period –1929–1941 – was unprecedented in the history of the country. It was not a random event that reflected an absence of market forces or market failure. Markets were doing everything possible to stabilize the economy. Rather, Supreme Court

---

[16]  U.S. Treasury Press Release No. 9–20, December 20, 1936.

[17]  See, Timberlake, *Monetary Policy*, pp. 297–299. See also Melltzer, *ibid.*, pp. 518–529.

decisions of the past, leading up to and including the Gold Clause cases, had taken the creation of money out of the province of the gold standard and put it completely under the discretion of mortal men on the Federal Reserve Board, in Federal Reserve Banks and the U.S. Treasury. Gold continued to accumulate in Treasury vaults. By 1940, the sheer volume of the Treasury's gold stock was something over *19,000 tons.* Such a stagnant bulk of one of the Earth's most valuable commodities is almost unimaginable. In dollar terms, the Fed-Treasury gold stock grew from $3.28 billion in 1929, to $9.12 billion in 1935, and to $20.0 billion in 1940.[18] At the same time the economy's stock of common money, M1, which was $26.2 billion in 1929, declined under Fed-Treasury management to $25.7 billion by 1935, and then increased to only $39.7 billion by 1940.[19] Consequently, the change in the monetary gold stock had almost no effect on the community's stock of conventional money.

Putting the shoe on the other foot, imagine the gold standard conditions of, say 1910, and assume that gold still determined the economy's stock of money in 1940 in the same fashion as it had in 1910. In that early year, M2 at mid-year was $13.12 billion, and the gold stock giving rise to this total was $1.753 billion, implying a "gold multiplier" of 7.48.[20] Using this same gold "multiplier," a gold stock of $20.0 billion in 1940 would have generated an M2 money stock of $149.6 billion. In fact, the actual M2 money stock was $54.3 billion, or hardly more than one-third of what would have occurred with a true gold standard in place.[21]

It is certain that this counterfactual event would not have happened. The dynamics of monetary adjustment in markets would have interrupted any such simple expansion of gold and common money. Had a gold standard resumed in 1929 after Benjamin Strong's stable price level policy of the 1920s, the excess gold-money adjustment would have produced an increase in U.S. prices. Banks would have expanded their loans and investments on the base of their existing gold reserves, which would not have been locked up in Fed Banks, thereby increasing the volume of their outstanding deposits. Since bank deposits are a major part of the community's stock of money,

---

[18] *Annual Reports, Secretary of the Treasury, 1918–1942.* The gold-dollar values after 1934 reflected the greatly increased dollar price of gold due to the 1934 devaluation.

[19] Friedman and Schwartz, *Monetary History,* Table A-1, pp. 714–719.

[20] *Ibid.* That is, $13.12 / 1.753 = $7.48. For this example I am using the M2 money stock, which is accounted as M1 – currency outside banks and demand deposits adjusted – plus time deposits in commercial banks. The M1 measure is not available before 1917.

[21] *Ibid.,* Table A-1, p. 716, and, Department of Commerce, *Historical Statistics of the United States, Colonial Times to 1957,* GPO: Washington, 1960, Table x-299, p. 649.

the general price level would have begun to increase in 1930, triggering a price-specie-[gold]-flow to other countries, particularly Europe. As foreign institutions received the outflow of U.S. gold, their money stocks would have tended to rise, too. By successive approximations of gold movements, imports and exports of goods, services, and capital, a tendency toward equilibrium of production, spending, national money stocks, and prices would have occurred, all within a few years of 1929. Rather than a Great Contraction in the United States, with all its attendant hardships, a slight inflation and subsequent stabilization would have resulted in a ho-hum history of the period. No, the common money stock would not have multiplied to $149 billion by 1940, because the surplus gold stocks in the United States by that time would have been scattered to many other countries. No one knows what prices and incomes would have been in retrospect, because government policies had frozen or distorted so many causative variables that markets could no longer restore equilibrium.[22] The contrast of probable gold standard equilibrium at near stable prices with the constant disequilibrium of human-directed deflationary policies that were current in the 1930s is instructive.

Much monetary policy happened after 1940, but gold no longer had any determinate relationship to common money. With the onset of World War II, money and the economy came even further under government dominance. To control prices and outputs, Congress authorized government bureaus to manage statutory wage-and-price ceilings and rationing programs. All the economies of the world became politicized.

After the end of World War II, the Treasury-Fed control of the monetary system continued but with many internal conflicts. An occasional effort to restore the primacy of the gold standard surfaced in Congress, but gold had such an undeservedly bad reputation by this time that the effort was nothing much more than lip service and a nostalgic bow to convention.[23]

Private gold ownership was another matter. The price of gold was still fixed at $35 per ounce, the devaluation price of 1934, but no one was allowed to hold bulk gold. Even if the prohibition had not been there, the real price of gold was much too high for anyone to hold gold speculatively

---

[22] The view of this writer is that prices would have risen about five to ten percent if the New York Fed had cut loose its hands-on control in 1929, allowing gold to resume its function. Prices probably would have see-sawed around this slight increase through the 1930s. Neither a Great Contraction nor a Great Depression would have appeared.

[23] For an account of the political forces at work in the determination of monetary policy in the post-war period, see again, Friedman and Schwartz, *Monetary History,* Chapter 11, pp. 592–637, and Timberlake, *Monetary Policy*, pp. 309–331.

in anticipation of a price level increase. Yet, the instability of prices in the post-war era was an incentive for creditors to find some means to ensure the value of the medium of payment in satisfaction of contracts.

The Resolution abrogating gold clauses had specified gold *coins* as the medium not permitted in a gold clause. But what about gold *bullion* – some quantity of gold not in the form of coin, and therefore not a money? The gold clause Resolution did not prohibit that. Or what about other commodities or land, or even some kind of specialized service, as the means of guaranteeing true value at the consummation of a debt? Obviously, Congress could not outlaw all possible commodity guarantees in order to prevent the monetary system from being compromised by non-gold commodity clauses in contracts. As Professor John P. Dawson observed in his 1935 article, "The Gold Clause Decisions," "The gold-clause resolution would clearly not prevent the adoption of particular commodities or groups of commodities as standards of value in money obligations.... Nor does it seem that Congress could directly prohibit the resort to *non-monetary* standards of performance, even as the measure of money obligations.... [And Congress] is unlikely to do so, unless the widespread use of such devices clearly interferes with Congressional control of money."[24] Dawson noted the inferior nature of other commodities as payment media compared to gold. One acceptable substitute for a gold clause, he noted, was a price index. By estimating the change in the general price level, a price index inversely measures the opposite change in the value of the money-unit. "Any legislature," he concluded, "would be convicted of an arbitrary and destructive purpose in attacking such contractual provisions."[25]

## RE-LEGALIZATION OF GOLD OWNERSHIP

Until December 31, 1974, the New Deal prohibition of private ownership of gold and of gold clauses in contracts remained the law of the land. Two issues had appeared in the gold restrictions of the 1930s – ownership of gold, and the use of gold as money. Both were disallowed, and both prohibitions were in force for 41 years.

The use of gold as money allegedly interfered with the complete monetary powers that the Supreme Court had deeded to Congress by its successive decisions on monetary disputes in 1871 and 1884. Prohibition of gold

---

[24] John P. Dawson, "The Gold Clause Decisions," originally published in *Michigan Law Review,* and re-printed in Holzer, *The Gold Clause,* p. 87. (Emphasis in original.)
[25] *Ibid.,* p. 90.

ownership, however, was a newer intervention, and no more logical than prohibition of any ordinary commodity – precious stones, metals, land, or any other "thing" that people wanted to have and to hold. As people came to realize this fact, its political correction appeared in executive and congressional actions.

Prior to a relaxation of the gold restrictions, on August 15, 1971, Congress passed a bill, signed into law by President Nixon, fixing a system of wage-price controls on the U.S. economy, but also decreeing that gold no longer had any defining relationship to the U.S. dollar. Henceforth, the government would not redeem its foreign dollar obligations with gold. Within the domestic economy, gold had not had any such relationship since 1935, so the Act did not change any current realities between gold and the domestic dollar. However, the new policy had the indirect effect of eliminating any reason for denying ordinary citizens ownership of gold for their own use.

In 1973 and 1974, Congress passed Gold Ownership Amendments that repealed the prohibitions on gold ownership. They provided that no law, rule, or regulation "may be construed to prohibit any person from purchasing, holding, selling, or otherwise dealing in gold in the United states or abroad." The Amendments gave the President the opportunity to offer objection if he thought the Amendments would "adversely affect the United States' international monetary position." The second amendment provided for automatic effectiveness of repeal on December 31, 1974, if the President, who by this time was Gerald Ford, did not report an objection before that date. Since he did not do so, the amendment became law.[26]

Legal acceptance of private gold ownership raised the question of whether the new provision also implied that gold clauses would again be legal. To test this possibility, Congressman Philip Crane (R-Ill.) introduced a bill into the House of Representatives in June, 1975, that would have removed "all legal obstacles to the use of gold clauses." Crane clearly aimed to repeal the Joint Resolution of 1933.[27] His bill, however, was too strong a medicine to get very far, and it died in committee.

Nine months later, Senator Jesse Helms (R-NC) revived the issue by addressing a letter to Treasury Secretary William Simon and Fed Chairman Arthur Burns asking for their official positions on re-legalizing the gold clause. Secretary Simon responded that he was against such a proposal because repeal of the Joint Resolution "could call into question the strength of the dollar and undermine our efforts to control inflation and

---

[26]  Holzer, *The Gold Clause*, p. 122. By this time, Gerald Ford was President.
[27]  *Ibid.*, p. 133.

maintain confidence in our currency. In my view, its repeal would be unwise." Chairman Burns replied, however, that in the light of recent circumstances with economic recovery well under way, he would not object "to legislative action that would permit private citizens to make contracts containing legally enforceable gold clauses." He noted, however, that the full Fed Board was split on the question.[28]

Senator Helms subsequently introduced a bill in June 1976, "To declare the public policy of the United States to remove all legal obstacles to the use of gold clauses." In support of his bill, Helms noted that "gold clauses, along with other inflation-hedging arrangements, provide an indication of the health of our currency.... It is far better to have no inflation and no such devices [as gold clauses], but since we have inflation, we should have freedom to cushion its effects.... Anyone can enter into agreements which state that a sum of dollars will be paid on a certain date measured in the value of pork-bellies or any other commodity. But, because of this archaic provision on the books, we could not use gold as a measure of payment.... Once Congress repealed the prohibitions against gold ownership, gold clauses cannot consistently be prohibited."[29]

In August 1976, Helms offered an amendment to his bill that answered yet another question about repeal of gold nullification. Some people still owned bonds and contracts that were created before the Congressional gold abrogation of 1933. These contracts might have renewed gold legitimacy if nullification were simply repealed *en bloc*. To prevent that implication, Helms explained that his amendment to S. 3563 "would [only] make enforceable gold clause contracts entered into after the enactment of the amendment."[30] Helm's bill as amended thereby accepted all previous gold clause nullifications, but allowed for gold clauses in all future contracts. In effect, it decreed that the past was a closed book not to be re-opened, but that in the future gold clauses in contracts were again legal.

To get the bill passed, Helms did some political footwork with other Senators in the fall of 1976, and managed to get the amendment on another bill. The new combination passed the Senate and became law on October 28, 1977. After more than four decades, the gold clause was again legal.[31]

---

[28]  *Ibid.*, pp. 134–136, Letters of Simon and Burns to Senator Jesse Helms.

[29]  *Ibid.*, pp. 137–138, Helms' speech before the Senate, June 14, 1976, in support of S. 3563.

[30]  *Ibid.*, p. 142.

[31]  *Ibid.*, p. 144. While the gold clause is legal again for federal government obligations, its legalization in state courts is still a question. (See, *The Gold Clause*, Chapter 8. pp. 145–162, for further discussion of states' objections to the gold clause.)

The possibility of a revised gold-based monetary system prompted a conference of high-level economists and jurists at the Center for Studies in Law and Economics at the University of Miami School of Law in late 1974. The proceedings reflected current legal and juristic thinking, and were published as a conference volume in 1975.[32] Subsequently, however, no consensus of economists, jurists, legislators or "people" appeared in either professional journals or popular media, suggesting that a revised gold standard was either possible or desirable.

---

[32] Center for Studies in Law and Economics, University of Miami School of Law, *Gold, Money and the Law*. Aldine Publishing Co.: Chicago, 1975.

# TWENTY FOUR

# A Constitutional Monetary System

*An "automatic" gold currency is part and parcel of a laissez-faire and free trade economy. It links every nation's money rates and price levels with the money rates and price levels of all other nations that are "on gold." It is extremely sensitive to government expenditure and even to attitudes or policies that do not involve expenditure directly, for example, to foreign policy, to certain policies of taxation, and, in general, to precisely all those policies that violate the principles of [classical] economic liberalism. This [sensitivity] is the reason gold is so unpopular now [1948] and also why it was so popular in a bourgeois era. It imposes restrictions upon governments or bureaucracies that are much more powerful than is parliamentary criticism. It is both the badge and the guarantee of bourgeois freedom – of freedom not simply of the bourgeois interest, but of the bourgeois sense. From this standpoint a man may quite rationally fight for it, even if fully convinced of the validity of all that has ever been urged against it on economic grounds. From the standpoint of etatisme and planning, a man may not less rationally condemn it, even if fully convinced of the validity of all that has ever been urged for it on economic grounds.*

– Joseph A. Schumpeter [1]

Prior to the Civil War no one ever imagined that anything other than gold or silver could be constitutional money. The precious metals were the limited dietary nutrients of the monetary system. Many bankers, businessmen, and especially debtors chafed under this discipline, just as Schumpeter's epigram implied. However, all parties respected the precious metal limits to monetary growth as absolutely necessary, very proper, and sufficient. As one legislator exclaimed in 1870: "Gold and silver! They are the legal tender of Commerce and the Constitution … the legal tender of Almighty God, who has made it precious!"[2]

---

[1] Schumpeter, Joseph. *History of Economic Analysis,* (New York: Oxford University Press, 1954), pp. 405–406.

[2] Samuel Cox in the House of Representatives, *Congressional Globe,* 41st Cong., 2nd sess., June 7, 1870.

The Supreme Court formally decided the cases of *Knox v. Lee* and *Parker v. Davis* 1 May, 1871. In so doing, it affirmed that the full-legal-tender greenbacks issued during the Civil War were constitutional for payments of debts contracted before the Legal Tender Acts were passed (February 1862) as well as for those after. In making this decision it overturned a previous case, *Hepburn v. Griswold*, decided February 7, 1870, that found the greenbacks unconstitutional for debts contracted before the Legal Tender Acts were passed.[3]

The Court's majority decision in *Knox* argued further that if the greenbacks were not legal tender for debts made before the acts were passed, they could not be legal tender for debts afterward either; and, second, if they were not full legal tender, every creditor who held any debt, especially government debt, could demand precious metal from his debtor to pay off the debt. The decision reflected the practical political fact that, at this time, the federal government was the nation's largest debtor.

These arguments were both shallow and contrary to past experience. The majority opinion could easily have differentiated between debts incurred before February 1862 and after, as the *Hepburn* decision had done. Furthermore, even if the full-legal-tender feature had been declared unconstitutional, the greenbacks would have continued to circulate at par with the other fiat government currencies – old style Treasury notes, national bank notes, and silver currency. Not "legal tender" did not mean that the notes would cease to exist, or that they would lose any value in market transactions.

The majority's most important "finding" in the *Knox* decision, however, was its newly discovered *sovereignty* for the federal government. "The Constitution," the opinion presumed, "was intended to frame a government as distinguished from a league or compact." This sovereignty gave the government "general power over the currency ... especially when considered in connection with the clause which denies to the states the power to coin money, emit bills of credit, or make anything but gold and silver coin a tender in payment of debts." That is, the denial of money-creating powers to the states implied that such power was intended for a sovereign federal government. Then came the astonishing conclusion from Justice Bradley: "It follows as a matter of necessity ... that it is specially the duty of the [federal] government to provide a national currency." The last legal tender decision in 1884, *Juilliard v. Greenman*, developed further this particularly fallacious misjudgment. Justice Gray, who rendered the *Juilliard* opinion,

---

[3]  U.S. 12 Wall, 457.

contended that the *McCulloch* decision in 1819 established a precedent for Congress's power to issue bills of credit and make them legal tender for all private debts. No matter what kind of magnifying glass an investigator uses, he will never find any words in the constitutional debates, the Constitution, the *McCulloch* decision, or any other official document that remotely supports this allegation.[4]

The *Knox* and *Juilliard* decisions used a line of reasoning that might best be described as *subjunctive syllogism*. First, the argument presumed that the federal government is sovereign, without any reference to the sovereignties of the states or the people. Next, Congress as the legislative agency of this sovereign government had the power to issue legal tender paper currency, a power, Justice Gray contended, that was "universally understood to belong to sovereignty in Europe and America at the time of the framing and adopting of the Constitution." Therefore, the Framers – and here is the syllogism – *would* have known of their own sovereign powers in 1787, and *could* have written a Constitution that *would* have included "the power to make the notes of the government a legal tender in payment of private debt." Gray did not add that the Framers had not acknowledged any such "sovereignty," nor written such a constitution. Rather, he constructed an argument on the presumption that he and the other majority Justices knew what the Framers were thinking when they wrote the actual Constitution that the Court was supposed to interpret.[5] Such an imagined document could include anything.

Justice Field, the only dissenter, objected strenuously to the presumptive interpretations of both the 1871 and 1884 judgments. "There is no such thing as a power of inherent sovereignty in the government of the United States," he stated flatly. "It is a government of delegated powers, supreme within its prescribed sphere but powerless outside of it. In this country, sovereignty resides in the people, and Congress can exercise no power which [the people] have not, by their Constitution, entrusted to it; all else is withheld."[6] In any Supreme Court convening before 1860, his arguments would very likely have been the majority decision. But in 1884, his were the arguments of a constitutionalist lost in a crowd of nationalists. This decision, it turned out, was the beginning of the end of constitutional money in the United States.

---

[4]  Once a highly placed authority makes such a statement, unwary laymen presume that the force of his argument and his very office sanctify the validity of the assertion. Here was a perfect example of the fallacy of that presumption.

[5]  U.S., pp. 449–451.

[6]  *Ibid.*, pp. 467–68.

In the years after 1884 and through the turn of the century, many jurists, historians, political scientists, and economists critically discussed the reasoning of the Court's final legal tender decision. All of the commentaries, except those coming from legal journals, were critical of the sovereignty presumption, and denied its validity, but to no avail. Congress did nothing either to gainsay its Court-approved powers, or to exploit them. It did, however, put the monetary system back into its gold standard clothes, in spite of much controversy over what other constraints the monetary system should include. Passage of the [Gold] Currency Act of 1900 seemed to imply that, whether Congress had all those monetary powers or not, the gold standard was in place and would be forever.[7] The stock of outstanding greenbacks was frozen, and would remain so. No matter what Congress might do, as long as the gold standard stayed operational and the stock of government fiat money virtually constant, Congress's discretionary monetary powers would never be used. That seemed to be the general consensus.

Throughout the 30 years between the *Juilliard* decision and the beginning of World War I, the gold standard worked as intended. Incorporation of the Federal Reserve System in December 1913, however, provided a new vehicle for the implementation of Congress's monetary powers.

The initial Federal Reserve system, as legislated, appeared innocent enough. It was nothing more than a group of predominantly private super-commercial banks that could provide a line of credit defense as lenders of last resort (LLRs) for the bulk of ordinary commercial banks. Nothing in the Fed Act, or in the congressional debates prior to its passage, referred in any way to the absolute monetary powers that the legal tender decisions had granted Congress. No congressman recalled them in the debates on the Fed Act in 1912–1913.

The Federal Reserve banks in practice were never LLRs. During World War I they were tied to the Treasury Department, and governed by Treasury policies. As soon as their wartime role ended around 1920, they promoted and endured the recession of 1920–1922. They then fell into line behind the dominant Federal Reserve Bank of New York, whose governor, Benjamin Strong, promoted informally what amounted to a stable price level policy by means of open market operations and discount rate manipulation that controlled the quantity of common money – currency in circulation

---

[7]    Silver by this time was a subsidiary coinage metal because of the rapid decline in its real value after large discoveries in the American West, and for other reasons. However, it was still a prominent subsidiary, and no laws prevented its use. Gold was, in any case, sufficient in its role for defining a constrained monetary base.

plus demand deposits in commercial banks. The Fed was no longer a gold standard central bank. Gold had become a medium that the Fed, through the agency of the Federal Reserve Bank of New York, manipulated to maintain a stable price level. While this policy was eminently successful, it emphasized the fact that the New York Fed had co-opted the gold standard.

If the New York Fed could initiate and manage a stable price level policy, some similar agency of the Fed could initiate and promote a policy that might be disruptive to the private sector. The "direct pressure" policy of the Fed Board, begun in 1929 following Strong's stable price level policy, was even worse than disruptive; it was disastrous. Its deliberate target was the stock market "speculator" who, through the ages, has been a scapegoat for financial problems. The Board's anti-speculation policy from 1929 to 1932 was so successful that financial markets and the banking system were virtually obliterated. By the time the carnage ended in early 1933, no one could be certain from the financial rubble whether there had even been a speculative bubble. If all new enterprise is destroyed by the strangling of bank credit, it is not possible to distinguish what businesses might have been successful and productive from those that might have been shallow and unsound.

The fallout from the Great Contraction did not lead to a re-examination of the wisdom of authorizing a central bank to manage the economy's money supply. To begin with, virtually no one knew how the Fed worked. However, everyone knew that the gold standard was supposed to govern the monetary system. So, if something did not work, it must have been the institution that was supposed to be guiding the system rather than the appendage central bank that almost no one could comprehend. By this line of reasoning, the gold standard that had been in place for over 100 years received most of the blame for the disaster. Federal Reserve spokesmen aided and abetted this notion, claiming that their attempts to "save" the gold standard in 1932–1933 hobbled their recovery policies.[8]

Financial institutions everywhere, both public and private, demonized gold. To prevent it from doing further "harm," the federal government forced the sale of much privately held gold to the U.S. Treasury, whereupon it was melted down, converted into twenty-seven–pound ingots that could not be used for anything, and stored deep in the ground where no one could see it or count it, let alone use it. While some of it has since been exported at various times in the past 75 years to promote different Treasury-Fed policies,

---

[8]  See, for example, Ben Bernanke, 1993. "The World on a Cross of Gold," *Journal of Monetary Economics* 31: pp. 251–267.

8,000-plus tons of it are still in the possession of the U.S. Treasury, and accounted on the Fed's Consolidated Statement of Condition at $42.22 per ounce, even though the market price of gold is now thirty-eight times this Treasury "price."

The Gold Clause cases of 1934–1935 focused attention on the "complete control over the monetary system" that both jurists and legislators claimed for Congress.[9] Both the five-man majority and the four-man minority of the Hughes Court believed that the decisions in the legal tender cases of 1871 and 1884 properly sanctioned sweeping monetary powers for Congress. The Court held that since Congress had such powers, it could establish any monetary system it wished, and that the Fed it had created in 1913 properly reflected such powers. In fact, Congress passed the Federal Reserve Act on very different grounds that had nothing at all to do with any "complete control over the monetary system." Nonetheless, if this "complete-control" power was valid, Congress *could* have legislated an omnipotent Fed as the Court suggested, and as the decisions in the Legal Tender Cases implied. But no Justice denied or even questioned this false analysis.

The review here of the Court's logic and the reasoning it used in deciding the 1871 and 1884 legal tender cases finds that the majority decisions in those cases were invalid: Congress does not have the complete monetary power the Court gave it, and a central bank – a Federal Reserve System – dependent for its legitimacy on those decisions cannot be constitutional.

To return to a constitutional system, Congress must provide measures for a monetary framework that feature legitimate constitutional constraints. To do so, both it and the Supreme Court must revisit the legal tender cases of 1871 and 1884, using valid monetary analysis together with traditional jurisprudence. Fortunately, the Court's procedure in reversing *Hepburn* established a precedent that provides an unexceptionable *modus operandi* for re-argument. It reflects the obvious principle that should govern all such cases: no Supreme Court decision can unequivocally answer an important question at issue for all time.

Ironically, Justice Strong, who wrote the questionable majority decision in the 1871 legal tender cases, himself recommended the possibility of review and re-argument of controversial cases. Being in the majority that had just reversed *Hepburn*, Strong could comfortably offer such re-argument as a

---

[9] Holzer, *The Gold Clause*, pp. 123–456. Vieira concludes on this issue: "Correctly interpreted, neither *Knox v. Lee*, nor *Juilliard v. Greenman*, nor any of the Gold Clause Cases provides the least rational support for the claim that Congress may constitutionally emit legal-tender *fiat* currency irredeemable in silver or gold coin, or delegate such a power to the corporative-state Federal Reserve System," *Pieces of Eight*, pp. 383–384.

general principle for the Court to follow. "These [Legal Tender] cases," he stated, "are constitutional questions of the most vital importance to the government and to the public at large.... Even in cases involving only private rights, if convinced we made a mistake, we would hear another argument and correct our error. And it is no unprecedented thing in courts of last resort, both in this country and in England, to overrule decisions previously made. We agree this should not be done inconsiderately, but in a case of such far-reaching consequences as the present, thoroughly convinced as we are that Congress has not transgressed its powers, we regard it as our duty so to decide and to affirm both these judgments."[10]

What's sauce for the goose is sauce for the gander! Just as Strong and the other four majority justices overruled *Hepburn*, so the Hughes Court, when faced with the impossible decision that it had to deal with in 1935, could rightfully have re-examined these earlier cases. Only with such a tradition of re-argument does a Supreme Court admit its human dimension. Decisions made in lower courts can be appealed up the chain, but no court is higher than the Supreme Court. Therefore, the check-and-balance to its decisions must be some later Court that has occasion to use the decision at issue in some complementary case. Controversial cases must always be subject to re-argument. Otherwise, improper past decisions serve as precedents that bias future ones. The precariousness of the principles still remaining in the U.S. Constitution at the present time is warning enough.

Between 1935 and 1975, ownership of monetary gold was prohibited to private citizens. The impropriety of that law finally resulted in its repeal, and since 1975 private households and business firms have been allowed to own and deal in gold, not as money – that is, not as a general medium of exchange – but as a barterable commodity. Moreover, since Congress has ceded its monetary powers to a central bank, gold cannot legally be money. Only paper Federal Reserve notes – modern "bills of credit" – are *legal tender*. They are the only legal money.

Federal Reserve policies in the twenty-first century have exhibited the complete power over the monetary system that the decisions of the tragically mis-argued legal tender cases sanctioned. In response to the Great Recession of 2008–2009, and with the approval of Congress and both the Bush and Obama Administrations, the Fed enlarged its money-creating activities by trillions of dollars. The results in the real economy have been between nil and nothing, not because monetary policy is powerless but

---

[10] U.S. p. 554.

because the problems are in the real economy and not in the monetary system.

Good or bad, such unbridled discretion has induced many observers to look for some check-and-balance to the Fed's power, including thoughts of a return to a gold standard. This possibility merits further consideration, especially in view of the 100-plus year history of the gold-silver standard in the United States from, say, 1800 to 1912, compared to the Fed's subsequent 99-year history of control from 1913 to 2012. The purchasing power value of the dollar under the gold-silver standard rule of law was essentially constant over that 100-year span, while the value of the dollar during the human-controlled Fed's 99 years has declined by more than 95 percent. That comparison is difficult to ignore. It amounts to a 50 percent decline in the value of the money-unit every generation

## REINSTITUTION OF A REAL GOLD STANDARD

Schumpeter's eloquent epigram that began this chapter implies that the strictures accompanying a gold standard ramify into many avenues of government policy. It inhibits wars; it discourages fiscal extravagance; its formal workings keep both governments and people civilized. Most to the point, it provides a constrained – and thus constitutional – monetary system. However, for its re-vitalization a gold standard must have a serious public consensus, a general commitment to its discipline, a public *ethos*, and a practical program for its workings. At this time, only a limited such movement exists, and often the notion is ridiculed with arrogant ignorance. If, however, a substantial effort for a gold standard were to gain momentum, the necessary practical conditions for its implementation and subsequent operation would need to include the following changes to the existing banking and monetary framework.

First, the revamped gold standard would have to be acknowledged the exclusive creator of money. As Milton Friedman observed many decades ago, the term "gold standard" cannot be applied as a gimmick to disguise the current central banking system. A new "gold standard" managed by a central bank would be just a façade for the existing Federal Reserve System, which would continue on its inflationary de-stabilizing ways.[11] Therefore, as a first step, the present-day Federal Reserve would have to be stripped of its money-creating powers. Fed Banks could become bank-holding

---

[11]   Friedman, Milton. "Real and Pseudo Gold Standards," 1961, *Journal of Law and Economics* 4, No.4, pp. 66–79.

companies for their titular owners, the member commercial banks, while the Fed Board and Federal Open Market Committee would be abolished altogether.

The ex-Federal Reserve Banks, without the "Federal Reserve" label, would then perform all the necessary check-clearing operations that their predecessors, the clearing-house associations, did 100 to 150 years ago when the commercial banking system functioned as a viable free enterprise institution. Here, also, it would make economic sense for Congress to abolish the many stultifying restrictions and regulations that made, and still make, the American banking system so fragile and vulnerable to bank panics.

Second, the 8,000-plus tons of gold – roughly 260 million ounces – in the U.S. Treasury's possession would have to be separated from Treasury ownership and made available for new money creation. One simple way to distribute it would be through the tax system. In some given year the federal government would issue Gold Certificates, each Certificate representing one ounce of pure gold, as tax rebates to all taxpayers and their dependents as listed on their IRS 1040 forms for that year. This graceful gesture would cost the government nothing since the Certificates would be claims on a stock of gold that is already in the Treasury's possession, cost the government almost nothing to acquire, costs real resources to maintain, and has been idle for decades. To avoid the issue of the many millions of income earners who do not pay income tax or file returns, for this one year every householder would file a return listing dependents. Then, whether any tax was paid or not, the Treasury would return a one-ounce Gold Certificate to the tax filer for each dependent.

Recipients of the Gold Certificates would not immediately get the actual gold. Before they could do so, the bulk gold in Ft. Knox and other depositories would have to be distributed to wholesalers who would get it by buying with current Fed dollars enough Gold Certificates from taxpayer-recipients to claim a twenty-seven–pound gold bar from the Treasury. At the current price of $1,600 per ounce, such an ingot would have a market value of almost $700,000. However, the New Gold Act would authorize the Treasury to sell the gold bars only for the Gold Certificates that had been rebated to taxpayers, not for Federal Reserve dollars. So the wholesaler would have to collect $27 \times 16 = 432$ Gold Certificates to claim one gold bar.

Gold wholesalers would now have the legal right to divide the gold bar or bars into any units of coinage that fit the prescribed coinage values for weight and fineness that Congress by this time would have specified. However, the coins would not yet have fixed dollar values because the market value of one ounce of gold would be somewhat variable until the gold had been in private markets for some months. Many people would simply cash in their Gold Certificates immediately for whatever dollar value the gold market established. It would not be $1,600, because certificate-buyer-wholesaler-distributors would have to realize competitive returns for their marketing functions.[12]

People who wanted to use the gold as money would deposit their Certificates in commercial banks that would then collect the gold from the Treasury just as gold wholesalers had done. On the basis of their newly acquired deposits of Gold Certificates or the actual gold, the banks would initiate gold-deposit accounts, which would be strictly limited to payments and clearings in gold. The gold depositor's checkbook would have a balance in gold ounces, not dollars, that the gold depositor could check against. Henceforth, as the banks made new loans and investments, increases in their gold-based deposits would provide for modest increases in the stock of common money.

At the same time, the existing monetary base of paper currency and bank reserves would need to be frozen statutorily at its current level. A department of the U.S. Treasury, say, the Comptroller of the Currency, would hereafter manage this base to keep its dollar value constant. Federal Reserve notes that compose the paper currency of the monetary base serve vital functions of exchange as hand-to-hand currency. Nothing would be gained by destroying this currency, even if its original issue was "based on nothing." All its costs have already been capitalized. No Federal Open-Market Committee, or any other government agency, however, would have any further discretion over the dollar quantity of this currency or of the bank reserves that make up the rest of the base. The notes would become again *Treasury notes* – a tender for all government dues and payments, and everybody would use them routinely for transactions as the nonlegal tender Treasury notes were used in the nineteenth century.

As gold checking accounts became more widely used, the market price of gold in dollars would stabilize – not necessarily at $1,600 per ounce, but

---

[12] For a slightly different approach to reinstituting the gold system, see, Lawrence H. White, "Making the Transition to a New Gold Standard," *Cato Journal*, Vol. 32, No. 2 (Spring/ Summer 2012), pp. 34–43. White conjectures that several factors would influence the price of gold to go in alternate directions. If done properly, however, he argues that the transition would be benign, and would greatly benefit all money users. White ably discusses several other factors in the transition that the interested reader can ponder, such as the use of subsidiary currency issued by commercial banks. See also, Richard M. Salsman, *Breaking the Banks: Central Banking Problems and Free Banking Solutions.* American Institute for Economic Research: Great Barrington, Mass., 1990. Salsman emphasizes Free Banking enterprise, in conjunction with a gold-based banking system.

probably at some price close to it. When a "world" gold price seemed established, Congress could set an official price in dollars to fit it, and at that price the government would accept gold as payment for government dues. However, a legal tender feature would not be necessary, and I, following William Brough and other nay-sayers including most monetary libertarians, would recommend against it.[13]

The transition forward to a truly operational gold standard would require political commitment and time. However, it is not the only option for a system that limits human discretion. One possibility that retains a central bank would require that institution keep a weighted general index of prices absolutely constant. This policy would be the easiest to implement, but it would still require a money-creating agency to operate it. Since the world has witnessed the evolution of such an undesirable agency over the last 200 years into the ubiquitous all-powerful central banks of the present day, this option is surely not optimal. However, it would be better than the "complete control" central bank that we have now.[14]

Another possibility is one that, instead of defining the dollar's value in terms of gold, defines it in terms of a bundle of commonly known and priced goods and services, and then allows monetary flexibility by means of growth in the total product that defines the money-unit. One such system, and the most market directed, is Greenfield and Yeager's (G-Y) privatized multicommodity standard.[15] It is similar to a gold standard but uses several commodities as "the" standard commodity. The new monetary unit of account, Yeager explains,

… would be defined by a bundle of goods and services comprehensive enough for the general level of prices quoted in it to be approximately stable. Private banks would issue notes and checkable deposits, and they might also offer checking privileges against equity mutual funds. The quantities of these media of exchange would accommodate themselves to the demand for them at the price level corresponding to the definition of the unit. Incipient imbalances would trigger corrective arbitrage. This automatic equilibration of demand for and supply of media

---

[13] White also argues against a legal tender property for gold. *Ibid.*, p. 3. His article also covers many other details of a switchover to gold.

[14] Many economists and much of the general public support this policy because of its simplicity and verifiability. Other more sophisticated proposals would have the price level declining by a few percent per year – specifically at the rate of growth in real output. (See, Milton Friedman, *The Optimum Quantity of Money and Other Essays.* Aldine Publishing Co.: Chicago, 1969, Ch. 1, "The Optimum Quantity of Money." Also, George Selgin, *Less Than Zero, The Case for a Falling Price Level in a Growing Economy.* Institute of Economic Affairs: London, 1997.)

[15] Yeager, Leland, "Privatizing Money," *Cato Journal*, 30 (3): 417–438.

of exchange at a stable price level would prevent price inflation and major reces-
sions....With the proposed reform in effect, ordinary persons would no more
need to understand what determined the purchasing power of the unit of account
than they needed to understand how the gold standard worked before World War I
or than they need to understand Federal Reserve operations and the rest of today's
unsatisfactory process of determining the purchasing power of the fiat dollar....
The particular reform just sketched ... illustrates what a fundamental monetary
reform would be, in contrast to superficial tinkering with the arrangements under
which undefined national currencies trade against each other.[16]

Redemption of the money-unit in the G-Y system requires a somewhat
more complex arrangement than one in which only one very recognizable
commodity (gold) is the monetary vehicle. But that, too, is its advantage – it
does not base the creation of money only on the growth of the gold stock.
The G-Y system also includes a private enterprise commercial banking
system, in which the production of money is treated similarly to the free
market production of all other goods and services.[17] Several other proposals have emphasized a rethinking and reordering of the monetary policy
framework that would revive the constitutionality of the system.[18]

This review of Supreme Court decisions on the monetary system does
not suggest necessarily the re-establishment of a gold standard, but that
some set of rules for monetary order be put in place – rules that remove the
hands-on "guidance of human wisdom" from any positive control over the
system. As James Buchanan stated the matter:

Clearly, some defined process and institutional structure must be established, with
genuine constitutional authority, over and beyond that of democratic majoritar-
ian politics. Something analogous to the independent judiciary, under the Supreme
Court, seems required – a monetary authority that is independent of politics, but
which remains itself bound by the parameters set out in the constitution... The
Constitution remains the ultimate sovereign authority rather than the government
as such.[19]

---

[16] This precis of the system is from Leland Yeager, "The International Monetary System in
Retrospect," in *Money and the Nation State*, p. 103.

[17] Greenfield, R. L., and Yeager, L. B., "A Laissez-Faire Approach to Monetary Stability,"
*Journal of Money, Credit, and Banking* 15 (3), pp. 302–315.

[18] "The Search for Stable Money: A Historical Perspective." In *The Search for Stable Money*, pp.
1–28. "Stable Money and a Market–Liberal Order." In *Money and Markets in the Americas*,
pp. 1–18. Edited by J.A. Dorn and Roberto Salinas–León. Vancouver, B.C.: The Fraser
Institute, 1996. "The Limits of Monetary Policy." In *Cato Handbook for Policymakers*, 7th
ed.: pp. 365–375. Washington: Cato Institute, 2009.

[19] Buchanan, James, "The Constitutionalization of Money," *The Cato Journal*, Spring–Summer
2010, pp. 256–258. In his reference here to a "Supreme Court" Buchanan was undoubtedly
thinking of an *ideal* Supreme Court, not subject to the political pressures that have sullied
the decisions of that institution in the past as well as the present.

By way of contrast, the Federal Reserve System now in place operates without any effective congressional oversight or control. It has no rigorous and exclusive rule for price level stability, but only a smorgasbord of "good" things it might promote – "price level stability and economic growth" – in spite of the fact that it cannot produce a toothpick. Its creativity is limited to money, and only money, and, unfortunately, it can create far too much of that.

The Fed's public image reflects its monetary omnipotence. Financial market participants wonder what the present Fed chairman will say at the press conference after the next meeting of the FOMC. What countenance will he present? Will he "raise" or "lower" interest rates? Will he use terms such as "irrational exuberance" and send stock market prices tumbling? Or will he show benign blandness and leave observers completely uncertain of what he is thinking, and what new policy action may be imminent? Will he approve another trillion-dollar stimulus, just as if he and the FOMC were a government unto themselves? Or will he sanguinely allege that recovery is proceeding "appropriately"?

With a constrained system of rules in place, such as a gold standard or a G-Y system, no Fed Board would be making decisions about money. No Fed Chairman would make pronouncements that paralyzed or puzzled the financial world. Such a system of rules would feature thousands of people and hundreds of institutions spontaneously making millions of decisions for its operation in an unbounded system of markets. None of the participants would deliberately assume a stabilizing role, but by their perceived ordering of priorities, all of them would determine the optimum quantity of money that would make the economy work most efficiently within the framework of a stable price level.

# Index

Abandonment of gold standard, 185–186
Abrogation of gold clauses by Congress
  generally, 183–184, 209–210
  Fifth Amendment and, 188
  gold bullion and, 217
  Gold Clause Cases and, 204
  gold devaluation of 1934 and, 186, 189
  *Norman v. Baltimore & Ohio Railroad Co.*
    and, 192–193
  *Perry v. United States* and, 201–202
Absolutism, 142
Aldrich, Nelson W., 162, 163
Aldrich-Vreeland Act, 162–163
Allison, William, 117
*The American Economic Review,* 174
Anderson, Benjamin M., 210, 214
Andrew, A. Piatt, 160, 166, 177
Angell, James W., 184
Anti-speculation policy, 173–174, 176, 180,
  225

Bagehot, Walter, 163, 194
Baltimore & Ohio Railroad, 187, 188–189, 195
Bancroft, George, 124–125, 135–141, 145, 147,
  149, 201
Banking Act of 1935, 207, 208–210, 211, 213
Banking crises, 176
Bank of the Commonwealth of Kentucky, 47
Bank reserve requirements, 160–161, 179, 181,
  207, 210–211, 213–214
Bankruptcy, 95
Barrett, Don C., 65–66, 153
Barter system, 4–5
Benton, Thomas Hart, 40–41, 42, 43, 44
Bernanke, Ben, 225
Biddle, Nicholas, 27, 28

Bills of credit
  generally, 1–2
  *Briscoe v. Bank of Commonwealth of
    Kentucky* and, 48–49, 51–53, 55
  *Craig v. Missouri* and, 39–40, 41–44, 45–46
  defined, 44–45
  Framers on, 134–135
  greenbacks as, 135
  as legal tender, 54
  Legal Tender Acts *See* (Legal Tender Acts
    (1860s))
  Treasury notes compared, 41, 42
Bimetallic monetary systems, 10–15
  advantages of, 15
  coinage power and, 11
  as complete commodity-money system, 11
  decline of, 15
  defined, 10
  devaluation in, 13–14
  disequilibrium in, 11–15, 156–158
  exchange rates in, 10–11
  Gresham's Law and, 13, 14–15
  historical background, 10
  monometallic monetary systems,
    conversion to, 14, 117
  recoinage and, 12
  self-regulation of, 11
  in United States, 178
Bingham, John, 153
Blackstone, William, 131–132
Blaine, James M., 86
Bland, Richard, 117
Bland-Allison Act of 1878, 117–118, 119, 146,
  158
Bond issues as alternative to legal tender, 64,
  67–68

Bopp, Karl R., 173
Borrowing power
  *Juilliard v. Greenman* and, 121, 123,
    125–126
  Legal Tender Acts and, 64–65
Boutwell, George, 87–88, 98, 112–113,
  122, 132
Bradley, Joseph
  generally, 98–99
  *Knox v. Lee,* 105–107, 112–113, 191
  *Parker v. Davis,* 105–107, 112–113
  on sovereignty, 222
Branch banks, 23
Brandeis, Louis, 198
Breckenridge, John, 150
Breckenridge, Sophonisba P., 36, 37, 57,
  150–154, 172
Brett, Elizabeth, 151
Briscoe, George H., 47
Briscoe, John, 47
*Briscoe v. Bank of Commonwealth of Kentucky*
  (1837), 47–55
  attorneys in, 48
  constitutional powers and, 48–49
  *Craig v. Missouri* distinguished, 53
  dissenting opinion in, 53–54
  factual background, 47–48
  notes as bills of credit, 48–49, 51–53, 55
  opinion of Justices in, 51–53
  Tenth Amendment and, 50–51
Bronson (party in *Bronson v. Rodes*),
  72–73, 74
*Bronson v. Rodes* (1868), 72–78
  generally, 186
  coinage power and, 74
  coined money, payment in, 75–77
  contract not debt redeemable in legal
    tender, 76–77
  dissenting opinion in, 77–78
  factual background, 72–73
  legal tender, payment in, 73–77
  Legal Tender Acts and, 77–78
  *Norman v. Baltimore & Ohio Railroad Co.*
    distinguished, 190–191
  opinion of Justices in, 73–77
Brough, William, 135, 149–150, 230–231
"Bubbles," 173
Buchanan, James (economist), 232
Buchanan, James (President), 94, 108
Burns, Arthur R., 7–8, 218–219
Bush, George W., 227–228
Butler, Pierce, 198

Cardozo, Benjamin, 198
Carothers, Neil, 15, 36, 69, 102
Carson, Deane, 160
Catterall, Ralph C.H., 22, 56
Center for Studies in Law and Economics, 220
Central banks
  generally, 3
  reserves and, 59
  Second National Bank as, 22, 31–32, 33
Certificates of deposit, 66
Chandler, L.V. 170
Chase, Salmon P.
  generally, 81, 88–89, 94, 95, 98, 138, 153
  *Bronson v. Rodes,* 73
  evolution of position of, 93–94
  gold and, 61
  *Hepburn v. Griswold,* 89–90, 93–94
  *Knox v. Lee,* 98, 107–108, 112
  Legal Tender Acts and, 62–63, 65–66,
    67–70, 89
  Lincoln and, 66
  *Parker v. Davis,* 98, 107–108, 112
  resignation of, 71
  on sovereignty, 138
  *Veazie Bank v. Fenno,* 82
Checkbook banking, 80–81
China, silver standard in, 15
Civil War
  certificates of deposit during, 66
  debt from, 71
  expenditures during, 70
  financing of, 58–60
  greenbacks ( *See* Greenbacks)
  Legal Tender Acts *See* (Legal Tender Acts
    (1860s))
  payments to armed forces during, 69–70
  post-war contraction, 86–87
  printing money, financing through, 59–60
  tariffs, financing through, 59
  taxation, financing through, 59
Clay, Henry, 22, 48, 49, 52
Clearinghouse Association of New York City,
  159
Clearing-House Loan Certificates, 159
Clearing-house system, 159–161
Cleveland, Grover, 145, 146, 156–157
Clifford, Nathan, 81, 94, 98, 108–109
Coinage Act of 1873, 117, 158
Coinage power
  bimetallic monetary systems and, 11
  *Bronson v. Rodes* and, 74
  emergence of money and, 6, 7–8

in Greece, 7
as including paper money, 122–123, 126
*Juilliard v. Greenman* and, 122–123, 126
printing money contrasted, 90–91
in Rome, 7–8
Second National Bank and, 28, 31
Smith on, 133–134
Collamer, Jacob, 65, 107
*Commentaries* (Story), 29
Commodity Theory of Money, 207–208
Comptroller of the Currency, 79, 86, 88, 230
Conkling, Roscoe, 113, 136–137
Constitution. *See specific Clause or Amendment*
Constitutional Convention of 1787, 44–45,
    123, 127, 131, 136–137
Consumer Price Index, 169, 187
Contraction Act, 86
Contracts. *See* Impairment of contracts
Coolidge, Calvin, 172, 198
Cox, Samuel, 221
Craig, Hiram, 40
*Craig v. Missouri* (1830), 39–44
    attorneys in, 40–41
    factual background, 39–40
    federalism and, 43–44
    notes as bills of credit, 39–40, 41–44,
        45–46
    opinion of Justices in, 41
Crane, Philip, 218
Crawford, William H., 18, 19
Creditor-debtor relations
    *Knox v. Lee* and, 105, 107–108, 110
    *Norman v. Baltimore & Ohio Railroad Co.*
        and, 191
    *Parker v. Davis* and, 105, 107–108, 110
Currency, power of federal government
    regarding
    Federal Money Clause, 103–105
    Federal Reserve Act and, 226
    Federal Reserve System and, 224
    Gold Clause Cases and, 203
    *Juilliard v. Greenman* and, 121–122
    *Knox v. Lee* and, 103–105, 106–107,
        108–109, 112
    *Legal Tender Cases* and, 226
    *Norman v. Baltimore & Ohio Railroad Co.*
        and, 189–192
    *Parker v. Davis* and, 103–105, 106–107,
        108–109, 112
    *Veazie Bank v. Fenno* and, 82
Currency Act of 1900, 152, 156–161,
    165, 224

Dallas, Alexander J., 18–19
Damages, 197–198
Davis, David, 77, 82, 94
Dawson, John P., 217
Debt
    federal government as debtor, 97–98
    War of 1812 and, 17–18
Deposit banking, 80–81
Depression. *See* Great Contraction
Deprivation of property, 92
Devaluation
    in bimetallic monetary systems, 13–14
    in England, 36–37
    gold devaluation of 1834 *See* (Gold
        devaluation of 1834)
    gold devaluation of 1934 *See* (Gold
        devaluation of 1934)
Direct pressure policy, 174–176, 225
Direct tax, 81, 82
Disappearance of gold, 1–2
Disequilibrium in bimetallic monetary
    systems, 11–15, 156–158
Dunbar, Charles, 56, 86, 98–99
Dunne, Gerald T., 25, 89

Eccles, Marinner, 209, 210, 211, 214
Einaudi, Luigi, 12
Elizabeth I (England), 151, 152
Ellsworth, Oliver, 136–137, 138
Emergence of money, 4–9
    barter system and, 4–5
    coinage power and, 6, 7–8
    lack of state involvement in, 5–6, 7
    legal tender and, 6, 8–9
    "sanction of state," 6
    seigniorage and, 8, 9
    "significant improvement," 6
Emergency Banking Act, 182–183
England
    devaluation in, 36–37
    gold standard in, 15, 134
    legal tender in, 151–152
    paper money in, 137
Exchange rates
    generally, 3
    in bimetallic monetary systems, 10–11
    under Federal Money Clause, 35
Executive Order 6102, 183

Federal Home Loan Bank Act, 182
Federalism
    *Craig v. Missouri* and, 43–44

Federalism (*cont.*)
  Hepburn on, 147–149
*The Federalist* (No. 44), 134
Federal Money Clause (Art. 1, Section 8,
  clause 5)
  currency, power of federal government
    regarding, 103–105
  exchange rates under, 35
  gold standard and, 178
  *Norman v. Baltimore & Ohio Railroad Co.*
    and, 190–191
  *Perry v. United States* and, 200
  regulation of value under, 35, 37
  text of, 1
Federal Reserve Act
  generally, 172–173, 175
  currency, power of federal government
    regarding, 226
  drafting of, 145, 162–163
  enactment of, 165
  gold reserves and, 179, 180–181, 185
  gold standard and, 178–179, 181
  Hepburn on, 172
  *Legal Tender Cases* and, 166–167
  lenders of last resort and, 183, 224–225
  Real Bills Doctrine and, 165
  reserves and, 168
Federal Reserve Board, 163–164, 170–172,
  173, 176, 180, 208, 214–215, 228–229
Federal Reserve Open Market Committee
  (FOMC), 207, 208, 211, 228–229, 230,
  233
Federal Reserve System, 162–169
  generally, 214–215
  anti-speculation policy, 173–174, 176, 180,
    225
  bank reserve requirements, 207, 210–211,
    213–214
  currency, power of federal government
    regarding, 224
  direct pressure policy, 174–176, 225
  earning assets, 168, 169
  emergency powers, 170–172
  gold reserves of, 179, 180–181, 184, 185,
    193, 207, 208–209
  gold standard and, 167, 169, 170, 175–176,
    178–180, 181, 228–229
  inflation and, 167–168, 169, 228
  initial intention not to be central bank, 162,
    164–165
  lack of Congressional oversight or control,
    233

  *Legal Tender Cases* and, 166–167
  legitimacy of actions, 209–210
  lenders of last resort and, 224–225
  M1 money supply in, 171
  monetary liabilities, 168
  non-earning assets, 168
  open market operations, 168–169
  policymaking powers, 170–172
  political nature of, 167
  price stabilization policy, 170, 173, 179–180,
    215–216, 224–225
  under reinstituted gold standard,
    228–229
  Treasury Department and, 167
Fenno (party in *Veazie Bank v. Fenno*), 81
Fessenden, William P., 71
Fiat money, 1–2, 119, 156
Field, Stephen
  generally, 128
  *Hepburn v. Griswold*, 94
  *Juilliard v. Greenman*, 120, 127, 153–154
  *Knox v. Lee*, 98, 109–110
  on legal tender, 132
  *Legal Tender Cases*, 196, 201
  on sovereignty, 136, 147, 223
  *Veazie Bank v. Fenno*, 81–82
Fifth Amendment
  generally, 92
  abrogation of gold clauses by Congress
    and, 188
  Gold Clause Cases and, 188
  *Hepburn v. Griswold* and, 92
  *Perry v. United States* and, 198
First National Bank, 15–17
  generally, 16
  denial of recharter, 17
  historical background, 15–16
  interstate nature of, 17
  limited scope of, 16
  sovereignty and, 17
Fish, Hamilton, 138
Fisher, Irving, 170
FOMC. *See* Federal Reserve Open Market
  Committee (FOMC)
Ford, Gerald, 218
Fort Knox, 206, 208, 229
*Fractional Money* (Carothers), 15
France, paper money in, 137
Friedman, Milton, 14–15, 144, 174, 176, 211,
  214, 216, 228
"Full employment," 212–213
Fullerson, Abraham, 47

Germany, gold standard in, 15
Glass, Carter, 162–163, 164, 165,
    172–173, 182
Glass-Borah Rider, 182
Glass-Steagall Act, 182
Gold. *See also* Bimetallic monetary systems
    coins, 179
    delivery of private gold to government
        required, 183
    demonetization of, 225–226
    devaluation of 1834 (*See* Gold devaluation
        of 1834)
    devaluation of 1934 (*See* Gold devaluation
        of 1934)
    disappearance of, 1–2
    hoarding of, 193
    as legal tender, 230–231
    in monometallic monetary systems, 14, 117
    private ownership of, 216–220, 227
    resumption of payments, 114–118, 144, 145
    separation from Treasury ownership,
        229–230
    setting price of, 230–231
    stockpiling by government, 61
    valuation of greenbacks versus, 92–93
Gold bullion, 217
Gold Certificates, 184, 185–186, 206–207, 208,
    229–230
Gold Clause Cases, 182–205
    generally, 113, 209–210, 214–215, 226
    abrogation of gold clauses by Congress, 204
    amount of obligations under, 188
    currency, power of federal government
        regarding, 203
    factual background, 187–188
    Fifth Amendment and, 188
    *Hepburn v. Griswold* compared, 204–205
    judicial review and, 205
    *Juilliard v. Greenman* cited in, 204
    *Knox v. Lee* cited in, 204
    legal tender and, 226
    *Missouri Pacific Railroad Co., In re*, 187
    *Norman v. Baltimore & Ohio Railroad
        Co.* (*See Norman v. Baltimore & Ohio
        Railroad Co.* (1935))
    *Nortz v. United States,* 187
    *Parker v. Davis* cited in, 204
    *Perry v. United States* (*See Perry v. United
        States* (1935))
    sovereignty and, 204
Gold clauses
    generally, 72, 101

abrogation by Congress *See* (Abrogation of
    gold clauses by Congress)
*Bronson v. Rodes* (*See also Bronson v. Rodes*
    (1868))
    coined money, payment in as alternative,
        75–77
    legal tender, payment in as alternative,
        73–77
    reinstatement by Congress, 218–219
    in state courts, 219
Gold Coin Act of 1834, 35
Gold Currency Act of 1900, *See* Currency Act
    of 1900
Gold devaluation of 1834,
    generally, 35–36, 195
    gold devaluation of 1934 compared,
        194–195
    *Knox v. Lee* and, 102–103, 105–106
    Legal Tender Acts compared, 102–103
    *Parker v. Davis* and, 102–103, 105–106
Gold devaluation of 1934,
    generally, 184–185, 186, 195, 209–210, 215
    abrogation of gold clauses by Congress and,
        186, 189
    amount of, 188
    arithmetic of, 199
    gold devaluation of 1834 compared,
        194–195
    *Norman v. Baltimore & Ohio Railroad Co.*
        and, 193–194
    *Perry v. United States* and, 199–200
    Section 5, 185
Gold Ownership Amendments, 218
Gold Reserve Act, 184
Gold reserves
    Federal Reserve Act and, 179, 180–181, 185
    of Federal Reserve System, 179, 180–181,
        184, 185, 193, 207, 208–209
    fractional reserves, 179
    Great Contraction and, 180–181
    of Treasury Department, 157, 184, 193, 215
Gold standard
    abandonment of, 185–186
    defined, 177
    in England, 15, 134
    as exclusive creator of money, 228–229
    Federal Money Clause and, 178
    Federal Reserve Act and, 178–179, 181
    Federal Reserve System and, 167, 169, 170,
        175–176, 178–180, 181, 228–229
    in Germany, 15
    Great Contraction and, 225

Gold standard (*cont.*)
  inflation and, 178
  M1 money supply and, 178
  political commitment to reinstituting, 231
  Real Bills Doctrine compared, 165–166,
    179–180
  reinstitution of, 228–233
  separation from Treasury ownership,
    229–230
  State Money Clause and, 178
  Treasury notes and, 230
  in United States, 117
Government securities, 123, 156–157,
    168–169, 183
Grant, Ulysses S., 87–88, 98, 112–113, 115,
    138, 191, 205
Gray, Horace, 120–123, 222–223
Great Britain. *See* England
Great Contraction, 170–176
  gold devaluation of 1934 *See* (Gold
    devaluation of 1934)
  gold reserves and, 180–181
  gold standard and, 225
  "Recession-in-a-Depression," 214
Great Recession, 227–228
Greece (Ancient), coinage power in, 7
*The Greenback Era* (Unger), 87, 97
Greenback Party, 80
Greenbacks, 58–61
  as bills of credit, 135
  Breckenridge on, 154
  constitutionality only for debts to federal
    government as alternative to *Legal Tender
    Cases,* 129
  continued existence during post-Civil War
    period, 87–88, 144
  definitions relating to, 58, 101
  denominations of, 60
  as fiat money, 156
  gold resumption and retirement of, 115–116
  Hepburn on, 147
  *Hepburn v. Griswold* and, 90, 96, 222
  *Knox v. Lee* and, 99–100, 109, 222, 226
  as legal tender, 90, 96, 99–100, 109, 156, 222
  national bank notes compared, 109–110
  *Parker v. Davis* and, 99–100, 109, 222
  post-Civil War retirement of, 86–87
  pre-Civil War Treasury notes compared, 58,
    59–58
  valuation of gold versus, 92–93
  as wartime measure, 90–91, 96
Greenfield, R.L., 231, 232

Greenfield-Yeager system, 231–232, 233
Greenman (party in *Juilliard v. Greenman*),
    120
Gresham, Thomas, 13
Gresham's Law, 13, 14–15
Grier, Robert, 81, 94, 97
Griswold, Henry, 89–90, 93

Hamilton, Alexander, 16, 24, 134, 138
Hammond, Bray, 24, 27
Hardin (attorney in *Briscoe v. Bank of
    Commonwealth of Kentucky*), 48
Harding, Warren, 198
Harrison, Benjamin, 145
*Harvard Law Review,* 131
Hayes, Rutherford B., 117
Helms, Jesse, 218–219
Henry VIII (England), 36, 151, 152, 153–154
Hepburn, A. Barton, 79, 80, 144–149, 172
Hepburn (party in *Hepburn v. Griswold*),
    89–90, 93
*Hepburn v. Griswold* (1870), 86–96
  generally, 205, 226–227
  bankruptcy and, 95
  Breckenridge on, 153
  deprivation of property and, 92
  dissenting opinion in, 94–96
  Fifth Amendment and, 92
  Gold Clause Cases compared, 204–205
  greenbacks as legal tender, 90, 96, 222
  impairment of contracts and, 92
  implied powers of Congress and, 91–92, 96
  judicial review and, 95–96
  Legal Tender Acts and, 93
  Necessary and Proper Clause and, 91–92, 96
  opinion of Justices in, 90–94
  Tenth Amendment and, 95
  wartime measure, greenbacks as, 90–91, 96
Hetzel, Robert, 170
Historical background. *See* Emergence of
    money
*A History of Currency in the United States*
    (Hepburn), 145
*History of the Formation of the Constitution*
    (Bancroft), 124–125
*A History of the Greenbacks* (Mitchell), 62
*History of the Legal Tender Paper Money Issued
    During the Great Rebellion* (Spaulding),
    62
*History of the United States* (Bancroft),
    124–125
Hoarding of gold, 193

Holzer, Henry Mark, 187
Hoover, Herbert, 182, 198
Hopkinson, Joseph, 23–24
Howard, J.M., 65
Hughes, Charles Evans
  generally, 198, 205, 226, 227
  *Norman v. Baltimore & Ohio Railroad Co.,*
    189–194, 195
  *Perry v. United States,* 196, 199
Humphrey, Thomas, 165
Hunt, Alva R., 131–132

Impairment of contracts
  *Hepburn v. Griswold* and, 92
  *Juilliard v. Greenman* and, 127
  *Knox v. Lee* and, 110
  *Norman v. Baltimore & Ohio Railroad Co.*
    and, 191, 195
  *Parker v. Davis* and, 110
  *Perry v. United States* and, 195–203
Independent Treasury Act of 1846, 34
India, silver standard in, 15
Inflation
  Federal Reserve System and, 167–168, 169,
    228
  gold standard and, 178
  paper money and, 141
  Second National Bank and, 19
Inflation Bill, 183
Inflexibility of banks, 159

Jackson, Andrew
  generally, 40, 48
  on Second National Bank, 27
  veto of recharter of Second National Bank,
    28–30, 31–33, 34, 38, 56, 83
Jastram, Roy W., 13, 114, 178
Jay, John, 134
Jefferson, Thomas, 150
Johnson, Andrew, 87–88, 97, 130
Johnson, William, 41, 42
Jones, William, 23–24
Judicial review
  Bancroft on, 139–140
  Gold Clause Cases and, 205
  *Hepburn v. Griswold* and, 95–96
  *Juilliard v. Greenman* and, 123
  Legal Tender Acts and, 96
  *McCulloch v. Maryland* and, 95–96
Juilliard (party in *Juilliard v. Greenman*), 120
*Juilliard v. Greenman* (1884), 119–128
  Bancroft on, 135

borrowing power and, 121, 123, 125–126
coinage power as including paper money,
  122–123, 126
constitutional powers and, 127
currency, power of federal government
  regarding, 121–122
depreciation and, 128
dissenting opinion in, 124–128
factual background, 120
Gold Clause Cases, cited in, 204
Hepburn on, 146
impairment of contracts and, 127
judicial review and, 123
legal tender and, 226
*McCulloch v. Maryland* compared, 120
Necessary and Proper Clause and, 121
*Norman v. Baltimore & Ohio Railroad Co.*
  distinguished, 190–191
opinion of Justices in, 120–123
paper money as legal tender, 124–125, 126
sovereignty and, 120–121, 123, 125, 127,
  222–223
Tenth Amendment and, 127
wartime measure, paper money as, 125

Kettl, Donald F., 209
Klebaner, Benjamin, 145
*Knox v. Lee* (1871), 97–113
  generally, 191
  commentaries on, 112–113
  creditor-debtor relations and, 105, 107–108,
    110
  currency, power of federal government
    regarding, 103–105, 106–107, 108–109, 112
  dissenting opinions in, 107–112
  Gold Clause Cases, cited in, 204
  gold devaluation of 1834 and, 102–103,
    105–106
  greenbacks as legal tender, 99–100, 109, 222
  historical background, 97–98
  impairment of contracts and, 110
  Legal Tender Acts and, 98
  legal tender and, 226
  necessity and, 101–102, 105, 107, 109, 110
  opinion of Justices in, 99–107
  prospective application of Legal Tender
    Acts, 99, 100–101, 111
  retroactive application of Legal Tender
    Acts, 99
  sovereignty and, 103–105, 106–107,
    108–109, 112, 222–223
  Tenth Amendment and, 108

Lack of economic understanding in Supreme
    Court, 2–3
Laughlin, J. Laurence, 150, 152, 172–173
Legal tender
    bills of credit as, 54
    bonds as alternative to, 64, 67–68
    Breckenridge on, 150–154
    *Bronson v. Rodes* and, 73–77
    Brough on, 149–150
    contractual debts, payment of, 73–77
    emergence of money and, 6, 8–9
    in England, 151–152
    Field on, 132
    gold as, 230–231
    Gold Clause Cases and, 226
    gold clauses, payment in as alternative to,
        73–77
    greenbacks as, 90, 96, 99–100, 109, 156, 222
    Hepburn on, 145, 146–147
    *Hepburn v. Griswold* and, 90, 96, 222
    *Juilliard v. Greenman* and, 124–125, 126, 226
    *Knox v. Lee* and, 99–100, 109, 222, 226
    Ninth Amendment and, 131
    paper money as, 124–125, 126
    *Parker v. Davis* and, 99–100, 109, 222
    Second National Bank notes as, 23
    silver as, 156
    taxation as alternative to, 64
    Tenth Amendment and, 131
    Treasury notes as alternative to, 67
Legal Tender Act of 1933, 183–184
Legal Tender Acts (1860s), 62–71
    generally, 87, 113
    bonds as alternative to legal tender, 64,
        67–68
    borrowing power and, 64–65
    *Bronson v. Rodes* and, 77–78
    denomination of notes under, 68
    as *ex post facto* laws, 100–101
    first Act, 62–67
    gold devaluation of 1834 compared,
        102–103
    *Hepburn v. Griswold* and, 93
    historical background, 62
    initial temporary nature of, 67
    judicial review and, 96
    *Knox v. Lee* and, 98
    necessity and, 64, 65, 66–68
    *Parker v. Davis* and, 98
    prospective application of, 99, 100–101, 111,
        129–130, 222
    quantity of notes under, 68, 69

    retroactive application of, 99, 222
    second Act, 67–68
    taxation as alternative to legal tender, 64
    third Act, 69–70
    Treasury notes as alternative to legal tender,
        67
*Legal Tender* (Breckenridge), 36, 150
*Legal Tender Cases*
    generally, 30–31, 186–187, 203, 227–228
    *Bronson v. Rodes* ( *See Bronson v. Rodes*
        (1868))
    constitutionality of greenbacks only for
        debts to federal government as alternative
        to, 129
    currency, power of federal government
        regarding, 226
    Currency Act of 1900, incompatibility with,
        159
    Federal Reserve Act and, 166–167
    Federal Reserve System and, 166–167
    *Hepburn v. Griswold* (*See Hepburn v.
        Griswold* (1870))
    judicial commentaries on, 131–132
    *Juilliard v. Greenman* (*See Juilliard v.
        Greenman* (1884))
    *Knox v. Lee* See (*Knox v. Lee* (1871))
    Necessary and Proper Clause and, 130–131
    need to revisit, 226–227
    *Norman v. Baltimore & Ohio Railroad Co.*
        distinguished, 190–191
    *Parker v. Davis* (*See Parker v. Davis* (1871))
    *Perry v. United States* compared, 199–201
    political nature of, 130
    prospective application of Legal Tender Acts
        as alternative to, 129–130
    sovereignty and, 130–131, 142
    *Veazie Bank v. Fenno* (*See Veazie Bank v.
        Fenno* (1869))
Legal tender obligations (LTOs), 201
Lenders of last resort, 159–161, 168, 183,
    224–225
Lincoln, Abraham
    generally, 71, 77, 81, 87–89, 94, 130
    Chase and, 66
    Legal Tender Acts and, 67, 70

Madison, James, 17, 45, 134, 136
Manning, Daniel, 146–147
Marshall, John
    generally, 49, 53, 54, 95
    cited in *Juilliard v. Greenman*, 120, 124
    *Craig v. Missouri*, 41–42, 44, 45

*McCulloch v. Maryland,*53.10, 24–25, 26, 84–85
  post-*McCulloch,* 28–29, 30
  on sovereignty, 138
Martin, Luther, 23–24
McCulloch, Hugh, 65–66, 71, 86, 87–88, 113, 146
McCulloch, J. Huston, 36, 85, 103, 160
McCulloch, James, 21
*McCulloch v. Maryland* (1819), 21–27
  generally, 19–20
  attorneys in, 23–24
  authority to create Second National Bank under, 24–25
  constitutionality of Second National Bank under, 22–23
  factual background, 21
  impact of decision, 27
  issues in, 21–22
  judicial review and, 95–96
  *Juilliard v. Greenman* compared, 120
  necessity of Second National Bank under, 25–27
  opinion of Justices in, 24
  positions of Justices in, 26–27
  power to tax as power to destroy, 84–85
  Second National Bank and, 22–23, 24–27
  sovereignty and, 138
  state taxation of federal agency under, 22
  taxation and, 21
McLean, Angus, 202–203, 204
McLean, John, 41, 43–44, 51–52
McReynolds, James, 198, 199, 200–202
Meltzer, Allan H., 211
Menger, Carl, 5–7
Miller, Adolph C., 172–176
Miller, Samuel, 77–78, 94, 191
Minting facilities, 35
*Missouri Pacific Railroad Co., In re* (1935), 187
Mitchell, Wesley C., 62, 64, 65–66
Mondell, Frank, 164
M1 money supply, 171, 178, 215
Monetary affairs
  current condition of, 1–3
  1871–1883, 114–118
  1900–1914, 156–161
Monetary base, 156
*Monetary Mischief* (Friedman), 14–15
Monometallic monetary systems, 14, 117
Monroe, James, 23–24, 154–155
Moore, Ephraim, 40
Moore, John, 40

Morgenthau, Henry, 209, 213–214
M2 money supply, 215

National Bank Act, 69, 80, 85, 115
National banking system, 79–80, 88
National bank notes, 58, 109–110, 115
National Monetary Commission, 163, 164
National Reserve Association, 163
*The Natural Law of Money* (Brough), 135, 149
Necessary and Proper Clause.
    *See also* Necessity
  *Hepburn v. Griswold* and, 91–92, 96
  *Juilliard v. Greenman* and, 121
  *Legal Tender Cases* and, 130–131
  Second National Bank and, 25, 26
  Tenth Amendment and, 108
Necessity
  *Knox v. Lee* and, 101–102, 105, 107, 109, 110
  Legal Tender Acts and, 64, 65, 66–68
  *Parker v. Davis* and, 101–102, 105, 107, 109, 110
Nelson, Samuel, 81, 82–85, 94
Newcomb, Simon, 65–66, 113
Ninth Amendment
  legal tender and, 131
  Second National Bank and, 26
Nixon, Richard, 218
Norman (party in *Norman v. Baltimore & Ohio Railroad Co.*), 188–189, 194, 195, 199
*Norman v. Baltimore & Ohio Railroad Co.* (1935), 188–195
  generally, 187
  abrogation of gold clauses by Congress and, 192–193
  *Bronson v. Rodes* distinguished, 190–191
  creditor-debtor relations and, 191
  currency, power of federal government regarding, 189–192
  factual background, 188–189
  Federal Money Clause and, 190–191
  gold devaluation of 1934 and, 193–194
  impairment of contracts and, 191, 195
  *Juilliard v. Greenman* distinguished, 190–191
  *Legal Tender Cases* distinguished, 190–191
  opinion of Justices in, 189–194, 195
  sovereignty and, 197
*Nortz v. United States* (1935), 187

Obama, Barack, 227–228
Open market operations, 168–169

Panic of 1857, 159
Panic of 1873, 114–115
Panic of 1907, 161, 170
Paper money
  Bancroft on, 136–137, 140–141
  bills of credit (*See* Bills of credit)
  coinage power as including, 122–123, 126
  in England, 137
  Framers on, 134–135
  in France, 137
  greenbacks ( *See* Greenbacks)
  Hepburn on, 147
  inflation and, 141
  as legal tender, 124–125, 126
  as wartime measure, 125
*Parker v. Davis* (1871), 97–113
  commentaries on, 112–113
  creditor-debtor relations and, 105, 107–108,
    110
  currency, power of federal government
    regarding, 103–105, 106–107, 108–109,
    112
  dissenting opinions in, 107–112
  Gold Clause Cases, cited in, 204
  gold devaluation of 1834 and, 102–103,
    105–106
  greenbacks as legal tender, 99–100, 109, 222
  historical background, 97–98
  impairment of contracts and, 110
  Legal Tender Acts and, 98
  necessity and, 101–102, 105, 107, 109, 110
  opinion of Justices in, 99–107
  prospective application of Legal Tender
    Acts, 99, 100–101, 111
  retroactive application of Legal Tender
    Acts, 99
  sovereignty and, 103–105, 106–107,
    108–109, 112
  Tenth Amendment and, 108
Paterson, William, 136
*The People, The Sovereigns* (Monroe), 154
Perry (party in *Perry v. United States*),
    195–196, 198, 199
*Perry v. United States* (1935), 195–203
  generally, 187
  abrogation of gold clauses by Congress and,
    201–202
  damages in, 197–198
  dissenting opinion in, 198, 199–203
  factual background, 195–203
  Federal Money Clause and, 200
  Fifth Amendment and, 198

gold devaluation of 1934 and, 199–200
  impairment of contracts and, 195–203
  *Legal Tender Cases* compared, 199–201
  opinion of Justices in, 196, 197–198
  sovereignty and, 197, 198–199
  unjust enrichment and, 198, 203
"Pet banks," 33–34
*Pieces of Eight* (Vieira), 113
Pilon, Roger, 95
Pinkney, William, 23–24
*A Plea for the Constitution of the United States,*
    *Wounded in the House of Its Guardians*
    (Bancroft), 135, 141, 145, 201
Pledges of faith, 51
Polk, James, 82, 94
Price stabilization policy, 170, 173, 179–180,
    215–216, 224–225
*Principles of Economics* (Menger), 5
Printing money. *See also* Paper money
  Civil War, financing of, 59–60
  coinage power contrasted, 90–91
Private ownership of gold, 216–220, 227
Privatized multi-commodity standard,
    231–232, 233
Public choice economics, 7

Quantity Theory of Money, 207–208,
    211–212

Real Bills Doctrine, 161, 165–166, 169, 170,
    172–173, 174, 179–180
"Recession-in-a-Depression," 214
Reconstruction Finance Corporation, 184
Reconstruction Finance Corporation Act, 182
Reinstatement of gold clauses by Congress,
    218–219
Reserve Currency Association, 163
Reserves
  generally, 18
  bank reserve requirements, 160–161, 179,
    181, 207, 210–211, 213–214
  central banks and, 59
  Federal Reserve Act and, 168
  gold reserves *See* (Gold reserves)
  of Second National Bank, 23
  Treasury notes as, 57
Resumption Act, 115–116, 144
Resumption of gold payments, 114–118, 144,
    145
Roberts, Owen, 198
Rodes (party in *Bronson v. Rodes*), 72–73, 186
Rome (Ancient)

coinage power in, 7–8
sovereignty in, 142
Roosevelt, Franklin D., 182, 194, 203, 209

St. Louis, Iron Mountain & Southern Railway,
   189
Salsman, Richard M., 230
Schumpeter, Joseph A., 221, 228
Schwartz, Anna J., 144, 174, 176, 211, 214, 216
Second National Bank, 18–20
   arguments against constitutionality of,
      37–38
   authority to charter, 24–25
   branches of, 23
   as central bank, 22, 31–32, 33
   circumstantial powers of, 27–28
   coinage power and, 28, 31
   constitutionality of, 22–23
   general theory of, 18–19
   inflation and, 19
   *McCulloch v. Maryland* and, 22–23, 24–27
   as monopoly, 23
   Necessary and Proper Clause and, 25, 26
   necessity of, 25–27
   Ninth Amendment and, 26
   notes as legal tender, 23
   reserves of, 23
   separation of powers and, 30–31, 33
   Tenth Amendment and, 25, 26
   veto of recharter by Jackson, 28–30, 31–33,
      34, 38, 56, 83
Seigniorage, 8, 9, 60, 63, 133, 151
Separation of powers
   Monroe on, 155
   Second National Bank and, 30–31, 33
Shaw, W.A., 12
Sheffey (attorney in *Craig v. Missouri*), 40
Sherman, John, 65
Sherman, Roger, 138
Sherman Silver Purchase Act, 156–157
Silver. *See also* Bimetallic monetary systems
   certificates, 58
   in China, 15
   decline in value of, 13
   as fiat money, 156
   in India, 15
   as legal tender, 156
   parity status, 88
   premium in, 114
   renewed interest in, 116–117
   as subsidiary coinage metal, 224
   Treasury Department holdings of, 157

Simon, William, 218–219
Smith, Adam, 16, 133–134, 140
Sound Money League, 145
Southard (attorney in *Briscoe v. Bank of
   Commonwealth of Kentucky*), 48, 49–51,
   53, 82
Sovereignty
   generally, 132–133
   Bancroft on, 136, 137–139
   Bradley on, 222
   Breckenridge on, 153
   Chase on, 138
   criticism of argument, 224
   evolution of concept, 142–143
   Field on, 136, 147, 223
   First National Bank and, 17
   Framers on, 143
   Gold Clause Cases and, 204
   judicial commentaries on, 131–132
   *Juilliard v. Greenman* and, 120–121, 123,
      125, 127, 222–223
   *Knox v. Lee* and, 103–105, 106–107,
      108–109, 112, 222–223
   *Legal Tender Cases* and, 130–131, 142
   Marshall on, 138
   *McCulloch v. Maryland* and, 138
   Monroe on, 154–155
   *Norman v. Baltimore & Ohio Railroad Co.*
      and, 197
   *Parker v. Davis* and, 103–105, 106–107,
      108–109, 112
   *Perry v. United States* and, 197, 198–199
   in Rome, 142
   Smith on, 133
Spaulding, Elbridge G., 62, 63–66, 67, 94–95,
   113, 153
Speculation, 173–174, 176, 180, 225
Sprague, O.M.W., 160, 161
State Money Clause (Art. 1, Section
   10, clause 1)
   enactment of, 45
   gold standard and, 178
   text of, 1
Steagall, Henry, 209
Stevens, Thaddeus, 69–70
Stone, Harlan, 198
Storing, Herbert J., 26
Story, Joseph, 29, 53–54
Strong, Benjamin
   generally, 172
   in Federal Reserve System, 170, 175–176
   money supply and, 173

Strong, Benjamin (*cont.*)
  price stabilization policy, 173, 174, 179–180,
    215, 224–225
Strong, William
  generally, 98–99
  *Knox v. Lee,* 99–105, 112–113
  *Legal Tender Cases,* 226–227
  *Parker v. Davis,* 99–105, 112–113
Subjunctive syllogism, 223
Subsidiary coin, 104
Supreme Court. *See specific Case or Justice*
Sutherland, George, 198
Swayne, Noah Haynes, 77, 94

Taft, William H., 198
Taney, Roger B., 28–29, 48, 88–89
Tariffs, financing of Civil War through, 59
Taxation
  as alternative to legal tender, 64
  Civil War, financing of, 59
  direct tax, 81, 82
  *McCulloch v. Maryland* and, 21
  as means of regulating lawful enterprise,
    82–85
  power to tax as power to destroy, 84–85
  of state bank notes, 80–81
  state taxation of federal agency, 22
Tenth Amendment
  generally, 153
  Bancroft on, 138
  *Briscoe v. Bank of Commonwealth of
    Kentucky* and, 50–51
  *Hepburn v. Griswold* and, 95
  *Juilliard v. Greenman* and, 127
  *Knox v. Lee* and, 108
  legal tender and, 131
  Necessary and Proper Clause and, 108
  *Parker v. Davis* and, 108
  Second National Bank and, 25, 26
  *Veazie Bank v. Fenno* and, 81, 83
Thayer, James Bradley, 131
Thomas, Elmer, 183
Thomas Amendment to the Agricultural Relief
  Act, 183
Thompson, Smith, 41, 42–43
Timberlake, Richard H., 4, 16, 36, 165, 209,
  216
Treasury Department
  bank reserve requirements, 213–214
  Document No. 1086, 11
  Federal Reserve System and, 167

gold reserves of, 157, 184, 193, 215
separation of gold from Treasury ownership,
  229–230
silver holdings, 157
Treasury Note Act of 1890, 158
Treasury notes
  as alternative to legal tender, 67
  bills of credit compared, 41, 42
  denomination of, 56–57
  dual nature of, 57
  greenbacks compared, 58, 59–58
    (*See also* Greenbacks)
  pre-Civil War, 56–57
  under reinstituted gold standard, 230
  as reserves, 57
  retirement of, 19
  War of 1812 and, 17–18, 50, 54
Tyler, John, 33, 94

Unemployment, 212
Unger, Irwin, 87, 88, 97
United Kingdom. *See* England
University of Miami School of Law, 220
Unjust enrichment, 198, 203

Van Devanter, Willis, 198
Van Dun, Frank, 142
Vannoy, Mason, 47
Veazie Bank, 81
*Veazie Bank v. Fenno* (1869), 79–85
  currency, power of federal government
    regarding, 82
  direct tax and, 81, 82
  dissenting opinion in, 82–85
  opinion of Justices in, 82
  state bank notes, taxation of, 80–81
  taxation as means of regulating lawful
    enterprise, 82–85
  Tenth Amendment and, 81, 83
Velocity of money, 212
Vieira, Edwin, 30, 113, 155, 226
Vreeland, Edward, 162

Wage-price controls, 218
*Wall* (legal publication), 89
Warburton, Clark, 175
War of 1812, 17–18, 50, 54
Washington, Bushrod, 26
Washington, George, 136
*The Wealth of Nations* (Smith), 16, 133
Webster, Daniel, 23, 24, 25

White, Horace, 61, 158–159
White, Lawrence H., 230, 231
White (attorney in *Briscoe v. Bank of Commonwealth of Kentucky*), 48
Wholesale Price Index, 169
*Why I Am a Republican* (Boutwell), 112–113
Wicker, Elmus, 169
Williams, John, 164

Willis, H. Parker, 172–173
Wilson, James, 136, 138
Wilson, Woodrow, 162, 165, 172, 198
Wirt, William, 23–24
World War II, 216

Yeager, Leland, 179, 231–232